THE
RUSSIAN
HERITAGE
COOKBOOK

THE
RUSSIAN
HERITAGE
COOKBOOK

*A Culinary Tradition Preserved
in 400 Authentic Recipes*

LYNN VISSON

THE OVERLOOK PRESS
New York, NY

This updated edition first published in paperback in the United States in 2018 by
The Overlook Press, Peter Mayer Publishers, Inc.

141 Wooster Street
New York, NY 10012
www.overlookpress.com

For bulk and special orders please contact sales@overlookny.com,
or wite us at the above address.

Library of Congress Cataloging-in-Publication Data

Visson, Lynn
The complete Russian heritage cookbook / introduced and compiled by Lynn Visson
p. cm.
Includes index.
1. Cookery, Russian.   I. Title.
TX723.3.V5t3   1982   641.5947   19 82011520

Layout and type formatting by Bernard Schleifer
Printed in the United States of America
ISBN 978-1-4683-1687-2
1 3 5 7 9 8 6 4 2

contents

❖   throughout the text indicates new recipe

dedication

This book is dedicated to the memory of my mother, Mirra-Renée Visson, who did not like to cook but actively supported this project, to my husband, Boris Rabbot, who was a critical taster of most of the recipes, to all the Russians whose hints and ideas were of such benefit, and, above all, to the more than forty men and women whose generous sharing of their recipes and advice made this book possible: Alexandra Baker; Irene Balaksha; Eugenie Belsky; Tatyana Bogrash; Lia Brodsky; Catherine Cheosky; Leonora Chernayakhovskaya, Mirra Frankfurt; Sofia Gellman; Janna Geoffrey; Anne Jalbert; Maria Gerstman; Jenny Grey; Riba Kaldor; Rosa Kavenoki, Boris Khazanov; Elena Koreneva; Marina Medvedeva-Khazanova; Oksana Kujbida; Mrs. L.; Olga Lang; Victoria Martin; Professor M.; Frank Miller; Sofia Nabokova; Mery Odesser; Rose Raskin; Elisavietta Ritchie Farnsworth; Ariadna Sosinskaya; Galina Sultan; Suzanne Tumarkin; Vera Vengerova; Alla Vinogradova; Bertha Vinogradova; Jacqueline Visson; Mirra-Renée Visson; Vivian Weil; Tamara Weinschenker; Irene Wolheim; Catherine Woronzoff; Manya Yavitz; Mrs. Yu.

acknowledgments

I am grateful to Professor Maurice Friedberg of the University of Illinois at Urbana-Champaign, Professor Simon Karlinsky of the University of California at Berkeley, and the late Rose Raskin for their valuable advice. I also wish to thank Edward Schneider for his culinary and editorial comments.

preface

In the twenty-five years that have elapsed since the first edition of this cookbook was published the Soviet Union collapsed, the Russian Federation emerged in its place, and Russian cooking began to flourish. A new interest in the national cuisine was fostered by the decline in shortages and in hours spent on line in food stores, along with the emergence of a market economy and a wide variety of products including Russian and imported fruit, vegetables, spices, meat and fish products and prepared foods. The ready availability of cooking equipment such as food processors and microwave ovens made cooking easier, simpler and faster. Prior to *perestroika* classical Russian cuisine had been primarily preserved and passed on from generation to generation by Russian émigrés scattered around the globe; no longer are the best Russian restaurants to be found in Paris or New York, as was the case after the revolution of 1917. Today Russians both inside and outside Russia share strong feelings of pride in their national cuisine, an integral part of their rich cultural heritage.

The drab and dull restaurants of the Soviet period have been replaced by an explosion of Russian eateries, ranging from local "bistros" serving Russian "fast food" including *blinchiki, pel'meni, pirozhki* and composed salads to imports such as McDonald's and Sbarro's, and a plethora of restaurants serving everything from sushi to tandoori chicken. Many restaurants, however, are rediscovering the glories of old Russian cuisine, the magnificent beet and cabbage soups, the wonderful stuffed *kulebiakas* and *pirogs*, tender fish filets in sour cream and delicate beef and veal *kotlety*, the incredible variety of cakes and pastries. Access to domestic and foreign food products has led to a broad revival of interest in cooking, and bookstores are filled with cookbooks devoted to Russian and other cuisines. Russian émigrés are coming to Russia and Russians are going abroad, taking their native recipes with them as part of their cultural baggage. The gastronomic legacy so carefully preserved in emigration is merging with the heritage preserved at home, as Russian cuisine develops new dishes while continuing to treasure the old ones.

Most of the classical Russian recipes in the earlier editions of this book were provided by émigrés, but time has taken its toll, and many of them are no longer with us; all the more reason that I am glad to have contributed to keeping their culinary heritage alive. Many of the new recipes come from cooks living in both Russia and abroad who share the older generation's interest in classical Russian gastronomy, preserving old recipes and deriving new ones from cookbooks, journals and word of mouth.

But not everyone can go to Russia to enjoy these treats. So here they are! All of the recipes use the same kind of fresh, natural ingredients, and range from everyday fare to fancy party dishes. I would like to thank all those who generously contributed their recipes, time and culinary advice. May readers enjoy many happy hours cooking, and, as the Russians say, *priatnogo appetita* (bon appétit!)

introduction

Creamy pâtés and glistening jellied fish, steamy cabbage soup with small meat-stuffed pastries, jam-filled nut cake heady with wine–the aromas of these Russian dishes are as much a part of my memories of growing up in a Russian émigré home as the children's books with funny Cyrillic letters and drawings of witches' houses on chicken legs, the Russian language newspaper that blindly continued to worship the late tsar, and the old Cameo movie house on New York's Eighth Avenue where I spent many hours watching a soprano race through glaring yellow wheat fields while singing of her doomed love to the melodies of Tchaikovsky's opera *Eugene Onegin*.

As far back as I can remember, I absorbed Russian food and culture in delectable and unforgettable ways at the mahogany tables in the smoke-filled, high-ceilinged apartments of my parents' friends on West End Avenue. I was often the only American-born person at the table. My mother is from St. Petersburg, my father was from Kiev, and their friends came from all over Russia–Moscow, the Crimea, big cities, small towns.

These émigrés, who had left their native country before or during the 1917 revolution, spent the time around those tables discussing Russia's fate and rewriting Russian history with undaunted enthusiasm, and passion, and sorrow. Between sips of ice-cold vodka and bites of the thickly buttered black bread that was considered a sure antidote to intoxication, they argued about what might have happened if the Bolsheviks had not come to power, if the Provisional Government formed in the months prior to the Revolution had been stronger, if there had been no military uprising during the summer of 1917, if, if, if. . . They discussed food with the same deadly seriousness they devoted to any other topic. To them gastronomy was a creative discipline in no way inferior to painting, music or ballet. With equal excitement they would plunge into a discussion of a particularly fluffy almond cake that had been served at Marya Mikhailovna's last bridge party, a debate over the relative merits of visiting Soviet pianists, and a critique of a poetry recital at which an aging émigré writer with watery eyes had just tremulously declaimed his latest verses on the longings of the exiled Russian soul. As director of exhibitions at the Wildenstein Gallery, my father was the resident art expert, and all questions on painting were referred to him. A piano teacher who gave lessons to all the children in the Russian community was the final authority on every concert in New York. But *everybody* was an expert on food. Often while savoring a particularly tasty morsel, a guest would begin dreamily reminiscing about a lemon pudding he had eaten the previous week at someone else's home, and this would set off an immediate chain of gastronomic recollections from all present.

"You may forget father and mother, but you'll not forget to eat," runs a Russian proverb. The Russian approach to food is direct. Food is necessary to life, a major part of life, and its preparation is to be taken seriously. Moreover, Russians derive a positively sensual enjoyment from merely talking about food. A novel way of baking eggplant, a new recipe for *pirozhki* dough, or a cousin's secret of tea brewing will lure any émigré away from the most fascinating conversation on any subject. (I know no faster way to disrupt a peacefully chatting group of Russian ladies than to ask them how to translate *brusnika* or *kliukva* into English. The thought of those untranslatable cranberry-like acidic berries is sure to start up an hour of nostalgic reminiscences.)

In Russian the verb *popravit'sia*–to get well, recover, improve–also means "to put on weight." "You've gained weight" is a compliment meaning "you're looking well," and not a hint that a bit of dieting might be in order. Another of the hundreds of Russian proverbs "the Russian appetite balks at nothing"–may be a slight overstatement but it is firmly founded on the national character.

Over and over, Russian nineteenth-century literature illustrates the Slavic love of eating. Take Chekhov's hymn to the appetite:

> A real wolf's appetite—that's when it seems that you could eat your own father . . .
> If you want to have dinner with a good appetite never think of anything intellectual
> . . . intellectual and rational things always do in your appetite . . . Philosophers and
> scholars eat worse than anyone, even the pigs eat better than they do . . . Once
> I closed my eyes on the way home and imagined a suckling pig with horseradish,
> and my appetite made me hysterical.[1]

Another example is to be found in Ivan Goncharov's popular novel *Oblomov,* in which life on the hero's parents' estate revolves around the kitchen:

> Their greatest concern was the preparing and eating of dinner. The entire house
> hold took part in the discussion. Everyone suggested his favorite dish—soup with
> noodles, or giblets, or tripe, or brawn, or red and white sauce. All suggestions
> were thoroughly discussed and then accepted or rejected by a final decision of
> the mistress of the house . . . For the inhabitants of Oblomovka food was the pri
> mary and most important concern in life.[2]

Devotees of Russian cooking have speculated that this intense interest in food may be the result of the harsh Russian climate. People tend to eat more for energy during long, bitter winters. The cold and the great distances may also explain the Russian love for pickled, preserved, and salted meat, fish, fruits and vegetables. These are the foods Russians would turn to when fresh products were not available, and which travelers would take along on trips between remote towns and villages.

While the Russian nobility traditionally gorged itself in unbridled gluttony, the peasants starved through bad harvests and years of famine. For many Russians, whether living in Russia or in emigration, the memory of starvation dates back to the severe famines following the Russian Civil War. According to psychological studies conducted after World War

II, Russians who suffered hunger during the war emerged from it with strong oral needs and an excessive preoccupation with food. My parents' friends could never forget the days when meat and butter were unknown and an egg was such an unexpected bounty it was gulped down raw. One former army officer told of living for a week on a jug of red wine he found hidden in a French barn while fleeing with his regiment from the advancing Germans.

The scars such hunger leaves create cravings which can be assuaged only by the assurance that food is not merely obtainable, but available in quantities such that no human being, no matter how gargantuan his appetite, could ever finish all that is set before him. My earliest childhood memories are of long afternoons spent at my parents' friends' houses at round tables decked out in white linen cloths and lace dollies and covered with an assortment of dishes that seemed to increase in number no matter how much the guests ate. As soon as one took a spoonful of chopped herring or a stuffed egg, yet another dish of *zakuski* (appetizers) popped up next to the slightly emptied bowl. Not having enough food for second and third helpings was the ultimate disgrace for a Russian émigré hostess. In urging their guests to eat, my mother's friends followed the traditional Russian ritual. The host insists that the guest have a bit more; the guest refuses; the host affects a very slightly injured "you-don't- really-like-it" look; the guest consents to take just the tiniest morsel and leaves half of it on his plate. The game has been played by the rules. The host has served the guest a bit more, and the guest has avoided the consequences of over-eating. And besides, as one Russian proverb says, "The more you eat, the more you want."

Though the Russian diet underwent various changes in the course of history, many of its contemporary staples go back to ancient times. Early Greek travelers in Russia commented on the abundance of different kinds of honey and sweet syrups, many of them derived from tree sap—cherry, currant, juniper, raspberry, and cloves. The sturgeon, a source of caviar, was mentioned by Herodotus: "Large fish are taken in it [the Dnepr river] of the sort called *antacaei*, without any prickly bones and good for pickling."[3] The food of Kievan Russia consisted primarily of wheat and rye breads and meat. Beef, lamb, pork, poultry, game, dairy products and fruits and vegetables such as apples, onions and beets were plentiful.

Russian food was subjected to successive foreign influences—Scandinavian, Tatar, Byzantine, Turkish, German and French. The allegedly Scandinavian Varangians, who were the first rulers of Russia, may be responsible for the introduction of fruit soups, smoked meats, cream sauces and herring. After St. Vladimir adopted Russian Orthodoxy as his country's religion in the tenth century, Byzantine foods such as lamb, eggplant, and raisins were brought to Russia. The Mongol invasion introduced the Russians to *koumiss* (fermented mare's milk) and other sour milk products, and to techniques for pickling cabbage.

By the fifteenth century, visitors to Russia were writing of "dishes with every delicacy, well dressed."[4] Tea was first introduced to Russia in 1638 by the Mongol Khan Altyn-Khan, who sent a present of 200 quarter-pound packages of wild dried tea to Tsar Mikhail Fedorovich. Nikolai Spafary, a scholar who was the Russian ambassador to

China forty years later, did much to promote the consumption of tea. In a long dispatch sent back to Moscow, he wrote that tea is "a good drink, and when you get used to it, much tastier." Tea was also praised for its ability to "refresh and purify the blood" and "to keep one awake during church services."

Tea was first grown within Russia at the beginning of the 1830s on the shores of the Black Sea, and cafés which served tea played an important role in Russian intellectual history. The Tsaregradskii Café, the Pechkina Coffee House, the Egorevskii Café were frequented by Gogol, Herzen, Belinsky and other famous Russian men of letters. Evidently the quantity of tea consumed was huge. The English traveler Sir Donald Mackenzie Wallace "looked in on some of the modest *traktirs* (café-bars) and gazed with wonder, not unmixed with fear, at the enormous quantity of weak tea which the inmates consumed."[5]

The image of Russian peasants sitting around their huts drinking cup after cup of tea is pure fiction. Tea was a luxury item until the twentieth century, since it was expensive and required a samovar, cups and saucers, sugar, and time for brewing. A folk poem describes how a peasant who was asked by his master to brew some tea hesitated a bit, threw some pepper, onion, and parsley into boiling water, and, on finding the result unsatisfactory, concluded it was because he had forgotten the salt.

The menus suggested by a sixteenth-century almanac-codex of religious and secular regulations, the *Domostroi*, show how little meat the peasant had, and how strictly the calendar of Church fasts regulated enjoyment of those bits that came his way: on meat days, bread and thick cabbage soup with lard; for supper: cabbage soup, milk, or kasha (porridge usually made from buckwheat groats or barley). On fast days, cabbage soup, thin kasha, sometimes with gravy, or peas and kasha. For Sunday and holiday dinners—a stuffed pastry or kasha with herring.

For the aristocracy, food was rich and plentiful. Feasts at the sixteenth-century court of Ivan the Terrible were legendary. One dinner the Tsar gave for 300 people consisted of an appetizer of five fowl and game courses including roasted peacock and cranes seasoned with ginger, three bouillons and three clear soups, and five main dishes including bear and reindeer loins and an entire calf.[6]

The nobility not only consumed large meals, but also gave away enormous quantities of food to monasteries in return for prayers. A donation made by one seventeenth-century family in partial payment for prayers for a boyar's soul consisted of twenty salted white sturgeon, 33 boiled pike, 130 carp, 40 pounds of cheese, 300 eggs, 16 gallons of mead, 100 pounds of butter, and 40 pounds of pressed caviar.

Many of today's dishes existed in their present form by the seventeenth century. The meal of one Russian noble consisted entirely of foods still served today by fine cooks of the old school: caviar, sturgeon, salted mushrooms, herring, *shchi* (cabbage soup), *ukha* (fish soup), a fish *pirog* (stuffed pie), and *olad'i* (fritters).[7] But despite a certain continuity, Russian cooking, like all aspects of Russian culture, has been subjected to two opposing trends during the past few centuries. Should Russia turn for inspiration to the West and borrow western foods, art, architecture, forms of government, literature, and even vocabulary, as was proposed by the nineteenth-century Westernizers, or should she rather look into the mirror of her own Slavic culture, based on Russian Orthodoxy, the peasant and his land, the commune, and Slavic linguistic and literary roots, as advocated by the so-called Slavophiles? The conflict between these two currents is strongly reflected in classical nineteenth-century Russian literature.

Russian peasant or "Slavophile" food was simple and earthy, consisting of products the peasant could easily grow and prepare. Cabbage, kasha, bread, stuffed pies, soups with a bit of meat and potatoes or cabbage and dishes using calves' or pigs' feet or liver, tongue, and kidneys are examples.

An army of proverbs attests to the widespread use of kasha: "He's got kasha in his head" (he's confused), "the kasha got cooked" (a mess started up), "you won't be able to cook kasha with him" (you won't get anywhere with him). According to an Arab traveler's tale, the last proverb dates from a Russian custom of sharing a meal of kasha with their former enemies as a sign of alliance and friendship when concluding a peace treaty.

The "westernizing" reforms of Peter the Great had as great an effect on cooking as they did on all other aspects of Russian life. While the Tsar disdained the excesses of his royal predecessors, he was not indifferent to gastronomic pleasures. He brought a French cook back with him from Paris and introduced coffee-drinking to Russia. From Holland and Germany he brought back Dutch-style apple cake, fried steaks, schnitzels, sausages, sauerkraut, and the custom of eating meat and game with fruits and jelly.[8]

Swiss and French chefs had begun to make their appearance in eighteenth-century Russia. However, it was during the first decades of the nineteenth century—due to the Napoleonic wars and a strong Russian interest in France—that Russian cooking was most greatly influenced by classic French cuisine. In this period such dishes were created as soup Bagration (cream of veal over asparagus, although the name was sometimes given to a puree of filet of sole), saddle of veal Prince Orloff (veal layered with mushrooms and onions), and pheasant Souvaroff (pheasant with truffles and *foie gras* under a pastry crust). The so-called Charlotte Russe was actually created in 1815 for Alexander I by the French chef Antoine Carême, who supervised the Tsar's kitchen in Paris in 1814–15 and at the Congress of Aix-la-Chapelle, and later spent a year in the Tsar's employ in St. Petersburg. French influence on Russian food remained strong until the 1917 Revolution. One of the best known Russian dishes, *Salat Olivier* (also known as Russian salad), was invented by the French chef who worked for the last tsar, Nicholas II. Many of the dishes created under French influence in the nineteenth century, such as soup Bagration or pheasant Souvaroff, underwent a second emigration and became part of the French classic repertory rather than the Russian.

By the mid-nineteenth century, the chic thing for a Russian noble to do was to import his own chef from Paris and teach him to adapt classic French cooking to Russian tastes. It became the fashion among Russian aristocrats to steal each other's chefs. One dignitary tried to get ahead of his competitors by sending a serf to Paris for culinary training only to receive the following note from the man: "I shall stay in France and you, sir, may make your own sauces or go without."

Upon returning home from Russia, several French chefs opened their own Russian restaurants and for years Paris was–and in the opinion of many gourmets still is–home to some of the best Russian food in the world.

Alphonse Petit was one of the many French chefs who worked in Russia. Upon his return to Paris from his post as cook for the Russian Minister of Justice, Count Panin, he wrote a fascinating little reference work for French cooks planning to enter Russian service. Petit alerted his colleagues to the fact that many Russians traveling in Italy, Germany, Switzerland, and France were actively looking for French chefs to take back with them. He warned of the language difficulties, and provided a lengthy French and Russian glossary of culinary terms, along with store addresses, and lists of recipes. "Furnished with this work," he concluded, "the cook arriving in St. Petersburg or Moscow will have no more problems than someone who has lived there for several years."[9]

Petit's book offers delightful glimpses of Russian eating habits during the mid-nineteenth century. While warning the prospective chef that Russians observe their many church fasts strictly, he stressed that foodstuffs were abundant in Russia. In St. Petersburg, he wrote, it was easy to obtain "all kinds of preserved vegetables, fruits, lobsters, oysters, *pâtés de foie gras*, cheeses, English and Westphalian hams, truffles, wines and liquors. English sauces, etc., are at all the groceries of the capital, along with native chicken game, fish, cereals, vegetables, spices, butter, eggs, milk and cream."[10] Some of the Russian products were quite novel for French tastes. Two of Petit's colleagues, Urbain Dubois and Emile Bernard, the personal cooks of the King and Queen of Prussia, commented in a weighty tome entitled *La Cuisine Classique: Etudes pratiques, raisonnées, et démonstratives de l'école française appliquée au service de la Russie*,[11] that while the reindeer tongues sold in St. Petersburg in winter were usually frozen stiff, they were no less prized by gourmets. Petit advises chefs planning to work in Russia that at dinnertime, plates of *hors d'oeuvre* including radishes, anchovies, sliced sausages, caviar, and a few hot dishes were set out not in the dining room, but in an adjacent room. Petit noted that if caviar was served, Russian custom dictated that it be accompanied by a small plate of chopped scallions. Such chopping, he noted, is beneath the dignity of the master chef, and should be relegated to the *Maître d'hôtel* or *buffetier*.

Often called on to produce meals for large households, cooks such as Petit did not spare ingredients. All of his recipes are intended for ten people. His "Slavonic Soup" consisted of two kinds of fish stewed with fifty sautéed oysters, pike dumplings, and a bottle of Sauternes. One of his typical fast day menus included a clear sturgeon soup with vegetables, a large pie stuffed with small fish, sterlet aspic with horseradish sauce, fried fish cutlets and lentils *à la Maître d'hôtel*. A pear and prune compote completed this frugal repast.

Hundreds of menus of lunches, dinners, suppers and buffets served at the homes of Russian nobility and royalty are cited in *La Cuisine classique* and in a contemporary work by A. Lobanov-Rostovskii, *Tablettes Gastronomiques de St. Petersbourg, redigées par un amateur et précédées des ouvrages à consulter*.[12] French dishes far outnumber Russian ones, which are often merely classic French recipes adapted to make use of native Russian foodstuffs, such as the fresh fish much admired by visiting chefs.

The rivalry between elegant Gallic fare and Slavophile Russian food is reflected in fiction as well as in fact. In Alexander Pushkin's novel in verse, *Eugene Onegin*, the hero, a rarified Westernized dandy, eats rare roast beef and imported delicacies such as truffles, *foie gras*, Limburger cheese and pineapples, washed down by Bordeaux and French champagne. In contrast, the family of the heroine, Tatiana (the incarnation of the pure Russian soul), serves pickled mushrooms, *bliny* (pancakes), *kvas*, an over-salted *pirog*, and Russian champagne. Onegin's neighbors find his habit of drinking red wine rather than vodka quite bizarre. Forty years later, in *Anna Karenina*, Leo Tolstoi describes how Konstantin Levin, the author's mouthpiece for his ideas on Russian attachment to the land and to the "Russian" way of life, thinks to himself that he would much prefer *shchi* (cabbage soup) and kasha to the French white wine (Cachet Blanc) and imported Flensburg oysters which Anna's brother Oblonsky orders for him at lunch in an elegant restaurant.

In Chekhov's play *The Three Sisters*, "Russian" food symbolizes the morass of mediocre provincial life from which one character dreams of freeing himself: "I see how my children and I will be freed from idleness, from *kvas*, from goose with cabbage, from vulgar parasitism."[13]

By the end of the nineteenth century, Russian cooking was a blend of the Slavic, so-called "peasant," tradition that made heavy use of cabbage, sour cream, pork, potatoes, kasha and bread puddings, and the French cuisine with its refined sauces, delicate seasonings, and products new to Russia (such as almonds), new dishes (such as mousses), and new techniques such as poaching fish dumplings in court bouillon.

The classic Russian cookbook, Elena Molokhovets' *The Gift to Young Housewives, or the Means of Reducing Household Expenditures*, published around 1870, offers recipes for both frugal Russian dishes and French *haute cuisine*. This collection of over 4,000 recipes is a veritable encyclopedia of Russian food. It gives a fascinating picture of the life of a young housewife who is obliged to serve up elegant nine-course dinners for twenty-five people and must then worry about how to make economical use of dried calves' stomachs (store cheese in them) or of water used to boil rice (a good hand lotion).[14]

The struggle between the pure Russian tradition and foreign influences is still going on. Soviet cookbooks warned of the danger of excessive nationalism in gastronomic matters and stressed that so- called "foreign borrowings" such as sausage, cabbage, cutlets, rich sauces, and mousses should be accepted as part of Russian cooking, while purely "peasant" but non-nutritive pre-revolutionary "Russian" dishes such as *tiuria* (a thin concoction of *kvas*, onion, and dried bread) or soups made from onion-flavored barley grass should not be retained by modern Russian cooks out of misguided feelings of national pride. One author warns that "these dishes are as inappropriate to our lives as an old cart on the streets of a modern city or a wooden plow on kolkhoz fields."[15]

The severe economic setbacks that followed the war, heavy work schedules and long lines in stores did not make cooking a popular pastime. Soviet cookbooks stressed the need for good nutrition and tried to educate the population in the basic principles of food preparation and home economics. Cooking was treated primarily as a science of health (the kitchen is a "home laboratory") rather than as an art. One cookbook from this time recounts crop statistics for the past five years. Others stress table manners, and one recipe book informs us that "it is not recommended that one eat off the end of a knife, for in so doing, it is possible to cut the lips or even the tongue. . . . The napkin is for wiping the mouth and not for blowing the nose . . ."[16]

For political and ideological reasons, Soviet cookbooks paid great attention to the cuisines of non-Russian nationalities such as the Uzbeks, Georgians, Armenians and Balts. The extent to which the cuisines of those and other nationalities had become integrated into one huge "Soviet" cuisine was heavily stressed. The "Russian" dishes found in Soviet publications basically consist of the same limited assortment to be found in most of the Russian cookbooks printed abroad. My own gastronomic experiences during numerous trips to the USSR and in compiling a guide to Moscow restaurants,[17] convinced me that the rigidly planned and inefficiently run Soviet restaurant industry provided little opportunity for rebirth of the old Russian cuisine.

Today, however, there is a resurgence of interest in gastronomy in Russia, and many foreign cookbooks have been translated. New Russian cookbooks and histories of Russian gastronomy are contributing to the effort to preserve the national heritage, and a spate of new restaurants offer a variety of Russian and foreign dishes. However, some of the recipes which emigrated have still not found their way home, and many of the food products sold in stores and served in restaurants are extremely expensive, making gastronomic experimentation impossible for many.

The wide range of superb dishes that my parents' friends used to make constituted a unique and fairly complete representation of nineteenth-century Russian cooking. Their hundreds of recipes, carefully recorded for generations and easily adaptable to modern conditions, were not available in either Soviet or western books on Russian cooking.

As I recalled the long afternoons of my childhood, I realized the urgency of collecting and preserving these "recipes in emigration." Quite a few of the cooks I knew were well into their seventies and eighties and there was a real possibility that the historical heritage of Russian cooking which they had so carefully kept alive might pass on with them. Sadly, many of the contributors of recipes to the earlier edition are no longer with us.

Though I did not realize it as a child, my parents' friends were the last of a unique generation. Born under the tsars, tossed about the globe by events of history, fabulously rich one month and desperately poor the next, educated with a year of French *pension* here and German boarding school there, they were all fluent in Russian, English, French and German—cosmopolitans in the true sense of the word. They took their recipes (and their mothers' and grandmothers' recipes) with them as they emigrated from one country to another. Wherever they went, they adapted their Russian dishes to the cultures and circumstances in which they found themselves. While some of them worked, they were wives, mothers and cooks first. For them, cooking was a matter of pride, a measure of their own self-respect and the esteem in which their friends held them.

These women had another trait in common—a unique dignity. It was the dignity of having survived and having retained a cultural and spiritual identity and integrity. They were always elegantly dressed for their long afternoons of tea and talk. In fact, they were perfectly dressed even when they went to the grocery store or the hairdresser, in rustling black silk dresses with a single strand of matched pearls and earrings or gold pendants and cameos, seamed stockings and bright red lipstick, with lacquered hair and tapered eyebrows, perfectly manicured hands playing with gold and white cigarette holders. The Russian maids who helped them serve—and there seemed to be an unlimited number of these women ready and willing to help bake cabbage pies and nut cakes or skim stocks and chop mushrooms—were small, rotund, middle-aged ladies with thick upper arms who wore sleeveless print dresses even in mid-winter as they spent days near a hot oven, padding back and forth to the kitchen in flat felt shoes and rumpled aprons, dirty-blond hair pulled back in tight buns from wide foreheads.

I loved watching them cook, and our wonderful Austrian housekeeper could imitate any Russian dish by tasting it once or even from a description. For years I watched her bake, fry, and stir, and as I became increasingly interested in Russian culture my interest in this unusual cuisine also grew.

Some of the women who contributed recipes to this book were famous cooks within the Russian community. Several had served as food consultants for magazines and television programs dealing with Russian culture. Others were shy and retiring souls who were quite surprised that anyone would be interested in their mothers' recipes.

The émigré ladies gave me their recipes in long sessions over their kitchen and dining room tables set out with tea, cakes and liqueurs. Out of their desk drawers emerged small brown-covered notebooks and scraps of paper on which their mothers had jotted down recipes, sheet after sheet of carefully noted and hastily scribbled instructions ranging from detailed directions and comments that "this dish is especially tasty" to statements such as "put in as much flour as fits into the dough." Some recipes were crossed out because they had failed the cook one time too many. Sometimes recipes listed only basic ingredients, or read "put in some butter" or "as much sugar as you like." They were written in the old Russian orthography, which gave them an archaic tinge somewhat akin to Victorian English. Through guesswork, trial and error, and long hours of testing, I struggled to recreate these dishes. Comments and tastings by a wide group of Russian-American friends and by the contributors themselves were of great assistance.

While sharing their treasured recipes they loved to talk about the past. They talked about the twenties in Paris when princes were driving cabs and counts were waiting on tables, when you could stay up all night going from one Russian restaurant to another and end up at Les Halles with a bowl of thoroughly un-Russian onion soup. They recalled the years spent in Berlin, the days sipping coffee with whipped cream in cafés on Kurfürstendamm Street. They spoke of Prague with its abundance of Russian newspapers and journals, and where over breakfast, lunch, tea and dinner they chatted, joked and sighed, waiting for the political disturbances in their motherland to calm down so that they could go home.

But these émigrés with whom I was raised in America knew that they could not go home. They always spoke of that event which had shattered their lives a second time and brought them together in America–World War II. In 1941, my father abandoned a promising career as a movie director in France to start life over in the museum world, while my mother put her knowledge of French to good use at the French Cultural Services in New York. Whenever they met friends, conversation would turn to the war–to the fear inspired by night-time air-raid sirens, the spread of wild rumors. They recalled the hours wives spent waiting, trying to find out the fate of their soldier husbands. They remembered how they had stood in endless lines in musty offices, waiting in more lines in the American Consulate for their visas, wondering if the affidavits would come from an uncle or friend in America. And there were more lines as they clutched their ration cards and gazed at the bare shelves of empty stores.

And a minute later, sitting in their well-stocked American kitchens, they would be discussing sour cream dough and short pastry. Sometimes one of them would describe a dish for which she had no precise recipe. Then she would try to find the recipe in a collection of old, tattered, out-of-print Russian cookbooks, packed away on dusty closet shelves between crumbling issues of *Novoe Russkoe Slovo*, the émigré Russian newspaper, and piles of old photos.

Recipes from such books were not always helpful, however, for they often gave either vague or incredibly gigantic quantities of ingredients, such as 36 hard-boiled egg yolks for a dessert. "Tschy à la russe" made use of "2–3 kilograms beef, 1 duck, 1 chicken, 6 small smoked sausages, carrots, onions, and cabbage"[18] among other ingredients. A "capricious baba" was described as "delicious when successful, which rarely happens." I have not tried to adapt for American kitchens a recipe which entails digging a hole in the backyard, entombing a large salted ham in it for six months, and then sending the maids out to dig it up. I have also omitted a recipe for marinating bear paws at least forty-eight hours before grilling and serving them with sweet-and-sour sauce. But many of the dishes suggested by the ladies, and many of the recipes in their old cookbooks can be easily reproduced in American kitchens and require neither special skills nor fancy equipment. Indeed, many can be made more easily and quickly today, thanks to machines such as blenders and food processors that perform in minutes formerly time-consuming tasks such as chopping nuts or grating chocolate.

These traditional Russian dishes are both simple and elegant, economical and luxurious, though some of the most delicious are made with plain, natural ingredients–dishes such as fillet of fish covered with lightly seasoned sour cream, a fluffy dessert of black bread, apples, and jam, or an appetizer of carrots and green pepper.

There should be no substitution for top quality natural products in making these recipes. While some of those given to me specified time-saving canned vegetables, frozen or fresh products may, of course, be used instead to better advantage. Using a sugar substitute or replacing butter with margarine may qualitatively affect the recipes, but either salted or unsalted butter may be used unless otherwise specified. Fat-free or low-calorie sour cream should not be used in doughs and sauces because they do not retain their consistency properly when heated.

In my attempt to preserve traditional Russian cooking, I collected over 400 recipes. Many of those included here were given to me by Russian friends, and the source of each is gratefully acknowledged. The rest are my adaptations of old Russian recipes. I have tried to include recipes representative of all aspects of classic Russian cooking, while omitting those that are totally impractical or unlikely to appeal to American tastes.

The book is divided into seven sections: *zakuski*; soups; *pirogs* and pancakes; fish; meats and poultry; vegetable, grain, cheese and egg dishes; desserts. A separate section follows on jams, sauces and drinks.

The *zakuski*, or appetizers, that precede almost any meal are a peculiarly Russian tradition. They are often presented on platters on a table in a room adjoining the dining room. There the guest is received, inspired by his first shot of vodka, and reassured by the array of *zakuski* that there is going to be plenty of food. Such a table of appetizers may easily be mistaken for an entire meal, and for the normal, non-Russian appetite, would be quite sufficient, but the Russian proceeds to dinner, which inevitably begins with soup, accompanied by bread—white, black, and plenty of it, or stuffed pastries, small (*pirozhki*), or large (*pirog*). The variety of these pastries is astonishing. The doughs may be made with yeast, sour cream, cream cheese, or potato, and the fillings may contain ground beef, veal, liver, fish, cabbage, sauerkraut, carrots and mushrooms. There are still other ingredients, some of which are included in the rhapsody to a *pirog* spoken by one of Gogol's characters in *Dead Souls:*

> "Make a four-cornered fish pie," he was saying, smacking his lips. . . "in one corner put a sturgeon's cheeks and dried spinal cord, in another put buckwheat porridge, little mushrooms, onions, soft roes, and brains and something else. . . and see that the crust on one side is well browned and a little less done on the other. . . and as a garnish for the sturgeon, cut a beetroot into little stars and put in some smelts and mushrooms, and, you know, a turnip and carrots and kidney beans and something else . . ."[19]

Huge and filling as the *pirog* may be, it is not considered substantial enough for a main course and will be succeeded by fowl or meat. There has always been a variety of meat in Russia, but because it is expensive, Russians have invented many ways in which to stretch a small quantity. There are croquettes, puddings stuffed and unstuffed, meat rolls in sauce, pot roasts with vegetables, meat loaves, and stews. Many of these dishes are extremely convenient for the cook because they taste better reheated the next day. Cheese and egg dishes have always been popular in Russia because of the meatless fast days. Some of the recipes for these dishes, such as cottage cheese pudding or egg pudding, are suitable for light, one-dish meals. Eggplant stuffed with mushrooms and a few other vegetable dishes can also constitute the main dish of a light meal. That staple of Russian fare, kasha can be served plain, with fried mushrooms, or baked with cottage cheese into a sweet pudding.

It is perhaps in the area of desserts, particularly cakes, that Russians triumph. The desserts are extraordinarily varied. There are puddings, mousses creams, ices, and a wide assortment of cakes, cookies, and candies. If the dessert is cake, there will be more than one on the table because Russians feel that serving just one cake for dessert is rather stingy.

Dessert is always accompanied by tea, without which no meal is complete. While cup after cup is drunk at a meal, tea is never drunk alone. The notion of drinking "naked tea," tea without at least a tidbit to eat, is inconceivable, and there is therefore a constant supply of cakes and cookies in the house to serve along with tea at any hour of the day or night.

A variety of fruit liqueurs, often homemade, may be served after dinner. There are punches of wine, champagne, and brandy, and there are a few more typically Russian drinks, such as *sbiten'* and *kvas* to warm you when it is cold or refresh you when it is hot.

As the Russians say, "To your health!. . . *Za vashe zdorov'e!*"

NOTES

1. Anton Chekhov, "The Siren," *Collected Works* (Moscow: Khudozhestvennaia literatura, 1962), V, 337. Author's translation.

2. Ivan Goncharov, *Oblomov*, in *Collected Works* (Moscow: Gosizdat. 1959). IV, 93–94. Author's translation.

3. Quoted in John Lawrence, *A History of Russia* (New York: Farrar, Strauss, and Cudahy, 1960), pp. 11–12.

4. Harold Lamb, *The March of Muscovy* (New York: Doubleday, 1966), p. 73.

5. Sir Donald Mackenzie Wallace, *Russia on the Eve of War and Revolution* (New York: Random House, 1961), p. 196.

6. Marie Markevitch, *The Epicure in Imperial Russia* (San Francisco: 1941), p. 3.

7. Nina Selivanova, *Dining and Wining in Old Russia* (New York: Dutton, pp. 13–14.

8. Vasili Klyuchevsky, *Peter the Great* (New York: Random House, 1958), p. 44.

9. Alphonse Petit, *La Gastronomie en Russie* (Paris: Emile Mellier, 1960), p. vii.

10. *Ibid.* p. 10.

11. *La Cuisine Classique: Etudes pratiques, raisonnées, et démonstratives de l'école française appliquée au service de la Russie* (Paris: E. Dentu: Palais-Royal, 1874).

12. A. Lobanov-Rostovskii, *Tablettes Gastronomiques de St. Petersbourg, redigées par un amateur et précédées des ouvrages à consulter* (St. Petersbourg: Edouard Prat, 1856).

13. I am grateful to Professor Emeritus Simon Karlinsky of the University of California at Berkeley for this reference.

14. Simon Karlinsky, "The Vanished World of Elena Molokhovets," *University Publishing*, No. 8, Fall 1979. A poem by Arsenii Tarkovskii written during the famine of the 30s and 40s raises the question whether Molokhovets is continuing to give her advice to the shades in the next life or is being gnawed by worms. Molokhovets's cookbook, *Classic Russian Cooking: A Gift to Young Housewives*, has been beautifully translated and edited by Joyce Toomre (Indian University Press: Bloomington & Indianapolis, 1992).

15. *Russkaia kulinariia* (Moscow: Ekonomika, 1972).

16. See *Kniga o vkusnoi i zdorovoi pishche* (Moscow: Pishchepromizdat, 1952), and *Priglashaem k stolu* (Dnepropetrovsk: Promin: 1970).

17. Lynn and Wesley Fisher, *The Moscow Gourmet: Dining Out in the Capital of the USSR* (Ann Arbor: Ardis, 1974).

18. *La Cuisine Classique*, p. 20.

19. Nikolai Gogol, *Dead Souls*, trans. David Magarshack (New York: Penguin Books, 1978), p. 311.

zakuski

z a k u s k i

The best zakuska, if you want to know, is herring. You eat a piece of it with a little onion and with mustard sauce–right away. . . While you still feel the sparks in your stomach, eat caviar, plain or, if you wish, with a bit of lemon, then a bit of salted radish, then again some herring, but best of all. . . saffron milk-cap mushrooms–if you chop them up as fine as caviar, and see, eat them with onion, with olive oil. . . What a feast!
—ANTON CHEKHOV, *The Siren*

The *zakuski* which begin a Russian meal may be no more than one or two simple dishes –cucumbers in sour cream and a few slices of pickled herring, or an entire table spread with a buffet-style meal of countless small plates.

Caviar, the most elegant of the *zakuski*, is served cold with no garnish except, perhaps, an accompanying plate of chopped hardboiled eggs and finely minced onions. Some people like to add a squeeze of lemon juice, but for many Russians this is heresy–or a way of masking the taste of a poor quality product. The finest is pale gray caviar from the *beluga* sturgeon. The next best is the darker and slightly smaller-grained *sevriuga*. Caviar from the still smaller *osetrina* is also of excellent quality, but most Russians prefer a good red caviar (*ketovaia*) to pressed or lumpfish black caviar, for unless the pressed caviar is made from good sturgeon roe, it is primarily useful as a decoration with a pretense to elegance.

An assortment of *zakuski* usually includes a variety of small, open-faced sandwiches: cold smoked fish (whitefish, sturgeon, or lox), anchovies or sardines (plain or mashed into a paste with butter and mustard), cold tongue and pickles, and ham, sausages, or salami. Vegetable canapés are made from combinations of tomatoes, cucumbers, radishes or scallions with sour cream. Cold fresh fish may be served in spiced tomato sauce and eaten with black bread. Herrings are preserved in wine, bathed in sour cream and mustard, or chopped with a variety of ingredients including apples, hardboiled eggs, olive oil and sour cream.

Onions, cucumbers and mushrooms are marinated or pickled. Eggplant, squash and mushrooms are chopped fine, fried in oil, simmered to a soft consistency, and served very cold on black bread. Veal, pigs' feet or fish are served jellied, with vegetables cut into attractive patterns set into aspic. A hot *zakuski* array might include mushrooms, kidneys, or chicken livers in sour cream, small meatballs, frankfurters in tomato sauce or *pirozhki*.

Eggs appear stuffed with anchovies, caviar, ham, liver, onions, horseradish, tongue or sardines. Cream cheese and cottage cheese are blended with assorted spices into a wide variety of dips and spreads. Molded pâtés of calf or chicken liver may be decorated with slices of hardboiled egg or sprigs of parsley. Any proper *zakuski* table also includes an assortment of salads, though the Russian word *salat* is not associated with leafy greens, but with combinations of chopped vegetables, meats, or fish bound by mayonnaise or sour cream sauce. The smaller the pieces, the more elegant the salad. For best results, food should be cut into one-quarter-inch cubes (the size of miniature dice). Fortunately, a food processor or chopper makes the cutting easy.

The pickles used should be kosher dills or any sour kind (do not use sweet pickles). Herbs should be fresh unless otherwise indicated. Paprika should be sweet (Hungarian, if possible). The vinegar should be wine vinegar unless otherwise specified. If whole herring fillets are unavailable, prepared jarred herring (such as the Vita brand) may be used instead. Commercially prepared white or red horseradish is used in most recipes (if you use freshly grated, reduce the amount to taste). Dressing should be added to salads at the last minute and in small quantities in order to ensure that the sauce does not overpower the other ingredients or become watery. Bear in mind that the ingredients in salads can be varied and that salads provide a tasty and economical way to use leftovers of all sorts.

COLD ZAKUSKI

open-faced small sandwiches

Canapés are a central part of any *zakuski* table. They are usually made up of no more than two or three ingredients, carefully chosen for color, flavor, and texture contrast. While a few sprigs of fresh parsley may be added to the serving tray, it is not customary to garnish *zakuski* with herbs or chopped spices.

A tray of mixed small canapés might include the following toppings, spread on small squares of pumpernickel or rye bread:

1) Grated Parmesan cheese mixed with an equal amount of butter and sprinkled with freshly ground black pepper and topped with mashed sardines.

2) Smoked salmon, topped by a thin slice of hardboiled egg.

3) Tiny pieces of smoked fish such as whitefish or smoked sturgeon.

4) Cream cheese topped with red caviar and a sprinkle of lemon juice.

5) Cream cheese, lumpfish caviar and a sprinkling of chopped onion.

6) Thinly sliced boiled ham, topped with chopped or thinly sliced hard boiled egg.

7) Equal amounts of butter and horseradish, covered with thin slices of tongue and a sliver of dill pickle.

8) Hardboiled eggs mixed with an equal amount of chopped and drained tomatoes, minced parsley, dill, sugar and salt, bound with just enough mayonnaise to hold the mixture together.

9) Chopped cucumbers blended with an equal quantity of hardboiled egg yolks, chopped parsley, salt and pepper, blended with just enough mayonnaise to make a paste. (These should be made at the last minute or cucumbers will give off water.)

10) 4 grated radishes, blended with 1 chopped hardboiled egg, 1 Tbsp. sour cream, 1/2 tsp. chopped dill, and salt to taste. (This should be done at the last minute or the radishes will give off water.)

11) 2–3 grated carrots blended with 1 1/2 tsp. mayonnaise, 1 clove minced garlic, 1/4 tsp. sugar, and salt and pepper to taste.

12) 2–3 chopped hardboiled eggs blended with 1 tsp. horseradish, 1 Tbsp. sour cream, 1/4 tsp. sugar, 1/4 tsp. vinegar and salt to taste.

13) 2 hardboiled egg yolks, mashed with 1 Tbsp. grated Swiss cheese, 1 tsp. butter, 1/2 tsp. mustard, and salt and pepper to taste.

stuffed eggs

These are favorite Russian zakuski. The basic idea is half a hardboiled egg, yolk removed, stuffed with a combination of the yolk and other ingredients. Preferably the yolk should be sieved, but if you are short on time this step can be omitted.

1) Stuff hardboiled egg halves with a mixture of the yolks and equal amounts of butter and cooked chopped chicken livers, blended with minced scallions (green part) and salt and pepper to taste.

2) To each 2 hardboiled egg yolks add 1 Tbsp. chopped cooked chicken livers, 1/2 tsp. minced onion, 1 tsp. butter, 1/2 tsp. chopped dill, 1/2 tsp. chopped parsley, 1/2 tsp. cognac and salt and pepper to taste.

3) Mix 2 hardboiled yolks with 1 Tbsp. chopped ham, 1 tsp. grated Parmesan cheese, 1/2 tsp. mustard, 1/2 tsp. chopped parsley, 2 tsp. sour cream and salt and pepper to taste.

4) To each 2 hardboiled yolks add 1 chopped sardine or 1 Tbsp. chopped herring, 1 tsp. butter, 1/2 tsp. chopped parsley, and 1/2 tsp. minced scallions.

5) To each 2 hardboiled egg yolks add 1 minced anchovy and 1 tsp. butter.

6) Blend hardboiled egg yolks with an equal amount of butter; season with sharp mustard and pepper to taste.

7) To each 2 chopped hardboiled egg yolks add 1 tsp. grated Parmesan cheese, 1 tsp. butter, 1/2 tsp. mustard, and salt and pepper to taste.

8) Mix 2 chopped hardboiled yolks with 1/2 tsp. grated horseradish, 1/2 tsp. lemon juice, 1 tsp. light cream, and salt to taste.

smoked salmon and red caviar torte

A first course for an elegant dinner

DOUGH:
3 eggs, separated
½ tsp. salt
1¾ cups flour
1 cup sour cream

FILLING:
3 eggs
¼ lb. (1 stick) unsalted butter
2 scallions
Pinch salt
3½ oz. smoked salmon
3½ oz. red caviar
½ cup sour cream

To make dough:
Beat egg yolks well with salt. Add alternating spoonfuls of flour and sour cream, beating well, until all of the mixture is used up. Beat egg whites stiff and carefully fold into mixture. Grease two 8-inch cake pans and divide mixture between them equally. Bake in 350-degree oven for 15–20 minutes until dough is puffy and knife inserted in center comes out clean.

To make filling:
Hardboil eggs and chop finely. Cream butter and blend in chopped eggs until smooth. Chop scallions (both green and white parts) and mix with egg-butter mixture. Add pinch of salt and blend.

When dough layers have cooled remove from pans and invert so that smooth side is on top. Spread first layer with ½ of butter cream and cover with thin slices of smoked salmon. Spread puffy side of second layer with cream and press down tightly over salmon-covered first layer. Reserve one tablespoon of red caviar. Mix sour cream with rest of caviar and spread over top layer. Put reserved caviar in a small mound in center. May be decorated with additional strips of scallions or thin slices of lemon peel.
Serves 8.

❖ red caviar torte

This is simpler to make than the smoked salmon and red caviar torte, and is also an elegant beginning to a meal

7 hardboiled eggs, peeled
¼ lb. butter, softened
1 small onion, peeled and finely diced
Small pinch cayenne pepper
½ cup sour cream
5 oz. red salmon caviar

Chop 5 eggs into very small pieces; put the other 2 through a food processor until nearly powdery. Blend the butter with the onion and cayenne, and add the eggs. Reserve one teaspoon of chopped egg. Place the egg mixture on a plate and mold into a flat round, about one inch thick. Chill for one hour in refrigerator

Using a large spatula, cover the top of the egg mixture with the sour cream and smooth it over until eggs are no longer visible. Using two spoons, carefully place the caviar in the center so that there is a border of sour cream around the edge of the plate. Sprinkle the reserved chopped eggs in the center of the caviar, and chill again until you are ready to serve. *Serves 8.*

herring snacks
 WEIL

2 fillets Matjes herring
12 miniature rye slices, or 3 whole slices rye bread
½ cup sour cream
1 Tbsp. fresh minced dill

Toast bread lightly. Slice herring into 12 equal pieces. Combine sour cream and dill. Spread a thin layer on each toast, cover with a piece of herring, and top with more sour cream. If using whole rye bread, cut into quarters. *Makes 12 herring snacks.*

stuffed celery
ODESSER

Stuff wide celery stalks with cream cheese and sprinkle with sweet paprika. Top with a thin layer of red caviar. Sprinkle lightly with salt and pepper.

stuffed cucumbers

2 cucumbers
2 eggs, hardboiled, peeled and chopped
8 radishes, finely chopped
1 Tbsp. chopped parsley
1 Tbsp. chopped dill
⅔ cup sour cream
Salt to taste

Peel and halve cucumbers; remove seeds. Halves should form large shells. Combine all remaining ingredients and fill cucumber shells.

NOTE: *Do not make this too long in advance or radishes will water. Serves 4.*

baklazhannaia ikra (eggplant caviar)

B. VINOGRADOVA

1 medium eggplant
1 medium green bell pepper
1 small onion, chopped
¼ cup vegetable oil
1 8½-oz. can tomatoes
1 tsp. salt
Pinch pepper
1–2 Tbsp. lemon juice

Prick eggplant in several places and wrap loosely in foil. Wrap green pepper in foil and bake both vegetables in 350-degree oven for 25 minutes until soft. Cool. Peel eggplant and chop fine; seed, derib and chop pepper and combine with eggplant. Sauté chopped onion slowly in oil until soft; add drained tomatoes, and cook over low heat for 5 minutes. Add eggplant, green pepper, salt, pepper, and lemon juice to taste, and simmer 15 minutes. Taste for seasoning. Puree for a few seconds in blender until smooth but still thick. Serve very cold on black bread. *Serves 6–8.*

b a k l a z h a n n a i a   i k r a   I I
NABOKOVA

2 large eggplants
1 onion, peeled and finely chopped
½ cup vegetable oil
1 Tbsp. tomato paste
1 clove garlic, peeled and minced
1 Tbsp. sugar
½ tsp. salt, or to taste
1 Tbsp. minced dill
¼ tsp. red wine vinegar

Prick eggplants with fork; wrap loosely in foil and bake 20–35 minutes in 350-degree oven until quite soft. Let cool. Peel and puree pulp lightly in blender or food processor. Heat oil in saucepan and sauté onion; cook for 5 minutes until onion is light golden color. Add eggplant pulp and all other ingredients; simmer for 10 minutes, stirring constantly. Taste for seasoning. Chill until very cold, and serve with black bread. *Serves 6–8.*

b a k l a z h a n n a i a   i k r a   I I I
MARTIN

1 medium eggplant
1 onion, peeled and finely chopped
1 clove garlic, peeled and minced
2 Tbsp. olive oil
1 8-oz. can tomato sauce
3 Tbsp. ketchup
Juice of ½ lemon
1 Tbsp. sugar
Salt and pepper to taste

Prick eggplant; cover loosely with foil and bake in 350-degree oven for 35–40 minutes. Cool. Remove skin and chop pulp coarsely. Cook onion and garlic in olive oil until soft and transparent. Add all other ingredients and simmer, covered, for 20 minutes, stirring occasionally. Taste for seasoning, and add lemon juice, salt and pepper as needed. Chill and serve with black bread. *Serves 4–6.*

squash caviar

2 lbs. yellow squash or zucchini, scrubbed
1 onion, peeled and chopped
¼ to ⅓ cup vegetable oil
3 Tbsp. tomato paste
1 tsp. red wine vinegar
1 tsp. sugar
½ tsp. salt
Pinch pepper
2 scallions, chopped (green parts only)

Scrub but do not peel zucchini. Slice thinly. Sauté gently with onion in oil until quite soft. Add tomato paste, vinegar, sugar, salt, and pepper, and simmer 5 minutes. Puree in blender and taste for seasoning. Chill until very cold and sprinkle with chopped scallions. Serve on black bread. *Serves 6.*

squash and eggplant caviar

1 small eggplant
1 zucchini, scrubbed
1 onion, peeled and chopped
½ cup shredded cabbage
2 carrots, cleaned and sliced
2 scallions, chopped (green and white parts)
½ cup vegetable oil
2 Tbsp. tomato paste
2 tsp. red wine vinegar
Salt
Pepper

Prick eggplant with fork. Wrap it and zucchini loosely in foil, and bake in 350-degree oven for 40 minutes. Slowly fry onion, cabbage, carrots and scallions in oil. Add tomato paste, and simmer until soft. Peel eggplant; chop eggplant and squash and add to vegetable mixture. Simmer 10–15 minutes; add vinegar, salt, pepper, and taste for seasoning. Puree ⅔ of mixture in blender, and combine with remaining mixture. Chill. Taste for seasoning, and serve very cold with black bread. *Serves 6.*

beet caviar

1 8½-oz. can beets
1 Tbsp. commercially prepared or 1 tsp. freshly grated horseradish
½ tsp. caraway seeds
Pinch salt
1 tsp. sugar
1½ Tbsp. red wine vinegar
1½ Tbsp. vegetable oil

Drain beets and puree in blender. Add all other ingredients and mix. Chill for several hours, and serve as a dip or spread on black bread. *Serves 4–6.*

mushroom caviar

¼ lb. mushrooms
3 small onions, peeled
2 Tbsp. vegetable oil
1 Tbsp. white vinegar
1 tsp. Dijon-style mustard
1 Tbsp. minced dill
Salt
Pepper

Wash mushrooms. Boil in salted water to cover until soft, about 5–10 minutes. Drain and chop fairly fine. Chop onions and mix with mushrooms. Combine oil, vinegar, mustard, dill, salt, and pepper, and blend well. Combine with onion-mushroom mixture and chill until very cold. Serve with black bread. *Serves 4.*

marinated mushrooms

BAKER

A tasty cocktail accompaniment, these will keep for 2–3 days in the refrigerator

1 lb. mushrooms
¾-1 cup vegetable oil
3 Tbsp. red wine vinegar
¼ cup minced parsley
2–3 cloves garlic, peeled and minced
1 tsp. salt
½ tsp. pepper

Mix all ingredients except mushrooms. Wash mushrooms; if large, cut into two or three rough pieces. Put mushrooms in a glass bowl and pour marinade over them. Refrigerate for at least 3–4 hours. Turn once to be sure the mushrooms marinate on all sides. Serve on lettuce leaves with some of the marinade poured over them. (Can also be served on cocktail picks.) *Makes 4 appetizers, or cocktail snacks for 6–8.*

pickled mushrooms
ODESSER

½ lb. mushrooms
1 cup water
1 Tbsp. salt
½ cup white vinegar
3 peppercorns
3 cloves
½ tsp. sugar
1 bay leaf
3 Tbsp. vegetable oil

Clean mushrooms; if very large, cut in half. Boil in water and salt for 5 minutes; add all other ingredients except oil and simmer another 15 minutes. Cool slightly, and pour into glass jar. Cover with thin layer of oil. Close jar and keep in refrigerator for at least 2 days. Will keep for about 1 week in refrigerator. *Serves 4–6 as cocktail snacks.*

pickled cucumbers

6–8 small cucumbers (no more than 5–6 inches long)
Water
1 Tbsp. salt
1 Tbsp. chopped dill
½ tsp. pepper
1 clove garlic, peeled and chopped
½ tsp. fresh chopped tarragon, or ¼ tsp. dried
½ cup white vinegar

Cover cucumbers in bowl with hot salted water and let stand for 20 minutes. Drain. In glass jar combine 3 cups hot water and all ingredients except cucumbers. Add cucumbers and keep in refrigerator, covered, for about 5 days. *Serves 6.*

marinated cucumbers
WORONZOFF

3 medium cucumbers, peeled and cut into 2-inch strips
3 Tbsp. vegetable oil
3 Tbsp. red wine vinegar
¼ cup minced parsley
2 cloves garlic, peeled and minced
½ tsp. salt
½ tsp. pepper

Combine all ingredients except cucumbers and beat well. Add cucumbers and marinate in refrigerator for at least 4 hours. Drain and serve on toothpicks or on black bread. *Serves 6.*

cucumber appetizer
MILLER

These sweet-sour sticks can be a salad if served on lettuce or a good accompaniment to drinks

3–4 medium cucumbers, peeled and seeded
2–3 tsp. salt
¼ cup white vinegar
2 cloves garlic, peeled and coarsely sliced
½ tsp. sugar
1 Tbsp. chopped dill

Slice cucumbers into thin 1-inch length sticks. Place on flat plate and sprinkle with salt. Let them "sweat" for 1 hour. Drain off liquid and reserve ¼ cup. Combine cucumber liquid with vinegar, garlic, sugar and dill. Pour over cucumbers in shallow dish and marinate in refrigerator for 2 hours or longer. *Serves 4–6.*

cucumber mousse

2 envelopes unflavored gelatin
3 Tbsp. cold water
½ cup boiling water
3 small cucumbers, peeled, seeded and chopped
2 scallions, green and white parts, diced
2 Tbsp. chopped parsley
2 Tbsp. chopped dill
1 cup mayonnaise (fat-free is fine)
2 tsp. lemon juice
½ tsp. salt
¼ tsp. black pepper
⅛ tsp. cayenne pepper

Soften the gelatin in a small bowl in the cold water for five minutes, and add the boiling water, stirring until gelatin is dissolved. In a large bowl combine the cucumbers, scallions, parsley, dill, mayonnaise and lemon juice and beat well. Add salt, black and cayenne pepper, and taste for seasoning. Transfer to a mold and chill for at least four hours. *Serves 6–8.*

mixed vegetable appetizer
PROFESSOR M.

4 green bell peppers
1 eggplant
3 tomatoes
8 carrots, peeled
2 onions, peeled
2 stalks celery
2 cloves garlic, peeled and minced
2 Tbsp. minced parsley
Salt to taste
¼ cup vegetable oil

Remove inside ribs, tops and seeds from green peppers. Peel eggplant and cut into round slices ½-inch thick. Chop tomatoes. Chop carrots, onions, celery, and mix together. Add garlic, parsley and salt to chopped carrot mixture.

In a 2-quart casserole (it must be large enough to accommodate the peppers snugly), place a layer of chopped mixed vegetables. Cover with a layer of eggplant lightly sprinkled with salt. Fill the peppers with the chopped onion-carrot-celery mixture. Place peppers on layer of vegetables in pot and cover spaces between them with layer of chopped tomatoes. Continue to alternate layers of vegetable mixture, tomatoes, and eggplant until all of the vegetables are used up. Pour oil evenly over casserole. Cover tightly and simmer over fairly low heat for about 1½ hours until most of the liquid has been absorbed. Do not allow to become too dry. Excellent hot or cold. *Serves 4.*

❖ spicy vegetable appetizer
CHERNYAKHOVSKAYA

3 medium eggplants
2 large red bell peppers
1 large onion, peeled and sliced into thin half-moon rounds
Salt and black pepper to taste
Pinch cayenne pepper
Oil for frying
3 cloves garlic, peeled and minced
¾ cup minced cilantro

Peel the eggplants and bell peppers, and cut into one-inch cubes. Stir-fry the eggplants in hot oil on fairly high heat, and then allow to drain in a sieve, discarding excess oil. In a clean pan repeat this process with the peppers, and then with the onion, but do not discard the oil used in frying the onion. Reduce heat, add the eggplants, peppers and garlic to the pan and simmer on low heat for five minutes, adding oil to keep the mixture from burning. Add salt and black pepper to taste, and the cayenne. Taste for seasoning, and stir in the cilantro.

Can be eaten hot, or allowed to cool and served as a cold appetizer (in that case, be sue to drain off excess oil). *Serves 4-6*

ratatouille I
BALAKSHA
A cold vegetable appetizer

1 eggplant, washed and peeled
1 green bell pepper, seeded and deribbed
1 carrot, peeled
1 small onion, peeled
1 zucchini, scrubbed
½ cup vegetable oil
1 8-oz. can tomato sauce
1 Tbsp. red wine vinegar
¼ tsp. sugar
Optional: salt

Cut up all vegetables finely. Heat oil and fry onion until soft. Add the remaining vegetables, adding more oil if necessary. When vegetables are soft add tomato sauce, vinegar and sugar, and simmer on low heat for 10 minutes. Serve very cold with black bread. Sprinkle with salt if desired. *Serves 6.*

ratatouille II

MRS. L.

This version of the dish is equally good hot or cold

1 eggplant, unpeeled and diced
¼ cup red wine vinegar
⅔ cup water
½ cup vegetable oil
1 zucchini, diced
4 tomatoes, diced
½ small green bell pepper, seeded, deribbed and diced
1 Spanish onion, peeled and finely chopped
3 Tbsp. tomato paste
1 tsp. lemon juice
Salt

Soak eggplant in vinegar and water to cover for 10 minutes. Drain. Heat oil, add vegetables and tomato paste, and simmer on very low heat for 50–55 minutes. Add lemon juice and taste for seasoning. Add salt to taste. Serve hot or cold. *Serves 6.*

cottage cheese appetizer

MILLER

1 lb. (2 cups) cottage cheese
½ lb. sweet butter, softened
3 cloves garlic, peeled and coarsely chopped
¼ cup parsley, minced
½ tsp. freshly ground pepper
Salt

Combine all ingredients except salt and puree in food processor or bit by bit in blender. Add salt to taste. Chill in refrigerator for at least 2 hours before serving. Excellent with thin rye crackers. *Serves 8–10.*

spiced cottage cheese

1½ cups cottage cheese
¼ cup sweet butter
3 Tbsp. sour cream
2 Tbsp. caraway seeds
½ tsp. salt
Pepper

Blend cottage cheese, butter, sour cream and 1 Tbsp. caraway seeds in blender or food processor. Taste for seasoning and add salt if needed. Place in glass dish and sprinkle with freshly ground pepper and remaining 1 Tbsp. caraway seeds. Chill and serve very cold on rye bread or crackers. *Serves 6–8.*

beet and cottage cheese spread

1 8½-oz. can beets, well drained
½ tsp. salt
½ tsp. caraway seeds
½ cup cottage cheese
1 Tbsp. milk
¼ tsp. sugar
½ tsp. lemon juice

Combine all ingredients in blender or food processor and puree until smooth. This can be served as a dip or spread on rye crackers. *Serves 6–8.*

chopped herring I

KALDOR / JOFFE

1 herring fillet, coarsely chopped
¼ cup shelled walnuts
1 apple, peeled, cored, and cut into chunks
2 Tbsp. lemon juice
Black olives

Combine all ingredients except olives in food processor or blender and puree until just smooth. Place in a glass bowl and chill thoroughly. Decorate with sliced black olives and serve on black bread. *Serves 3–4.*

chopped herring II
VENGEROVA

2 herring fillets
½ cup milk
1½ slices white bread, crusts removed
2 Tbsp. white vinegar
2 Tbsp. water
½ apple, peeled, cored, and coarsely chopped
2 Tbsp. vegetable oil
1 tsp. sour cream
1 small onion, peeled and coarsely sliced
Pinch sugar
1 hardboiled egg, peeled and sliced

Soak herring in milk for 2 hours. Discard milk. Soak bread in vinegar and water for 15 minutes; squeeze dry. Put all ingredients except hardboiled egg in food processor or blender and puree until just smooth. Chill for several hours until very cold. Decorate with sliced hardboiled egg. Serve on rye crackers or black bread. *Serves 4–5.*

pickled wine herring
VENGEROVA

HERRING:
2 large herring fillets
2 bay leaves
10 black peppercorns
2 tsp. pickling spice
1 cup dry white wine

OPTIONAL DECORATION:
1 hardboiled egg, peeled and sliced
Black olives
Scallions (green and white parts)

Combine bay leaves, peppercorns, pickling spice and wine and mix; pour into glass jar and add herring. Close jar tightly and leave in refrigerator for 1 week. Herring may be decorated with olives or hardboiled egg slices; serve with minced scallions. *Serves 4.*

herring in sour cream and mustard

2 herring fillets, cut into bite-sized pieces
2 tsp. mustard
2 tsp. sugar
2 tsp. white vinegar
1 tsp. sour cream
1 scallion, minced (green and white parts)

Put herring in shallow glass dish. Combine mustard, sugar, vinegar, sour cream and scallion. Pour over herring fillets and let stand in refrigerator overnight. Spread sauce on squares of black bread and place a piece of herring on top of each. *Serves 6.*

herring with a fur coat

2 hardboiled eggs, peeled and coarsely chopped
1 small onion, peeled and finely chopped
2 carrots, peeled, boiled, and finely chopped
1 small apple, peeled, cored and chopped
8 oz. herring fillets, cut into 1-inch pieces
4 small red potatoes, peeled and thinly sliced
1 15-oz. can beets, well drained and finely chopped
½ cup sour cream
½ cup mayonnaise
Salt and pepper

Combine eggs, onion, carrots and apple, and sprinkle with a little salt and pepper. Place the potato slices in one layer in a buttered glass baking dish (9 x 12 inches, or a 10-inch pie plate); some of the slices may overlap. Place the pieces of herring on top of the potatoes, and cover with the vegetable mixture. Scatter beets on top. Add salt and pepper to sour cream and mayonnaise (be careful not to oversalt because the herring is quite salty). With a spatula spread the sour cream mixture over the beets. Chill mixture in refrigerator for at least 4 hours, or overnight. *Serves 6–8.*

jellied (zalivnaia) fish

MARTIN

1½ lbs. fish fillets (cod, pike, sturgeon, or any white-fleshed fish), cut into small servings
3 cups water
2 carrots, peeled and sliced
1 bay leaf
1 onion, peeled and sliced
½ tsp. salt
Pinch pepper
½ tsp. lemon juice
1 envelope powdered gelatin
½ lemon, sliced
1 hardboiled egg, peeled and sliced
6 black olives
Optional: horseradish

Bring water to a boil with 1 of the carrots, bay leaf, onion, salt, pepper and lemon juice. Add fish and simmer till just tender, about 8–10 minutes. Remove from heat and carefully remove fish pieces to a deep platter. Strain fish broth and add lemon juice and gelatin, stirring constantly till gelatin dissolves. Pour a thin layer of aspic over fish and chill for 45 minutes or until gelatin is slightly thickened. Lightly cook the remaining carrot until the pieces are soft (5–7 minutes), and arrange them together with thin slices of lemon, hardboiled egg, and olives on top of thickened gelatin layer and carefully pour remaining aspic over it. Chill for 5 hours until aspic is set and fish is very cold. May be served with horseradish. *Serves 6.*

studen'

ODESSER

1 lb. pigs' feet
½ lb. stewing veal, cubed
7 cups water
1 bay leaf
1 carrot, peeled and sliced
1 tsp. salt
Pinch pepper
2 cloves garlic, peeled and minced
1 Tbsp. chopped parsley
1 envelope powdered gelatin
1 Tbsp. lemon juice
Optional: Mustard or horseradish

Bring water to a boil with bay leaf, carrot, salt, pepper, garlic and parsley. Simmer 15 minutes. Add meat and simmer for about 1½ hours, on very low heat, until meat is very soft. Strain off bouillon and reserve. Chop pigs' feet and place with veal in bottom of deep dish. Add gelatin and lemon juice to 4 cups of strained bouillon, mix well and pour over meat. Chill for several hours until set. Serve with mustard or horseradish. *Serves 4.*

pashtet I
MARTIN

An elegant but easy pâté

½ lb. calf liver
8 Tbsp. butter
1 hardboiled egg, peeled and chopped
1 small onion, peeled and finely chopped
Salt and pepper to taste

Sauté calf liver in 4 Tbsp. butter until tender, a few minutes on each side. Cool and put through meat grinder or food processor. Add hardboiled egg, onion, remaining butter, salt and pepper and work with a wooden spoon until very smooth. Chill for at least 1 hour. *Serves 4.*

pashtet II
MILLER

The carrots give a special flavor to this chicken liver pâté

1 lb. chicken livers
2 small onions, chopped
3 Tbsp. butter + ¼ lb butter
1 hardboiled egg, peeled and chopped
2 carrots, peeled, boiled and chopped
Salt
Pepper
Optional: 2 tsp. dry sherry

Sauté onions in 3 tablespoons butter until soft. Add livers, and cook until they are no longer pink. Remove from heat and cool. Grind chicken livers and combine with egg, carrots, ¼ lb. butter, and salt and pepper to taste. Add sherry if desired, and chill for at least 3 hours. *Serves 4.*

pashtet III
ODESSER

The sour cream and mayonnaise give the pashtet an exceptionally smooth consistency

1 lb. chicken livers
1 small onion, peeled and chopped
1 Tbsp. butter
2 hardboiled eggs, peeled and chopped
3 Tbsp. sour cream
1 Tbsp. mayonnaise
Salt
Pepper

Boil chicken livers in water to cover until they are soft—about 7 minutes. Fry onion until golden in 1 Tbsp. butter. Grind livers, and combine with onion, hardboiled eggs, sour cream, mayonnaise and salt and pepper to taste. Chill until firm. *Serves 4.*

HOT ZAKUSKI

vol–au–vent with brains and mushrooms
ODESSER

4 vol-au-vent patty shells, baked
1 medium onion, peeled and chopped
1 Tbsp. butter
½ lb. mushrooms, coarsely chopped
Water
4 Tbsp. lemon juice
¾ cup sour cream
1 pair calf brains
Salt
Pepper
1 Tbsp. grated Parmesan cheese

Fry onion in butter until soft. Stew mushrooms in water to cover with a pinch of salt until tender—about 8–10 minutes; drain, cool slightly, and mix with ¼ cup sour cream. Soak brains for 3 hours in water to cover and 3 Tbsp. lemon juice; drain, remove all membranes and blood. Simmer for 20 minutes in water to cover together with remaining Tbsp. lemon juice and a pinch of salt. Drain brains well and puree in food processor or blender.

Add remaining sour cream, onion, mushrooms, and salt and pepper to taste. Place in vol-au-vent shells and sprinkle with Parmesan cheese. Bake in 350-degree oven for about 15–20 minutes until shells are well browned and cheese is bubbly. *Serves 4.*

browned eggs

B. VINOGRADOVA

An attractive first course or, with a green salad, a light luncheon dish

2 hardboiled eggs, peeled
1 egg, raw
2 Tbsp. butter
½ tsp. salt
2 tsp. minced dill
2 tsp. minced parsley
2 Tbsp. + 1 tsp. bread crumbs

Carefully halve hardboiled eggs lengthwise and remove yolks. Melt 1 tsp. butter; remove from heat and sprinkle in chopped egg yolks. Add salt, chopped dill and parsley, 2 Tbsp. bread crumbs, and raw egg. Stuff whites with this mixture. Sprinkle with remaining crumbs; melt remaining butter and pour over eggs. Brown in 350-degree oven for 6–8 minutes or run under broiler for 2–3 minutes. Each egg may be baked in an individual ramekin, if desired. *Serves 2.*

mushrooms in sour cream

1 lb. fresh mushrooms
1 tsp. salt
2–3 Tbsp. butter
1 Tbsp. flour
½ cup sour cream
2 Tbsp. grated Swiss cheese
1 Tbsp. minced parsley

Clean mushrooms, place in sieve and pour hot water over them. Drain well. (If mushrooms are very big they may be cut in half.) Sprinkle with salt and fry in hot butter until soft. Sprinkle with flour, and cook, stirring constantly. Whisk in sour cream, and stir until smooth. Place in baking dish or individual ramekins, sprinkle with cheese, and bake in 350-degree oven for about 10 minutes until cheese browns. Sprinkle with parsley before serving. *Serves 4.*

meatless forshmak

A first course or lunch main dish

2 herring fillets
2 slices white bread, crusts removed
⅔ cup milk
1 Tbsp. butter
2 medium potatoes, peeled, boiled, and mashed
1 small onion, peeled and finely chopped
Pinch pepper
2 Tbsp. sour cream
3 eggs, separated

Preheat oven to 375 degrees. Wash herring fillets and cut into rough pieces. Soak bread in milk and squeeze dry. Grind bread and herring together or put through food processor for a few seconds. Add butter, potatoes, onion, pepper, and sour cream, and mix well. Beat egg yolks and add to mixture. Beat egg whites stiff and fold in carefully. Bake in lightly greased casserole in oven for 25 minutes until golden. May be served with sour cream mixed with a little mustard. *Serves 2.*

meat forshmak

An excellent way of using any leftover meat

1 small onion, peeled and chopped
5 Tbsp. butter
2 medium potatoes, peeled, boiled and mashed
1 lb. cold cooked beef, lamb, veal, or chicken, coarsely chopped
½ herring fillet
2 Tbsp. flour
3 Tbsp. sour cream
2 eggs, separated
Salt and pepper to taste
1 Tbsp. grated Swiss or Parmesan cheese

Fry onion in 1 Tbsp. butter, and mix with potatoes. Grind meat and herring together. Add potatoes. Combine flour with sour cream and stir in 2 Tbsp. melted butter. Add to meat and herring mixture. Beat egg yolks and add to mixture along with salt and pepper to taste. Beat egg whites stiff and fold in carefully. Place in greased casserole, sprinkle the top with grated cheese and drizzle with remaining 2 tablespoons melted butter. Bake in 325-degree oven for 30–40 minutes until casserole is browned and shrinks from sides of dish. Can be served with sour cream or with tomato sauce. *Serves 4–6.*

dragomir forshmak

1 large onion, peeled and chopped
¼ lb. mushrooms, washed and sliced
2 Tbsp. butter
1 Tbsp. flour
½ cup beef broth
1 Tbsp. tomato paste
1 cup sour cream
¼ lb. cooked tongue, cut into julienne
¼ lb. ham, cut into julienne
Optional: ¼ lb. cold chicken, cut into julienne
4 medium potatoes, peeled, boiled, and mashed
2 kosher dill pickles, chopped
Salt
Pepper
2 Tbsp. grated Parmesan cheese

Sauté onion and mushrooms in 2 Tbsp. butter. Sprinkle with flour, and stir until smooth. Add beef broth, and whisk in tomato paste and sour cream, stirring until smooth. Remove from heat and blend with tongue, ham, chicken, potatoes, pickles, and salt and pepper to taste. Place in lightly greased casserole and sprinkle with grated cheese. Bake in 375-degree oven for 15–20 minutes until very hot and browned on top. *Serves 4–6.*

vegetable forshmak

2 large potatoes, peeled and boiled
1 cup chopped white cabbage, boiled
3 pieces white bread, crusts removed
½ cup milk
3 eggs, separated
1 cup sour cream
1 small onion, peeled and chopped
3 Tbsp. butter
1 anchovy, chopped
½ tsp. lemon juice
Dash Tabasco sauce
Salt and pepper
2 Tbsp. grated Swiss cheese

Mash potatoes and combine with cabbage. Soak 2 slices of white bread in milk, squeeze dry, and add to cabbage-potato mixture. Mix egg yolks with sour cream and blend in. Fry onion lightly in 1 Tbsp. butter and blend in. Add chopped anchovy, lemon juice, Tabasco, salt and pepper, tasting carefully for seasoning since anchovy is quite salty. Beat egg whites stiff and fold in. Place in greased casserole. Make fresh bread crumbs out of remaining slice of bread and sprinkle over casserole. Melt remaining 2 Tbsp. butter and drizzle over top. Sprinkle with grated cheese, and bake for 45 minutes in 350-degree oven until brown. May be served with sour cream. *Serves 6.*

salat olivier I

B. VINOGRADOVA

2 cups cooked chicken, cut into chunks
3 large potatoes, peeled, boiled and cut into chunks
3 hardboiled eggs, peeled and chopped
2 kosher dill pickles, diced
1 8½-oz. can small peas
2 Tbsp. chopped ham
2 Tbsp. mayonnaise
2 Tbsp. sour cream
½ tsp. mustard
½ tsp. lemon juice
2 hardboiled egg yolks, mashed
Salt and pepper

Combine chicken, potatoes, 3 hardboiled eggs, pickles, peas, and ham, taking care not to mash potatoes. Separately, combine mayonnaise, sour cream, mustard, lemon juice, and mashed hardboiled egg yolks. Lightly salt chicken mixture; season mayonnaise mixture with salt and pepper to taste. Just before serving lightly toss chicken mixture in mayonnaise sauce, making sure all of salad is coated. *Serves 6.*

salat olivier II

BALAKSHA

1 boiled chicken breast or 2 large drumsticks, diced
3 medium potatoes, peeled, boiled and diced
1 medium cucumber, peeled, seeded and diced
1 green pepper, deribbed, seeded and diced
1 large carrot, peeled, cooked and diced
½ cup cooked peas
3 hardboiled eggs, peeled and finely chopped
Salt and pepper
3 Tbsp. mayonnaise
3 Tbsp. sour cream
1 tsp. sugar
1 tsp. ketchup
1 tsp. lemon juice

Combine chicken, potatoes, cucumber, green pepper, carrot, peas and eggs. Add salt and pepper to taste. Mix mayonnaise, sour cream, sugar, ketchup, and lemon juice. Just before serving, combine with chicken mixture. *Serves 4–5.*

red salad

TUMARKIN

1 1-lb. can beets, drained
2 medium potatoes, boiled and diced
2 carrots, peeled, boiled and diced
1 8½-oz. can peas
1 kosher dill pickle, diced
2 Tbsp. red wine vinegar
2 Tbsp. vegetable oil
Salt
⅛ lb. black olives, pitted and sliced
½ fillet Matjes herring
¼ lb. boiled beef, diced
2 Tbsp. sour cream
1 Tbsp. mayonnaise
1 tsp. mustard

Combine beets, potatoes, carrots, peas, and pickle. Stir in vinegar and oil and salt to taste. Let rest for 10 minutes. Combine with olives, herring, and boiled beef; let rest for 20 minutes. Blend sour cream, mayonnaise and mustard. Just before serving mix into salad. *Serves 6–8.*

vinegret I

B. VINOGRADOVA

This filling salad could be a dinner first course or a light lunch dish

2 1-lb. cans mixed peas and carrots
1 1-lb. can red kidney beans
1 1-lb. can diced beets
8 hardboiled eggs, peeled
3 large potatoes, peeled and boiled
5 kosher dill pickles
1 tsp. capers
¼ cup black olives, pitted and chopped
2 Tbsp. vegetable oil

Rinse each can of vegetables carefully in cold water, draining thoroughly in sieve. Dry on paper towels. Dice hardboiled eggs with potatoes and pickles and mix gently with the vegetables, being careful not to mash potatoes–use a wooden spoon or hands. Add capers, olives and oil, and blend.

Serve with the following dressing:
⅔ cup mayonnaise
⅓ cup sour cream
2 tsp. paprika
½ tsp. salt
½ tsp. pepper
1 tsp. capers

Mix all ingredients and taste for seasoning. Add more salt if desired. Reserve ¼ cup of sauce and mix rest with salad. Spread thin layer of reserved sauce on top. May be decorated with quartered hardboiled eggs and olives. *Serves 8–10.*

vinegret II
WORONZOFF

1 8½-oz. can small peas, drained
1 1-lb. can beets, drained
4 medium potatoes, peeled, boiled and cooled
1 hardboiled egg, peeled and chopped
2–3 kosher dill pickles, finely chopped
2 apples, peeled, cored and diced
Optional: ½ cup minced mushrooms
Optional: 5 black olives, pitted and minced
1 medium onion, peeled and minced
1 Tbsp. minced dill

Dice all ingredients except peas very finely (pieces should be about 1⁄4 size of playing dice). Mix together and sprinkle with dill.

S A U C E :
⅓ cup mayonnaise
⅓ cup sour cream
Salt
Pepper

Combine mayonnaise, sour cream, salt and pepper. Before serving carefully mix with vegetables. *Serves 4–6.*

fish vinegret

PETIT

½ cup cold cooked salmon, flaked
1 medium pickle, diced
1 tsp. capers
4 black olives, pitted and diced
½ cup boiled and sliced mushrooms
2 medium potatoes, peeled, boiled and diced
1 8½-oz. can beets, drained and diced
1 small cucumber, peeled, seeded and diced
3 Tbsp. mayonnaise
½ tsp. vegetable oil
½ tsp. vinegar
1 tsp. chopped chives
½ tsp. minced parsley
¼ tsp. chopped chervil
¼ tsp. dried tarragon
Salt
Pepper

Combine salmon, pickle, capers, olives, mushrooms, potatoes, beets, and cucumber. Separately, mix mayonnaise with oil, vinegar, chives, parsley, chervil, tarragon, and salt and pepper to taste. Blend gently into fish mixture, being careful not to crush fish or potatoes. *Serves 4–5.*

salmon salad

1 14-oz. can salmon
2 hardboiled eggs, peeled and chopped
1 large cucumber, peeled, seeded and diced
1 cup boiled white rice
2 scallions, green and white parts, diced
1 small onion, peeled and diced
2 Tbsp. minced parsley
2 Tbsp. minced dill
4 Tbsp. mayonnaise
2 Tbsp. sour cream
Salt and pepper

Drain salmon and pick over to remove any skin, cartilage, or bones. Combine in a large bowl with eggs, cucumber, rice, scallions, onion, parsley and dill. Blend mayonnaise and sour cream and add to mixture, stirring to moisten well. Add salt and pepper carefully, tasting for seasoning, since if the salmon is salty not much additional seasoning may be needed. Chill for 1 hour before serving. *Serves 6.*

shrimp salad
TUMARKIN

5 cups water
Salt
1 lb. shrimp, cleaned
1 bunch fresh dill
5 hardboiled eggs, peeled and cut into eighths
½ cup mayonnaise
2 Tbsp. ketchup

Bring salted water and a few sprigs of dill to a rapid boil. Throw in shrimp and boil for a few minutes (no more than 4–5) until shrimp have turned pink. Drain in colander. Cool. Mix mayonnaise with ketchup and 3 Tbsp. minced dill. In a small bowl, put a layer of sauce, then a layer of shrimp and eggs. Sprinkle with dill. Cover with a layer of sauce, another layer of shrimp and eggs, and more dill. Repeat until all shrimp are used up. Sprinkle more dill on top of salad. *Serves 4.*

herring salad

1 small head of Boston lettuce
1 herring fillet, diced
2 hardboiled eggs, peeled and chopped
2 Tbsp. white vinegar
2 tsp. lemon juice
2 tsp. sugar
½ cup sour cream
1 Tbsp. chopped dill
1 Tbsp. chopped parsley

Wash lettuce. Reserve the largest leaves (about half the head) and tear remaining leaves into small pieces. Combine herring and eggs. In a bowl mix vinegar, lemon juice and sugar. Blend in sour cream. Mix with herring and eggs. Place reserved lettuce leaves on plate. Combine torn pieces of lettuce with eggs, herring, and sour cream mixture; pile up in a mound on large lettuce leaves. Sprinkle with dill and parsley. *Serves 4.*

russian salad
<small>MRS. L.</small>

2 medium potatoes, peeled, boiled and diced
1 stalk celery, diced
½ cup cooked peas
½ cup boiled mushrooms, coarsely chopped
2 small pickles, diced
¼ cup diced ham
¼ cup diced, cooked tongue
1 apple, peeled, cored and diced
⅓ cup sour cream
Salt and pepper
¼ tsp. lemon juice.

Mix potatoes, celery, peas, mushrooms, pickles, ham, tongue and apple. Blend sour cream with salt and pepper to taste, and lemon juice. Mix with vegetables. Can be served on lettuce leaves. *Serves 4–5.*

salade mixte
<small>MRS. L.</small>

1 1-lb can mixed carrots and peas, drained
2 medium potatoes, peeled, boiled and diced
1 large cucumber, peeled, seeded and chopped
1 kosher dill pickle, diced
½ apple, peeled, cored and diced
1 Tbsp. mayonnaise
3 Tbsp. sour cream
1 tsp. lemon juice
1 tsp. mustard
1 tsp. chopped dill
1 tsp. chopped parsley
Salt

Combine carrots and peas, potatoes, cucumber, pickle and apple. Mix mayonnaise, sour cream, lemon juice, mustard, dill and parsley; add salt to taste. Just before serving blend sauce with vegetables. *Serves 4.*

green salad

1 small head Boston lettuce
1 carrot, peeled and cut into julienne
2 tomatoes, diced
1 bunch radishes, thinly sliced
2 scallions, minced (both green and white parts)
1 large cucumber, peeled and thinly sliced
1 Tbsp. chives
2 hardboiled eggs, peeled and chopped
Salt

SAUCE:
½ cup sour cream
½ tsp. lemon juice
¼ tsp. sugar
Salt

Tear lettuce into small pieces. Combine with carrot, tomatoes, radishes, scallions, cucumber, chives, and eggs. Salt lightly and place in salad bowl. Combine sour cream, lemon juice, sugar, and pinch of salt. Pour over vegetables and serve immediately. *Serves 4.*

vegetable salad
KHAZANOVA

2 sour pickles, diced
2 apples, peeled, cored and diced
1 small onion, diced
1 8½-oz. can peas, drained
2 medium cucumbers, peeled, seeded and chopped
4 medium potatoes, peeled, boiled and diced
3 Tbsp. sour cream
3 Tbsp. mayonnaise
Salt

Combine pickles, apples, onion, peas, cucumbers and potatoes. Blend sour cream with mayonnaise, and salt to taste. Before serving toss vegetables with sauce. *Serves 4–6.*

onion and vegetable salad
BOGRASH

2 medium onions, peeled
2 hardboiled eggs, peeled and chopped
3 tomatoes, coarsely chopped
2 small cucumbers (such as Kirby),
    peeled and coarsely chopped
2 medium potatoes, peeled, boiled and cubed
2 large apples, peeled, cored and chopped
½ cup diced Swiss cheese (do not grate)
4 Tbsp. mayonnaise
2 Tbsp. sour cream
½ tsp. salt, or to taste
¼ tsp. pepper

Parboil onions by plunging them into boiling water for 60 seconds, and slice into thin rings. Combine with eggs, tomatoes, cucumbers, potatoes, apples and cheese, blending carefully to avoid mashing the potatoes. Blend mayonnaise with sour cream and salt and pepper, and add to vegetables. Serve at room temperature. *Serves 6.*

egg salad
KHAZANOVA

A Russian version of an American favorite

4 hardboiled eggs, peeled and chopped
2 medium onions, peeled and diced
2 scallions, diced (green and white parts)
2 apples, peeled, cored and diced
2–3 Tbsp. mayonnaise
Salt

Combine all ingredients (tasting carefully for salt). Let the salad sit in the refrigerator for at least 1 hour before serving. Excellent on lettuce leaves or spread on rye crackers. *Serves 4–6.*

beet or carrot salad
KHAZANOVA

1 1-lb. can beets, well drained, or 5 raw carrots, peeled
½ cup walnuts, coarsely chopped
2 cloves garlic, peeled and crushed (or less to taste)
⅓ cup sour cream
½ tsp. salt

Dice beets (if using carrots, chop coarsely). Combine beets or carrots with all other ingredients and chill for ½ hour. Can be served on lettuce leaves. *Serves 4.*

❖ raw beet salad
MILLER

An easy and very tasty no-cook recipe

1 lb. raw beets
1 large shallot
2 tsp. Dijon or Russian mustard
1 Tbsp. extra virgin olive oil
2 Tbsp. sherry or red wine vinegar
Large pinch minced dill, parsley, rosemary or tarragon
Salt and pepper to taste.

Wash and peel beets and shallot. Shred beets finely in food processor with metal blade or using mandoline (do not grate) and chop shallot finely.

Scrape beets and shallot into bowl and toss with all the remaining ingredients, mixing well. Chill slightly, and serve at room temperature. *Serves 4.*

beet and fruit salad
BOGRASH

An excellent and unusual accompaniment to chicken or pork

1 8-oz. can beets, drained and chopped
⅓ cup dark raisins, coarsely chopped
⅓ cup dried apricots, coarsely chopped
1 apple, peeled, cored and chopped
⅓ cup coarsely chopped walnuts
2 Tbsp. mayonnaise
2 Tbsp. sour cream

Combine beets, raisins, apricots, apple and walnuts and mix well. Blend mayonnaise with sour cream and stir into mixture. Chill for half an hour. Salad should be served at room temperature. *Serves 4.*

cucumbers with sour cream salad
ODESSER

5 large cucumbers, peeled and thinly sliced
5 scallions, minced (green and white parts)
⅓ cup buttermilk
⅓ cup sour cream
Salt
Lettuce leaves

Toss cucumbers with scallions. Mix buttermilk, sour cream, and salt. Place lettuce leaves on plate. Just before serving toss cucumbers with dressing—do not do this ahead of time or cucumbers will give off water. Serve on lettuce leaves. *Serves 4–6.*

lettuce, egg, and cucumber salad
PETIT

6 hardboiled egg yolks
½ cup sour cream
¼ tsp. salt
¼ tsp. pepper
½ tsp. white vinegar
¼ tsp. dried tarragon
¼ tsp. fennel seeds
¼ tsp. chervil
1 head Boston lettuce
3 large cucumbers, peeled, seeded, and chopped

Put egg yolks through sieve, and combine with sour cream, salt, pepper, vinegar, tarragon, fennel, and chervil. Wash lettuce; tear into small pieces. Toss lettuce with cucumbers. Before serving, toss cucumbers and lettuce with sour cream sauce. *Serves 4–6.*

tomato and cucumber salad

MILLER

2 tomatoes, diced
2 large cucumbers, peeled and diced
½ medium onion, peeled and diced
1 green bell pepper, deribbed, seeded and chopped
3 Tbsp. vegetable oil
1½ Tbsp. red wine vinegar
Salt
Pepper

Mix vegetables together. Combine oil and vinegar with salt and pepper to taste. Pour over vegetables and toss lightly. *Serves 4.*

tomato, apple, and scallion salad

ODESSER

½ head Boston lettuce
4 tomatoes
1 apple, peeled, cored and diced
1 scallion, minced (green and white parts)
¼ cup olive or corn oil
2 Tbsp. red wine vinegar
½ tsp. sugar
½ tsp. salt
Pinch pepper

Line bowl with lettuce leaves (washed and squeezed dry). Cut tomatoes into chunks. Mix with apple and scallion, and scatter over lettuce. Combine oil, vinegar, sugar, salt, and pepper. Just before serving pour over salad. *Serves 4.*

mushroom salad
MRS. YU.

1 lb. mushrooms, cleaned and coarsely chopped
6 medium potatoes, peeled and coarsely chopped
Water
2 small cucumbers, peeled, seeded and coarsely chopped
1 egg, hardboiled and peeled
1 tsp. sugar
Salt and pepper
1 tsp. mustard
¼ cup vegetable oil
2 tsp. white vinegar
1 cup sour cream
2 scallions, chopped (green and white parts)

Boil mushrooms and potatoes in salted water for 10 minutes. Drain. Cool and add cucumbers and chopped hardboiled egg white. Put egg yolk through sieve; combine with sugar, salt and mustard. Slowly beat in oil, and then vinegar. Add sour cream and blend well. Taste for seasoning and add salt, sugar and pepper as needed. Toss potato-mushroom mixture in sour cream sauce and sprinkle with scallions. *Serves 6.*

gribok (fake mushroom) salad

1 large lettuce leaf
1 tsp. minced dill
2 tsp. butter
1½ oz. cream cheese
1 clove garlic, peeled and mashed
¼ tsp. salt
Pinch pepper
2 cherry tomatoes

Cut the lettuce into thin strips; arrange on plate and sprinkle with dill. Blend butter and cream cheese to form a smooth mixture. Add garlic, salt, and pepper. Divide into 5 equal portions. Form 4 of these into small, cylindrical rolls, about 1 inch long and ¾ of an inch to 1 inch thick. Stand them up on the lettuce. Cut the cherry tomatoes in half. Squeeze gently to get rid of seeds and excess juice; hollow out the center slightly. Put the tomato half on the cheese "stem" to form the cap of the mushroom. Dot the mushroom with the remaining cheese mixture. Chill until ready to serve. *Makes 4 "mushrooms."*

carrot and apple salad

4 carrots, peeled
2 apples
2 Tbsp. sugar
½ cup sour cream
1 tsp. lemon juice
½ tsp. dill

Cut the carrots into julienne strips. Peel, core, and finely chop apples. Mix apples, carrots, sugar, lemon juice and sour cream. Sprinkle with dill. *Serves 4.*

radish and apple salad

5 radishes, diced
2 carrots, peeled and diced
2 apples, peeled, cored and diced
¼ tsp. grated lemon rind
3 Tbsp. sour cream
Salt if needed

Combine radishes, carrots, apples and lemon rind in a large bowl. Add sour cream, and stir to moisten. Add salt if desired (the sharpness of the radishes and acidity of the lemon rind require very little if any salt). *Serves 4–5.*

scallion and radish salad

6 scallions (green and white parts)
1 bunch radishes
2 hardboiled eggs, peeled
⅓ cup sour cream
1 Tbsp. minced dill
1 Tbsp. minced parsley
Salt
Pepper
Lettuce leaves

Mince scallions, radishes and hardboiled eggs, and combine. Blend sour cream with dill, parsley, salt and pepper. Put vegetable mixture on lettuce leaves and pour sauce over just before serving (otherwise radishes will give off water). *Serves 4.*

string bean salad

2 tomatoes, coarsely chopped
1 10-oz. package frozen French-cut string beans
4 medium potatoes, peeled, boiled and diced
¼ cup mayonnaise
2 tsp. white vinegar
½ tsp. sugar
1 Tbsp. chopped dill
Salt and pepper

Prepare string beans according to package directions (be careful not to overcook). Drain well and combine with potatoes and tomatoes. Chill. Blend mayonnaise, vinegar, sugar, dill, salt and pepper, and add to salad. Can be served on lettuce leaves. *Serves 4.*

soups

soups

Shchi must be hot, fiery. But best of all is beet borshch Ukrainian style, with ham and sausages. It's served with sour cream and fresh parsley and dill. Rassol'nik from entrails and young kidneys is also wonderful, and if you love soup, then the best kind is sprinkled with herbs and greens: carrots, asparagus, cauliflower, etc . . .
—Anton Chekhov, *The Siren*

The traditional pot of soup simmering all day on the stove was the final repository of whatever foodstuffs happened to be available in the house. At first, soups were called *pokhlebka* and the foreign word *sup* only appeared during the reign of Peter the Great. The sixteenth-century *Domostroi* codex mentions hot and cold chicken soups and fish and meat soups made with noodles, barley and vegetables. Served in clay pots know as *gorshki*, in old Russia these soups were eaten only with decorative wooden spoons.

According to Molokhovets's classic Russian cookbook, if a butter-flour roux, sour cream, or an egg-milk liaison is added to a broth, the result is a *sup* as opposed to a bouillon, which is a pure and transparent mixture. Molokhovets recommends bouillon made of beef shanks with rum for "weak children and for adults who are forced to live an active life and to be in constant motion." Soup becomes *borshch* with the addition of beets, a *shchi* if fresh and/or sour cabbage and a roux are added, and a *rassol'nik* if the bouillon is thickened with a roux and flavored with kidneys and pickles.

The bouillon which is the base for all borshchs and *shchis* is called yellow if the vegetables are fried prior to being added to the broth, red if both meat and vegetables are fried (since this imparts a red color to the soup), and white if the raw vegetables are put directly into the soup.

The bouillon for borshch or *shchi* is best prepared on a day when the cook must be at home for several hours. The soup does not require constant attention since, once it is simmering, the cook is free to do as he pleases. The longer the bouillon is allowed to simmer, the more flavorful it will be. Bouillon should be cooled thoroughly before other ingredients are added, so that all fat can be skimmed from the surface. (I prefer to leave the soup in the refrigerator overnight before skimming, if possible.) It is also advisable to blanch the soup meat by letting the meat and water reach a boil, pouring off the water, and bringing the meat back to a boil with fresh water. This procedure produces a clear, transparent broth free of scum.

Molokhovets suggests ten to twelve pounds of beef for six servings of soup, but such extravagance is hardly necessary. Two pounds of meat per ten cups of water should provide an extremely strong broth. If only one pound is used, a few drops of beef extract or a cup of canned beef broth may be added (though this would send shudders down the spines of many traditional émigré cooks). For extra color, one small grated beet may be added to the borshch 10 minutes before the end of cooking. This is particularly important if the cook has decided to "cheat" by using canned instead of fresh beets (canned vegetables lose their color rapidly.) Be careful not to put in vegetables such as potatoes too early in the cooking, for they will become mushy. The stock should have attained full strength before they are added. Blending a roux into a borshch or *shchi* is not really necessary. This touch was added by French chefs, but borshch derives quite enough substance from its vegetable and meat ingredients. All of these soups should be served piping hot, and sour cream should be passed separately because if it is added to the pot any leftover soup will be spoiled. Almost any borshch or *shchi* is better on the second day after flavors have had a chance to blend.

Great care should be used in adding salt. It is always easy to add, but very difficult to subtract, and ingredients like frankfurters or sauerkraut release a good deal of salt during the cooking process. It is best to add salt fairly late in the preparation of the soup and to check the seasoning again just before serving.

While any borshch must, by definition, contain beets, it can include almost anything else–white beans, frankfurters, pork, bacon, peas, dried mushrooms, sour apples–whatever pleases the cook's fancy. There are consequently as many recipes for borshch as there are grandmothers. The eleven borshch recipes given here use extremely varied ingredients, and the final results have little in common.

Shchi, Russia's second-most famous soup, is a cabbage soup made in some sixty variations with all sorts of meat, fish, mushrooms, greens, and herbs, even including nettles. Variations of both *shchi* and borshch can be served cold in summer.

One of the most popular cold soups, *okroshka*, is made with *kvas*, a fermented beverage that is not easy to make. (I have several permanent stains on my ceiling from bottles which blew their corks.) Fortunately, flat beer or a combination of white wine and club soda can be substituted easily and successfully.

A meat *solianka* that makes good use of sausages such as salami and organ meats such as liver and kidneys is an inexpensive dish as well as a tasty one. Also popular is the *rassol'nik* made from beef and kidney bouillon or chicken giblets and flavored with pickles and pickle juice. The combination may seem strange to Western palates, but the soup has a refreshing and pungent flavor. (Incidentally, Russians consider pickle juice the ideal cure for hangovers.)

During Lent, the so-called Lenten borshchs combining different kinds of vegetables, and soups of dried mushrooms and barley, squash, potatoes, cauliflower and spinach are particularly popular. The classic fish broth *ukha*, or fish *solianka* can be made from almost any white-fleshed fish. Fruit soups are refreshing as a first course or dessert in summer, and a blender performs in seconds the formerly tedious task of pureeing berries.

　　Note: in Russian cooking *solianka* is used to describe both a kind of soup such as the mixed or fish *solianka* included here, and a stew consisting of many ingredients—usually including cabbage (see the fish, mushroom and vegetable *soliankas* found in the fish and vegetable chapters).

HOT SOUPS

clear bouillon

8 cups water
2 large carrots, peeled and sliced
4 sprigs parsley, chopped
1 stalk celery, chopped
1 large turnip, peeled and chopped
Salt
Pepper
Optional: 6 frankfurters, cooked

Bring water to a boil. Add chopped vegetables and simmer uncovered for 15 minutes. Cover and simmer on low heat for 45 minutes, adding salt and pepper to taste. Strain. Can be served with noodles, cooked chopped beets, or croutons. A cooked frankfurter may be cut into thick rounds and added to each serving. *Serves 4–6.*

bouillon with crêpes
WEINSCHENKER

2 eggs, separated
1 cup milk
4 Tbsp. flour
1 recipe for clear bouillon (above)
1 tsp. butter

Beat egg yolks and slowly combine with milk. Whisk in flour, stirring constantly. Beat egg whites stiff and gently fold into mixture. Melt butter on very hot griddle and pour in batter to make small (4–6 inch) crêpes. Cool crêpes, and cut into thin, noodle-like strips. Heat bouillon and add crêpes just before serving. (Heat only until crêpes are warmed through). *Serves 6.*

potage moscovite
PETIT

An extremely rich soup of chicken broth with poached cheese dumplings

6 cups chicken broth
½ cup cream cheese
6 Tbsp. sweet butter, melted
2 eggs, separated
1 cup flour
2 Tbsp. sour cream
½ tsp. salt
½ tsp. sugar
½ tsp. grated lemon peel
1 Tbsp. heavy cream (if needed)
2 Tbsp. grated Parmesan cheese

Whip cream cheese until smooth. Add 4 Tbsp. melted butter, and continue to beat. Add egg yolks. Slowly add flour, sour cream, salt, sugar, and grated lemon peel. Beat egg whites stiff and add to mixture. Taste for seasoning and add salt, sugar, or lemon peel to taste. If mixture is thin, add a bit more flour; if too thick, add a few drops of heavy cream. Drop by the tablespoonful into simmering water which just covers balls and poach until they rise to the surface. Remove with a slotted spoon and place in lightly greased flat casserole. Dribble remaining 2 Tbsp. of melted butter over the top and sprinkle with grated Parmesan. Bake for 15 minutes in 350-degree oven. Serve in hot chicken broth. May also be eaten as a side dish with sour cream served separately. *Serves 6.*

soup with meatballs
MRS. YU.

1 lb. beef (chuck or brisket)
2 small onions, peeled
1 medium carrot, peeled and sliced
2 Tbsp. chopped parsley
Salt and pepper
7 cups water
2 slices white bread, crusts removed, soaked
    in ½ cup milk and squeezed dry

1 Tbsp. butter
1 egg
6 small potatoes, peeled and cut into bite-sized pieces

Cut off approximately ⅓ of the meat, choosing a piece free of fat, and set aside. Place the rest of the meat in a pot with the carrot, 1 Tbsp. parsley, 1 onion, quartered, salt, pepper, and 7 cups water and bring to a boil. Simmer for 50 minutes. Put the reserved meat, the remaining onion, chopped, parsley, soaked bread, egg, and butter through the meat grinder. Add salt and pepper to taste. Form into small, 1-inch balls.

When broth is cooked, skim fat and put in potatoes; simmer 10 minutes. Add meatballs and cook just until done (about 15–20 minutes). Before serving, cut the meat into small pieces. *Serves 6.*

soup with macaroni
MRS. YU.

2 medium onions, peeled and finely chopped
2 medium carrots, peeled and finely chopped
1 turnip, peeled and finely chopped
1 Tbsp. chopped parsley
3 Tbsp. butter + 1 Tbsp. melted butter
6 cups beef broth
1 cup cooked macaroni
⅔ cup sour cream
1 Tbsp. grated Parmesan cheese
2 egg yolks

Fry onions, carrots, turnip and parsley in 3 Tbsp. butter until soft. Add 1 cup beef broth, stir, and put mixture through blender or food processor. Return to the pot, put in remaining beef broth and macaroni, and heat through. Combine 1 Tbsp. melted butter, sour cream, grated cheese and egg yolks, and beat well. Add to broth but do not allow to boil. Simmer 5 minutes. *Serves 6.*

quick borshch

BAKER

A short-cut way of making authentic-tasting borshch

6 cups fresh or canned beef broth
2 cups tomato juice
1 1-lb. can beets with juice, sliced
1 small head of cabbage, shredded
1 medium onion, peeled and chopped
3 medium carrots, peeled and sliced
2 Tbsp. butter
Salt and pepper
2 cloves garlic
2 Tbsp. chopped dill
2 Tbsp. chopped parsley
Sour cream

Combine beef broth, tomato juice, and beets and their liquid. Bring to boil. Add shredded cabbage and cook until cabbage is soft but not mushy, 25–30 minutes. Sauté onion and carrots in butter until soft and add to cabbage mixture. Taste for seasoning; amount of salt needed will depend on saltiness of beef broth. Add salt and pepper to taste. Approximately 5 minutes before serving add chopped garlic, dill, and parsley to soup. Taste for seasoning, and serve with sour cream on the side. *Serves 8.*

anya's borshch

JALBERT

Easy and nourishing

10 cups water
2 lbs. beef (chuck or soup meat)
½ small head of cabbage, shredded
Salt and pepper
3 beets, peeled and sliced
4 medium carrots, peeled and sliced
2 medium onions, peeled and coarsely chopped
4 Tbsp. butter
2 large potatoes, peeled and cut in bite-sized pieces
1 Tbsp. chopped parsley
1 Tbsp. chopped dill
Sour cream

Boil meat, cabbage, water and salt to taste; simmer 50 minutes. Fry beets, carrots and onions in butter for 10–15 minutes until soft. Add vegetables to pot with meat and cabbage and continue to simmer for 30 minutes. Add potatoes and cook 15 minutes. Taste for seasoning and add salt and pepper to taste. Add parsley and dill. Remove meat, divide into portions and place one piece in each plate. Pour soup over meat and serve with sour cream. *Serves 8–10.*

russian borshch

NABOKOVA

A classic, hearty meat soup

10 cups water
3–4 lbs. lean beef (shank, chuck, soup meat)
1 large carrot, peeled and cut into 1-inch strips
1 parsnip, peeled and cut into strips
1 large leek, chopped
2 ribs celery, chopped
7 medium-sized red beets, peeled and cut in strips + 1 large beet, grated
2 Tbsp. butter
1 lb. cabbage, shredded
4 medium potatoes, peeled and cut in bite-sized pieces
4 tomatoes
2 Tbsp. tomato paste
1 Tbsp. salt
¼ tsp. pepper
1 tsp. red wine vinegar or lemon juice
1 garlic clove, peeled and minced
1 Tbsp. minced dill
Sour cream

Place meat and water in a heavy soup pot and bring to a boil. Skim off foam. Add salt, pepper, carrot, parsnip, leek, and celery; cover and simmer gently for 20 minutes. Sauté 7 beets in butter until shiny. Add to mixture and continue to simmer gently for 1¼ hours, gradually adding cabbage, potatoes, tomatoes and tomato paste. Remove meat and cut in bite-sized pieces. Return to pot. Hold remaining grated beet in sieve over the soup pot and pour 3 cups soup over it to give borshch a bright color. Discard beet. Add vinegar or lemon juice, garlic, and dill. Taste for seasoning. Serve with sour cream on side. This borshch is excellent with *pirozhki* and buckwheat kasha. *Serves 8–10.*

ukrainian borshch

NABOKOVA

The bacon and pork give this borshch a distinctive flavor

Water
1½ lbs. beef (shank or chuck)
2 lbs. pork
1 carrot, peeled and cut in strips
1 parsnip, peeled and cut in strips
2 ribs celery, peeled and cut in strips
1 large leek, chopped
2 medium onions, peeled and thinly sliced
½ cup dry white beans
1 lb. cabbage, shredded
4 medium potatoes, peeled and cut in bite-sized pieces
8 medium-sized beets, baked in skins for about 30 minutes
     in 350-degree oven and then peeled
5 tomatoes
3 Tbsp. tomato paste
2 green bell peppers, deribbed, seeded and sliced
1 tsp. lemon juice
4 slices smoked bacon
1 Tbsp. minced dill
1 garlic clove, peeled and minced
Salt

Remove as much fat as possible from pork. Put beef and pork in heavy soup pot, cover with cold water and bring to a boil. Add carrot, parsnip, celery, leek, onions, and beans. Simmer for 25 minutes. Add cabbage, potatoes, 7 beets cut into strips, tomatoes, tomato paste, and peppers. Simmer partially covered for 1½ hours. When beef and pork are tender remove them, cut in bite-sized pieces and return to pot. Grate the remaining red beet, sprinkle with lemon juice, and add to soup. Ten minutes before serving mince bacon and blend with dill and garlic. Add to soup. Taste for seasoning and add salt as necessary. Serve with sour cream, *pirozhki*, or kasha. *Serves 8.*

polish borshch

NABOKOVA

This tasty and unusual borshch even makes use of the beet leaves and stems

1½ lbs. beef (shank, chuck or flanken)
1½ lbs. smoked pork (butt or shoulder)
1 large carrot, peeled and cut into 1-inch strips

1 parsnip, peeled and cut into 1-inch strips
2 ribs celery, chopped
1 large leek, chopped
2 bunches (about 7–8) young red beets with stems and leaves
½ lb. cabbage, shredded
4 medium potatoes, peeled and cut in bite-sized pieces
4–5 tomatoes, cubed
2 Tbsp. tomato paste
1 garlic clove, peeled and minced
1 Tbsp. dill
½ Tbsp. lemon juice
2 frankfurters, sliced
Salt and pepper to taste

Put beef and smoked pork in a heavy kettle, cover with water (at least 12 cups) and bring to a boil. Pour off water, refill with fresh water, and bring back to boil. Add carrot, parsnip, celery and leek. Let simmer for about ¹/₂ hour. Peel and slice beets; chop leaves and stems. Boil 4 cups water and put in beets. Boil all except 1 beet for 25 minutes until beets are tender. Add sliced beets with their cooking liquid, chopped stems and leaves, cabbage, potatoes and tomatoes to kettle. Simmer on low heat for 1¹/₂ hours. When beef and pork are tender, remove, cut in bite-sized pieces and return to kettle. Add tomato paste, garlic, dill, salt and pepper. Grate the remaining beet, sprinkle with lemon juice and add to the soup for color. About 10 minutes before serving soup, add frankfurters. Simmer 10 minutes and taste for seasoning. Serve with sour cream. *Serves 8–10.*

mother's borshch

VENGEROVA

The smoked pork and the eggs give a deliciously rich character to this soup

10 cups water
1½ lbs. beef flanken
2–3 soup bones
¼ lb. smoked pork (a small hock will do nicely)
1 onion, sliced
2 carrots, peeled and sliced
1 stalk celery, peeled and sliced
7 beets, peeled
½ small cabbage, shredded
1 bay leaf
Salt and pepper
2 lbs. very ripe tomatoes (if unavailable use 2 lbs. canned tomatoes)
Pinch sugar
3 eggs

Combine water, flanken, soup bones, pork, onion, carrots and celery. Bring to a boil and simmer 1¼ hours. Strain broth; remove meat and cut into bite-sized pieces; return to broth. Grind beets coarsely and add them to the soup along with the cabbage, bay leaf, pepper and salt to taste (be careful since both the pork and cabbage are salty!). Simmer 30 minutes. Puree tomatoes in blender or food processor and add to soup. Simmer another 15 minutes. Add sugar and taste for seasoning. Beat eggs well. Be sure soup is not boiling. Just before serving, slowly beat a cup of soup into eggs and carefully pour back into soup pot. (The soup must be below boiling point or the eggs will curdle.) *Serves 6–8.*

borshch for an army or the neighbors

B. VINOGRADOVA

Flanken and sour salt give a unique taste to this borshch

1 lb. beef flanken
1 lb. short ribs
1 beef marrow bone
4 beets, peeled and diced
1 small head cabbage, shredded
1 small green bell pepper, deribbed, seeded and thinly sliced
½ stalk celery, chopped
2 medium potatoes, peeled and cut in bite-sized pieces
1 carrot, peeled and sliced
1 onion, peeled and chopped
1 1-lb. can tomatoes
1 8-oz. can tomato sauce
Salt and pepper
¼ tsp. sour salt

Put meat and bones in pot with cold water to cover. Add 1 tsp. salt and ½ tsp. pepper. Simmer for 1 hour. Remove bones and meat. Remove as much fat as possible, cut meat in small pieces and return to soup. Add 3 beets, cabbage, green bell pepper, celery, potatoes, carrot, onion and canned tomatoes. Stir. Add pinch of salt and pepper and sour salt. Simmer for ½ hour. Grate remaining beet and mix with tomato sauce. Ten minutes before serving add to soup. Taste for seasoning and add salt, pepper or sour salt if needed. Caution: sour salt should be added in small dashes. Serve with sour cream. *Serves 6–8.*

my special borshch

WEINSCHENKER

*This very Russian borshch makes use of such American products
as ketchup and brown sugar*

12 cups water
2 lbs. flanken
1 small lamb shank
1 marrow bone
1 large bunch beets (6–7), peeled and grated
4 tomatoes, pureed in blender or food processor
½ small head of cabbage, shredded
3 small onions, peeled and chopped
1 Tbsp. butter
2 1-lb. cans tomato sauce
1 8-oz. can string beans (or ½ cup frozen or fresh)
1 8-oz. can peas (or ½ cup frozen or fresh)
1 Tbsp. ketchup
2 tsp. brown sugar
1 Tbsp. salt
Pepper
1 clove garlic, peeled
3 eggs

Combine water, flanken, lamb shank and marrow bone and bring to boil. Add salt and pinch of pepper, skim foam, and simmer 45 minutes. Remove meat. Discard fat and bones; cut meat into bite-sized pieces and return to soup. Add beets, tomatoes, cabbage, and 1 chopped onion. Melt butter. Fry remaining onions until golden. Add tomato sauce and simmer 15 minutes. Add to soup. Simmer for about 50 minutes. Drain string beans and peas under cold water and add to soup. (If using fresh vegetables simmer another 25 minutes.) Add ketchup and brown sugar and taste for seasoning; add salt, pepper, sugar or ketchup to taste. Simmer 15 minutes. Just before serving rub a wooden salad bowl with split garlic clove. Beat eggs well in bowl. Be sure soup is not boiling. Slowly pour 1 cup of soup into eggs, blend thoroughly and pour back into soup. Do not allow mixture to boil. *Serves 8–10.*

green borshch

NABOKOVA

Though beetless, this traditional hearty soup is called borshch

3½ lbs. beef shank or chuck
10 cups cold water
1 medium carrot, peeled and diced
6 sprigs parsley, chopped
1 large leek, chopped
2 ribs celery, finely chopped
½ lb. sorrel leaves, chopped
   (if unavailable, increase spinach to 1 lb. and add 1 Tbsp. lemon juice)
½ lb. spinach leaves, chopped
Salt and pepper
4 small potatoes, peeled and diced
6 hard-boiled eggs, peeled and quartered
Sugar
Sour cream

Place meat in deep soup pot and add water. Bring to a boil. Add carrot, parsley, leek, celery, and salt and pepper to taste. Simmer for about 1½ hours, covered. Add sorrel and spinach (with lemon juice if not using sorrel) and potatoes; simmer, covered, for about 20 minutes. Remove meat, cut into bite-sized pieces and return to pot. Taste for seasoning, and add sugar to taste. Place hardboiled egg quarter on bottom of each plate and ladle in borshch. Serve with a spoonful of sour cream in each portion. *Serves 8.*

lenten borshch I

BALAKSHA

3–4 oz. dried mushrooms
1 8¼-oz. can lima beans
6 Greek black olives, pitted and chopped
10 cups water
3 beets, peeled and cut in strips
1 6-oz. can tomato paste
2 carrots, diced
2 potatoes, peeled and cut in bite-sized pieces
½ lb. cabbage, shredded, or ½ lb. sauerkraut, canned or in bag

1 medium onion, peeled and chopped
3 Tbsp. vegetable oil
Salt and pepper

Wash mushrooms with boiling water and allow them to soak for 40 minutes. Then combine lima beans, mushrooms with the water in which they were soaked, chopped olives, and 10 cups water. Simmer for 15 minutes. Add beets, tomato paste, carrots, and potatoes. Simmer ½ hour. Add cabbage or drained sauerkraut, and cook for 25 minutes. Fry onion in oil until golden and add to soup. Simmer for 5 minutes. Add salt and pepper to taste (if sauerkraut is used, be careful, since the soup will already be quite salty). *Serves 8.*

lenten borshch II

NABOKOVA

A somewhat spicier version of this Lenten soup

12 cups water
3–4 oz. dried mushrooms (boletus), imported from Poland,
    or 1½ lbs. domestic fresh mushrooms, thinly sliced
2 large carrots, peeled and thinly sliced
2 parsnips, peeled and thinly sliced
2 leeks, chopped
2 stalks celery, chopped
7 medium-sized beets, peeled and sliced
¼ lb. Greek or Italian black salt olives,
    or ¼ lb. canned domestic black olives, pitted and halved
1 lb. cabbage, shredded
5 medium-sized potatoes, peeled and cut in bite-sized pieces
5 tomatoes
2 Tbsp. tomato paste
2 medium onions, peeled and chopped
Vegetable oil
2 Tbsp. lemon juice
1 clove minced garlic
2 Tbsp. minced dill
Salt and pepper

If dried mushrooms are used, wash them and soak in 2 cups water for 2 hours; then bring to a boil and simmer 15 minutes. Remove mushrooms, reserving their liquid;

slice them and sauté in 2 tablespoons oil for 5 minutes. Put mushrooms, their cooking liquid, and 8 cups water in a soup pot. If using fresh mushrooms, sauté them in 2 tablespoons oil and then add to soup pot with 10 cups water. Add carrots, parsnips, leeks, and celery. Bring to a boil and simmer ½ hour, partially covered. Sauté beets in 2 tablespoons oil, stirring constantly until shiny. Add to soup and simmer along with olives, cabbage, potatoes, tomatoes and tomato paste for 45 minutes. Sauté onions in 1 Tbsp. oil until golden brown and add to soup. Simmer for 5 minutes. Add lemon juice, garlic, dill, and salt and pepper to taste. This is delicious served with cabbage- or kasha-filled *pirozhki*. *Serves 8–10.*

wine borshch

This unusual borshch is refreshing either hot or cold

6 cups water
1 carrot, peeled and sliced
1 stalk celery, sliced
1 small turnip, peeled and sliced
1 small onion, peeled and sliced
2 Tbsp. chopped parsley
2 Tbsp. chopped dill
½ cup juice from jar of pickles
1 1-lb. can of beets with juice
1 Tbsp. lemon juice
1 cup Sauternes
1 bay leaf
Salt and pepper

Combine water, carrot, celery, turnip, onion, 1 Tbsp. parsley, and pickle juice in a pot and simmer 30 minutes. Strain broth and discard vegetables. Drain and dice beets reserving juice; combine with lemon juice, Sauternes, and 1 Tbsp. dill. Place in pot and add strained bouillon. Add ½ cup beet juice, bay leaf, and a pinch of pepper. Simmer on low heat 25 minutes. Taste for seasoning and add salt if necessary. Remove bay leaf and sprinkle with remaining chopped parsley and dill. *Serves 6.*

shchi

8 cups fresh or canned beef broth
3–4 Tbsp. butter
½ lb. cabbage, chopped
1 medium onion, peeled and chopped

2 medium carrots, peeled and chopped
½ lb. sauerkraut, drained
3 medium potatoes, peeled and cut in bite-sized pieces
1 6-oz. can tomato paste
¼ lb. leftover boiled beef, cut in bite-sized pieces
½ clove garlic, peeled and minced
Lemon juice
Salt and pepper

Fry cabbage, onion and carrots in butter. Add bouillon, and bring to a boil. Add sauerkraut, and simmer for 15 minutes. Add potatoes, tomato paste, pepper and salt (if needed). Cook on low heat for 45 minutes, stirring occasionally. Add beef and simmer 10 minutes. Just before serving add garlic and a few drops of lemon juice. Serve with sour cream. *Serves 8*.

lazy shchi

PETIT

This version is more a cream soup than a traditional shchi

10 cups fresh or canned beef bouillon
1 lb. beef, cut in cubes
½ lb. cabbage, shredded
2 large carrots, peeled and sliced
1 medium turnip, peeled and chopped
1 leek, chopped
3 Tbsp. chopped parsley
Salt and pepper
2 Tbsp. butter
2 Tbsp. flour
½ cup sour cream

Put beef in boiling water to cover for 5 minutes; drain off water. Combine bouillon, beef, cabbage, carrots, turnip, leek and 2 Tbsp. parsley, and simmer for 50 minutes. Taste for seasoning, and add salt and pepper. Melt butter; add flour, and stir till lightly browned. Add 1½ cups of strained soup and whisk until thick. Whisk back into the soup mixture. Stir until smooth. Blend in sour cream but do not boil. Just before serving sprinkle with remaining tablespoon of chopped parsley. *Serves 8.*

shchi with mushrooms

3 oz. dried mushrooms
4 cups cold water
2 medium onions, peeled
1 carrot
1 Tbsp. chopped parsley
3 Tbsp. butter
½ small white cabbage
1 bay leaf
2 cups fresh or canned beef broth
Salt and pepper

Wash mushrooms well. Put into a pot with 4 cups cold water and 1 onion, finely chopped, and bring to a boil. Reduce heat and simmer 30 minutes. Chop remaining onion and carrot and fry in butter along with parsley. Wash cabbage in cold water and squeeze dry. Shred cabbage and add to vegetables along with 2 cups of the water in which mushrooms were cooked, the bay leaf, and salt and pepper to taste. Simmer for 20 minutes. Add remaining mushroom broth, chopped mushrooms, and 2 cups beef broth. Simmer another 20 minutes, and taste for seasoning. *Serves 4–6.*

❖ shchi with apples

ODESSER

The fruit gives a pleasant tang to this unusual starter

7 cups water
1 lb. beef (chuck or flanken), cut into 1-inch cubes
1 medium onion, peeled and chopped
2 medium carrots, peeled and chopped
½ lb. cabbage, finely shredded
1 28-oz. can crushed tomatoes
1 19-oz. can white beans (cannelloni), washed and drained
2 small apples, peeled, cored and diced (preferably tart apples)
Salt and pepper to taste

In a large pot boil the meat with the carrots and onion until meat is soft, about 30-40 minutes. Meanwhile, soak the shredded cabbage in boiling water to cover (off heat). When meat is done drain the cabbage, add it to the soup and simmer 15 minutes.

Add the tomatoes and beans to the soup, stir well and cook for five minutes. Mix in the apples, and cook for another ten minutes. Taste for seasoning and serve very hot. *Serves 6–8.*

mixed solianka

KHAZANOV

Other kinds of sausages or leftover meats can be substituted for those suggested

9 cups water
1½ lbs. beef (chuck or flanken)
1 smoked pork hock
2 large onions, peeled
4 medium carrots, peeled and sliced
2 ribs celery, chopped
3 Tbsp. tomato paste
¼ lb. ham, shredded
3 frankfurters
¼ lb. salami
¼ lb. liver (beef or calf), diced
1 veal or 2 lamb kidneys, diced
2 Tbsp. diced salt pork
2 Tbsp. vegetable oil
2 Tbsp. butter
1 tsp. capers
4 dill pickles, chopped
1 bay leaf
5 black olives, pitted and chopped
1 Tbsp. chopped parsley
1 Tbsp. chopped dill
Salt and pepper
1 lemon, sliced

Put beef and pork hock in 9 cups water, bring to a boil, pour out water, refill with fresh water and bring back to a boil. Add 1 tsp. salt, pinch pepper, 1 onion, quartered, 2 sliced carrots and 1 rib celery. Simmer 1½ hours. Strain broth and skim fat. Add remaining carrots and celery to broth. Simmer for 10 minutes. In oil and butter lightly fry the remaining onion, finely chopped. Add the tomato paste and ham, sliced frank-furters, chopped salami, liver, kidneys and diced salt pork. Simmer for 5–8 minutes and add to soup. Add capers, pickles, bay leaf and a pinch of pepper and simmer 20 minutes. Ten minutes before serving sprinkle in olives, parsley and dill. Taste for sea-soning and add salt and pepper as needed. Float a thin lemon slice in each portion and serve sour cream on the side. *Serves 6–8.*

rassol'nik

2 beef kidneys
8 cups beef bouillon
1 Tbsp. chopped parsley
1 stalk celery, chopped
1 small onion, peeled and chopped
1 turnip, peeled and chopped
4 Tbsp. butter
1 tomato, chopped
1 Tbsp. tomato paste
2 cloves garlic, peeled and minced
4 sour pickles, chopped
½ cup pickle juice
4 small potatoes, peeled and diced
1 bay leaf
Dill
Parsley
Salt and pepper
Optional: sour cream

Clean kidneys of all membranes and fat. Place in water to cover, bring to a boil, drain off water, replace with fresh cold water, boil again, drain off water, replace with fresh water, and boil 10 minutes. Dice kidneys and add them with their cooking liquid to beef bouillon. Fry 1 Tbsp. parsley, celery, onion, turnip, tomato, tomato paste, and garlic in butter for 5–10 minutes. Combine with the kidneys in the bouillon and simmer 30 minutes. Add pickles, pickle juice and potatoes, bay leaf and salt and pepper to taste. Simmer for 20 minutes. Taste for seasoning and just before serving sprinkle with minced dill and parsley. *Rassol'nik* may be served with sour cream on the side. *Serves 6.*

rassol'nik with spinach

This rassol'nik is a relative of "Green borshch"

2 beef kidneys
6 cups beef bouillon
2 Tbsp. chopped parsley
1 parsnip, peeled and sliced
1 stalk celery, sliced
1 medium onion, peeled and sliced

1 medium turnip, peeled and sliced
2 Tbsp. butter
4 sour pickles, coarsely chopped
½ cup pickle juice
1 bay leaf
Salt and pepper
½ lb. spinach leaves, washed and shredded
½ lb. lettuce, washed and shredded
3 egg yolks
⅔ cup milk
1 Tbsp. minced dill

Clean kidneys of membranes and fat; boil kidneys in cold water, changing water as in recipe for *Rassol'nik*. Chop kidneys and add them with their broth to beef bouillon. Fry 1 Tbsp. parsley, parsnip, celery, onion and turnip in butter for 5–10 minutes. Add to soup. Simmer on low heat for 10 minutes. Add pickles, pickle juice, bay leaf and dash pepper, and simmer 15 minutes. Put in spinach and lettuce and simmer 5 minutes; taste for salt and add only if needed. Beat egg yolks well with milk; be sure soup is not boiling. Pour a cupful of soup into egg mixture and slowly stir back into soup, beating constantly. Before serving sprinkle with remaining parsley and dill. *Serves 8.*

chicken rassol'nik

This soup is identical to *Rassol'nik* with spinach with the following exceptions: substitute 8 cups of chicken bouillon for beef bouillon. Do not add the water in which the kidneys were cooked to the soup. Add a package of chopped chicken giblets (except for liver) to the bouillon, along with the kidneys and vegetables.

puree of liver soup

Almost any kind of liver will do for this soup

1 lb. liver (beef, calf, chicken)
5 cups beef broth (if you use chicken livers use chicken broth)
6 Tbsp. butter
1 small carrot, peeled and chopped
1 medium onion, peeled and chopped
1 Tbsp. chopped parsley
2 Tbsp. flour
Salt and pepper

Clean liver, cut in small pieces and fry in 4 Tbsp. butter along with the onion, parsley and carrot. Add 1½ cups stock, cover, and simmer 25 minutes. Strain stock; puree liver in food processor or grind very fine. Melt 2 Tbsp. butter, whisk in flour, and stir to make a roux. Pour in the strained stock from the liver and cook till thick, stirring. Add the rest of the stock, the liver and salt and pepper to taste. Simmer 5 minutes. *Serves 4–5.*

ukha

This clear fish soup is still very popular in Russia

8 cups water
1 lb. fish heads, tails, and trimmings
1 lb. fresh fish such as halibut or cod
2 medium onions, peeled and thinly sliced
Salt and pepper
1 bay leaf
2 large potatoes, peeled and cut in bite-sized pieces
2 Tbsp. chopped parsley
1 Tbsp. butter
2 Tbsp. chopped dill
1 lemon, thinly sliced

Boil the fish trimmings in water with 1 onion, salt, and pepper for 30–40 minutes. Strain. Stir in remaining onion, bay leaf, potatoes and 1 Tbsp. parsley; simmer for 15–20 minutes. Gently lower in fresh fish, cut into serving pieces, and simmer for 8–10 minutes. Add butter, remaining parsley and dill. In each plate put 2 or 3 thin slices of lemon. *Serves 6.*

fish solianka

Almost any fresh fish can go into this broth

8 cups water
1 lb. fish trimmings
2 medium onions, peeled
1 large carrot, peeled and sliced
2 Tbsp. chopped parsley
Salt and pepper
1 Tbsp. butter
1 8½-oz. can tomatoes
1 lb. fresh fish, cut into 1-inch chunks
4 kosher dill pickles, chopped
½ cup pickle juice

1 Tbsp. capers
1 bay leaf
1 Tbsp. minced dill
1 lemon, thinly sliced
¼ lb. black olives, pitted and sliced

Boil fish trimmings in water with 1 coarsely sliced onion, carrot, parsley, salt and pepper. Simmer for 35 minutes; strain, discarding trimmings and vegetables and reserving broth. Brown remaining onion, peeled and chopped, in butter. Add tomatoes and simmer, then stir in fish, pickles, and pickle juice, capers, bay leaf, and pepper. Add stock and salt to taste, and simmer for 15 minutes. Just before serving, sprinkle with minced dill and put a few thin slices of lemon and olives in each soup plate. *Serves 6.*

vegetable puree

2 large carrots, peeled and coarsely sliced
2 medium potatoes, peeled and quartered
2 medium turnips, peeled and quartered
5 oz. frozen peas (½ of 10-oz. package)
1 tsp. salt
4 cups water

Bring water to a boil and put in vegetables and salt. Bring back to a boil and simmer on low heat, partially covered, for 35 minutes. Puree in blender. If too thick, thin out with a few tablespoons of water. Check seasoning and add salt to taste. *Serves 4.*

lentil soup

A more traditional version of this staple dish

8 cups water
1 smoked pork hock
½ lb. lentils
5 large carrots, peeled and sliced
2 Tbsp. minced parsley
1 turnip, peeled and chopped
1 medium onion, peeled and chopped
2 Tbsp. butter
1 Tbsp. flour
1 cup milk
Salt and pepper

Wash lentils. Cover with water, and bring to a boil along with pork hock, carrots, parsley, and turnip. Fry onion in 1 Tbsp. butter and add to soup. Simmer 45 minutes. Melt remaining 1 Tbsp. butter, blend in flour and stir till golden. Add milk and whisk until thick. Add sauce to soup; taste for seasoning and add salt. Remove pork hock, chop off meat from bone and return to soup. Puree soup in blender or put through food processor. Check seasoning and serve very hot. *Serves 6.*

lentil soup with everything

RITCHIE FARNSWORTH

1 bag lentils (1 lb.)
12 cups water
1 smoked pork hock
1 large onion, peeled and finely chopped
2 cloves garlic, peeled and minced
1 rib celery, chopped
2 large carrots, peeled and coarsely chopped
½ lb. leftover cooked lamb, beef or turkey, or 3 frankfurters,
    or any other cooked, leftover meat, coarsely chopped
4 tomatoes, coarsely chopped
½ small eggplant, peeled and diced
3 small potatoes, peeled and diced
2 tsp. Worcestershire sauce
2 tsp. lemon juice
Pinch cayenne pepper
1 tsp. curry powder
1 Tbsp. chopped parsley
Salt
1 lemon, thinly sliced
Sour cream
Yogurt

Bring lentils, water and pork hock to a boil. Simmer 45 minutes or until lentils are tender. Add chopped onion, garlic, celery, carrots, leftover meat, tomatoes, eggplant and potatoes, and stir gently. Stir in Worcestershire sauce, lemon juice, cayenne and curry. Taste for seasoning. If necessary add a pinch of salt. Simmer 1½ hours, partially covered, and taste again for seasoning; add curry, lemon juice, or cayenne as needed. The spicing should be snappy. Cook for at least an hour. If there is too much liquid, or if 10 more guests suddenly show up, throw in a handful or two of rice or grate in a peeled potato, and cook 20 more minutes. If it cooks down too much, add more water and/or bouillon, or give up and call it a casserole and thrust it in a 350-degree oven to finish cooking. Taste frequently and add more of whatever anyone says it still needs. Soup should be very thick. Remove pork hock, slice off meat and add to soup.

Just before serving, add a thinly sliced lemon and sprinkle with chopped parsley. Serve very hot with a bowl of sour cream and a bowl of yogurt on the side. *Serves 8–10.*

mushroom soup

2 cups hot water
¾ cup dried mushrooms
5 cups beef broth
½ cup carrots, peeled and chopped
½ stalk celery, chopped
1 onion, peeled and minced
Optional: 1 Tbsp. barley
4 Tbsp. butter
2 Tbsp. flour
½ tsp. salt
Pinch pepper
1 clove garlic, peeled and crushed
⅔ cup sour cream

Soak mushrooms for 45 minutes in 2 cups hot water, and then cook them in the soaking water until tender. Remove mushrooms and chop finely. Add beef broth to mushrooms and their cooking liquid. Fry onion in 2 Tbsp. butter, and add it along with carrots, celery and barley to mushroom soup. Partially cover and cook for 40 minutes on low heat. Melt remaining 2 Tbsp. butter. Add flour and whisk until smooth. Stir 1 cup of soup into roux; blend, and pour back into soup. Add salt, pepper, and garlic and taste for seasoning. Whisk in sour cream and blend until smooth, but do not boil. Correct seasoning. *Serves 6.*

❖ mushroom and barley soup

KAVENOKI

This is particularly good with porcini mushrooms

4 oz. dried porcini or white mushrooms, or 8 oz. fresh porcini mushrooms
3 Tbsp. pearl barley
2 medium potatoes, peeled and diced
1½ Tbsp. olive oil
½ cup minced sweet onion
Salt and pepper to taste
Minced dill (approximately ¼ cup)
Sour cream

If using fresh mushrooms, wash well and mince. If using the dried mushrooms, rinse quickly in a sieve with cold water to remove external grit, then soak for 30 minutes in enough cold water to cover mushrooms. Carefully drain off and reserve the soaking liquid, and put it through a fine sieve to remove any remaining sediment. Rinse the mushrooms well in a sieve under cold running water to eliminate any grit, and chop finely.

Place the barley in a pot and cover with 4 cups water. Bring to a boil, add the soaking liquid from the mushrooms, and allow to simmer on medium heat. While the barley is simmering fry the onions and mushrooms (either fresh or dried) in the olive oil for 5-8 minutes, until mushrooms are soft and onion is soft and takes on color. If necessary, add a few drops of olive oil; when the vegetables are done there should be no extra oil remaining in the pan.

Stir the mushrooms, onions and potatoes into the pot and add salt and pepper to taste. Simmer on medium heat for 20-30 minutes until the barley and potatoes are cooked through. Taste again for seasoning.

Serve very hot with sour cream and minced dill. *Serves 6.*

mushroom soup with potatoes

KORENEVA

1 cup dried mushrooms
2 large potatoes, peeled and cubed
2 large carrots, peeled and diced
1 parsnip, peeled and diced
2 Tbsp. pearl barley
1 medium onion, peeled and finely chopped
1 Tbsp. butter

1 tsp. salt or to taste
¼ tsp. black pepper
Sour cream

Place mushrooms in a sieve and run cold water over them to remove dirt and sandy particles. Bring washed mushrooms to a boil in 2 cups water and simmer on low heat for 15 minutes. In a separate pot bring the potatoes, carrots, parsnip, barley, salt and pepper to a boil in 4 cups water and simmer 10–15 minutes. Melt the butter and sauté onion until soft; add to the pot with vegetables. Strain the liquid from the mushrooms into the pot with the vegetables and chop mushrooms finely; then add them to the pot and simmer the soup another 10 minutes. Serve very hot with sour cream on the side. *Serves 6.*

cauliflower soup

6 cups beef broth
1 2–3 lb. cauliflower
2 Tbsp. butter
1 Tbsp. flour
2 egg yolks
1½ cups light cream
Salt and pepper

Wash cauliflower and cut into florets. Cook cauliflower with 1 Tbsp. butter in beef broth on low heat for 30 minutes until cauliflower is very soft. Puree in blender or food processor. Melt remaining Tbsp. butter, whisk in flour, and when smooth blend in 1 cup of soup. Pour back into soup pot and stir well. Blend egg yolks with cream. Be sure soup is not boiling. Whisk egg mixture into soup, stirring constantly. Do not allow to boil. Taste for seasoning and add salt and pepper as needed. *Serves 4–6.*

potato puree soup

10–12 small potatoes, boiled, peeled and quartered
½ tsp. salt
2 Tbsp. butter
1 Tbsp. flour
5 cups chicken bouillon
¼ cup chopped ham
½ cup light cream
2 egg yolks
Optional: chives

Mash potatoes with salt and 1 Tbsp. butter; blend until smooth. Melt remaining Tbsp. butter, and add flour. When smooth stir in 1 cup chicken bouillon and whisk until thick. Add potatoes, the rest of the bouillon, and ham. Taste for salt. Cook for 10 minutes on low heat. Blend egg yolks and cream; keep soup below boiling point. Whisk in egg mixture but do not allow to boil. If mixture is too thick, thin with a bit of chicken broth. May be served sprinkled with chopped chives. *Serves 6.*

potato and mushroom soup

1 lb. mushrooms, washed and coarsely chopped
1 large onion, peeled and coarsely chopped
3 Tbsp. butter
7 cups beef broth
8 medium potatoes, peeled and cubed
Salt and pepper
1 Tbsp. chopped dill
1 Tbsp. chopped parsley
Few drops lemon juice
Sour cream

Fry mushrooms and onion in butter until soft; sprinkle with salt and pepper. Place in beef broth along with potatoes, dill, and parsley, and simmer for 20–30 minutes. Add salt and pepper to taste. Add lemon juice and taste for seasoning. Serve very hot, with sour cream on the side. *Serves 6.*

potato and onion soup
CHEOSKY

3 quarts water
Salt
4 large potatoes, peeled and diced
3 large onions, chopped
¼ lb. salt pork, diced
4 Tbsp. butter

Cook potatoes in 3 quarts of salted water for 20 minutes. Fry pork in butter until brown. Remove with a slotted spoon and add to potatoes. Put onions in same pan in which pork was fried and cook until golden, adding more butter if necessary. Add onions to potato mixture and simmer ½ hour. *Serves 6–8.*

spicy potato soup
MRS. YU.

6 medium potatoes, peeled and cubed
7 cups chicken broth
1 tsp. salt
1 Tbsp. butter
1 Tbsp. flour
1 onion, peeled and minced
Generous pinch cayenne pepper
Black pepper
Sour cream

Boil potatoes in 7 cups broth with salt until tender (about 20 minutes). Pour off and reserve broth, and sprinkle flour over potatoes; stir in butter, being careful not to mash potatoes. Add onion, and black pepper to taste. Pour broth in which potatoes were cooked back into pot and bring to a boil, stirring. Add salt and cayenne and taste for seasoning. Put in soup plates and place a heaping Tbsp. of sour cream in each serving. *Serves 6.*

tomato and apple soup
An unusual and healthy vegetable combination

2 tomatoes, chopped
2 apples, peeled, cored, and chopped
½ tsp. salt
1 tsp. paprika
2 Tbsp. butter
2 Tbsp. flour
2 cups chicken stock
½ cup cooked rice
1 egg yolk
1½ cups milk or light cream

Sprinkle tomatoes and apples with salt and paprika. On low heat braise tomato-apple mixture in 1 Tbsp. butter. Stir constantly to prevent burning. Cook for 10 minutes. Melt remaining Tbsp. butter. Stir in flour, and when thick add chicken stock and stir till smooth. Add to tomato-apple mixture. Cook 15 minutes and stir in rice. Blend milk or cream with egg yolk and carefully stir into soup, taking care that mixture does not boil. Taste for seasoning and add salt if needed. *Serves 4.*

cheese soup

BELSKY

A very simple and elegant dish

¼ lb. hard cheese such as Cheddar, grated
4 Tbsp. butter
4 Tbsp. flour
3 cups water
1 egg, well beaten
Salt and pepper
Optional: croutons

Melt the butter and add flour. Blend until smooth. Whisk in water and blend until thick. Add grated cheese and continue to cook on low heat. Blend in egg, but do not boil. Taste for seasoning and add salt and pepper to taste. Soup will be thick. Serve in small cups with a sprinkling of croutons. *Serves 4*.

❖ cheese and vegetable Soup

CHERNYAKHOVSKAYA

It's hard to guess at all the ingredients in this unusual soup

5 cups water
4 oz. processed cheese, such as "Laughing Cow" brand, diced
6 oz. mushrooms, washed and chopped
1 Tbsp. vegetable oil
2 Tbsp. butter
1 small onion, peeled and chopped
2 medium carrots, peeled and chopped
2 medium potatoes, peeled and cut into one-half-inch cubes
¼ cup angel hair pasta, broken into pieces (you can also use orzo, but this will produce a very thick soup)
Salt and pepper to taste
1 Tbsp. minced parsley
1 Tbsp. minced dill

Bring the water to a boil in a pot large enough to hold all the ingredients, and add the cheese, stirring until the cheese is completely dissolved. Add the mushrooms, and simmer for five minutes. In the meantime fry the onion, carrots and potatoes in the oil and butter for 5-7 minutes, until vegetables are soft and the onion is starting to take on color.

Add the vegetables and the butter-oil mixture to the pot, and bring to a boil. Drop in the pasta, and simmer. Add salt and pepper; how much will depend on the amount of salt in your brand of cheese. Simmer for 20-25 minutes until the vegetables and pasta are cooked through.

Sprinkle with parsley and dill and serve very hot. *Serves 6-8.*

milk soup with noodles

1 cup flour
Salt
1 egg, beaten
2 Tbsp. water
4 cups milk
1 Tbsp. sugar
1 Tbsp. butter
1 tsp. cinnamon

Sift flour with a pinch of salt and form a well in center. Add egg mixed with water and form a stiff dough. Refrigerate 20 minutes. Roll out and cut into thin noodles. Simmer 10 minutes in boiling salted water. Remove from pot and let rest 10–15 minutes. Boil milk, add pinch salt, sugar and butter. Add noodles and simmer 5 minutes. Sprinkle each serving with cinnamon. *Serves 4.*

COLD SOUPS

vegetable okroshka

3 scallions, minced (green and white parts)
Salt
2 hardboiled eggs, peeled
½ tsp. mustard
1 tsp. sugar
3 Tbsp. sour cream
2 medium potatoes, peeled, boiled and diced
1 large carrot, peeled, boiled and diced
6 radishes, diced
1 large cucumber, peeled, seeded and minced
3 cups dry white wine
3 cups soda water, chilled
1 Tbsp. minced dill
1 Tbsp. minced parsley

Sprinkle scallions with salt, and combine with hardboiled egg yolks, mustard, sugar, and sour cream. Chop egg whites and mix with potatoes, carrot, radishes, cucumber, and a pinch of salt. Combine scallion mixture, potato mixture and wine and chill for several hours until very cold. Fifteen minutes before serving add soda water. Sprinkle each serving with chopped dill and parsley. *Serves 6.*

meat okroshka

½ lb. beef, cut into chunks
5 cups water
1 bay leaf
1 stalk celery, sliced
1 large carrot, peeled and sliced
½ tsp. salt
Pinch pepper
2 Tbsp. chopped scallions (green and white parts)
¼ tsp. dried tarragon
1 tsp. sugar
1 Tbsp. lemon juice
1 cup + 2 Tbsp. sour cream
1 Tbsp. Dijon-style mustard
1 Tbsp. pickle juice
½ large cucumber, peeled, seeded and chopped
2 small kosher dill pickles, diced
1 can (12 oz.) light beer
2 hardboiled eggs, peeled
Salt and pepper

Boil water, add bay leaf, celery, carrot, salt, pepper and beef, and simmer partially covered for 50 minutes. Remove from heat and skim fat from broth. Combine scallions, tarragon, sugar, lemon juice, sour cream, mustard and pickle juice and beat until smooth. Whisk mixture into 2½ cups strained broth. Add meat, cut in small pieces, cucumber and pickles, and stir until smooth. Taste for seasoning and add salt and pepper as needed. Add beer and leave in refrigerator for at least 5 hours, uncovered. Just before serving, chop hardboiled eggs and sprinkle onto each serving. *Serves 6.*

fish okroshka

6 cups beer
1 lb. cooked fish fillets, cut in 1-inch squares
   (cod, flounder or pike would be fine)
1 large herring fillet, cut in small pieces
1 8½-oz. can beets, drained and diced
4 scallions, minced
1 medium cucumber, peeled, seeded and chopped
1 Tbsp. prepared red horseradish
1 Tbsp. minced dill
Parsley

Combine all ingredients except minced dill and parsley, and chill for several hours. Sprinkle with chopped dill and parsley before serving. *Serves 6.*

cold beet and vegetable soup

MARTIN

5 cups water
1 small onion, peeled and quartered
2 medium carrots, peeled and coarsely sliced
⅓ cup chopped celery
1 scallion (green and white parts)
4 sprigs chopped parsley
1 Tbsp. chopped dill
1 tsp. salt
Pinch pepper
1 bay leaf
1 medium potato, peeled and quartered
1 1-lb. can beets with juice, sliced
3 tsp. sugar
1 tsp. lemon juice

GARNISH:
2 hardboiled eggs, peeled and sliced
6 scallions, chopped (green part only)
3 Tbsp. mixed chopped dill and parsley
4 radishes, chopped
¼ cucumber, peeled and coarsely chopped
⅔ cup sour cream

Simmer water, onion, carrots, celery, scallion, parsley, dill, salt, pepper, bay leaf and potato, partially covered, on low heat for 1 hour. Strain. Add beets with juice, sugar and lemon
juice; stir, and chill. Taste for seasoning and add salt or lemon juice if needed. Spoon into
4 bowls. Mix hard-boiled eggs, scallions, dill, parsley, radishes, and cucumber and add to
each bowl. Float a heaping Tbsp. of sour cream on top of each portion. *Serves 4.*

cold summer beet soup

This soup can be made in five minutes

1 1-lb. can beets with juice
7 scallions (green and white parts)
¼ small cucumber, peeled and seeded
1 cup yogurt
4 Tbsp. sour cream
1 cup buttermilk
¼ tsp. salt
Pinch pepper
2 tsp. lemon juice
1 tsp. sugar

Put all ingredients except for 3 scallions in blender or food processor, and puree until
smooth. Taste for seasoning and add salt, sugar, or lemon juice as needed. If puree is too
thick, thin with a little milk. Dice remaining 3 scallions and serve as garnish. *Serves 4.*

cold carrot soup

4 large carrots, peeled and very finely chopped
3 cups milk
¾ cup cottage cheese
4 Tbsp. sour cream
2 Tbsp. dark raisins
¼ tsp. salt
1 Tbsp. chopped parsley

The carrots should be finely chopped or grated; if using a food processor be careful not
to puree them. Pour milk into a pot, add carrots and bring slowly to a boil. Reduce heat
to very low, cover, and simmer 15 minutes. Remove from heat. Drain cottage cheese
and put through food processor along with sour cream and raisins, processing until
mixture is fairly smooth. Slowly stir cottage cheese mixture into carrots and milk, and

continue stirring until thoroughly blended. Add salt and chill for at least 3 hours. Taste for seasoning and serve sprinkled with chopped parsley. *Serves 4–6.*

spinach soup
ODESSER

1 10-oz. package frozen chopped spinach
1 tsp. salt
1½ cups water
2 cups chicken stock
½ tsp. pepper
1 cup sour cream
3 Tbsp. flour
½ cup milk
1½ Tbsp. lemon juice
3 hardboiled eggs, peeled and cut in half

Cook frozen spinach in water and salt for 7 minutes. Add chicken stock and pepper and simmer 5 minutes. Whisk flour into sour cream and beat until smooth. Add milk, stirring constantly, and pour into spinach mixture over low heat. Simmer 10 minutes. Add lemon juice. Pour half of mixture into blender and blend on low speed for 10 seconds. Pour back into rest of soup mixture and simmer for 10 minutes. Taste for seasoning and add salt, pepper, or lemon juice to taste. Chill until very cold. Taste for seasoning and add more lemon juice if necessary. Soup should be quite sour. Serve with half a hard-boiled egg and additional sour cream in each portion. Note: Soup may also be served hot. In that case, omit eggs and reduce lemon juice to 1 tsp. *Serves 6.*

zucchini soup
B. VINOGRADOVA

This easy-to-prepare soup is equally good hot or cold

5 zucchini
1 large onion, peeled and sliced
¼ lb. butter
1 cup chicken broth
Dash curry powder
½ tsp. salt
Dash pepper
1 cup heavy cream

GARNISH:
If served hot: 4 frankfurters, cooked and sliced
If served cold: 2 Tbsp. chopped chives

Scrub but do not peel zucchini; trim ends, slice, and put in pot with onion and butter. Cook, partially covered, on medium heat for 12–15 minutes until soft. Add broth, curry, salt and pepper, and cook for 5 minutes. Add cream and bring to a boil. Puree in blender and taste for seasoning. To serve hot: add sliced frankfurters, heat through and serve. To serve cold: chill until very cold and sprinkle each serving with chopped chives. *Serves 4.*

blueberry soup

ODESSER

Other berries can also be used for this summer soup

2 cups blueberries (1 basket), washed
½ cup sugar
½ cup rosé wine
2 cups water
2 tsp. lemon juice
½ cup sour cream

Reserve ¼ cup of blueberries. Heat remaining berries with sugar, wine and water to boiling point, then simmer on low heat 10 minutes. Remove from heat and add lemon juice. Put in blender for 10 seconds on low speed. Cool slightly and whisk in sour cream. Stir in reserved berries; chill thoroughly. May be served with croutons. *Serves 4–6.*

strawberry soup

This soup could be an unusual dessert as well as a first course

2 pint baskets strawberries, cleaned
1½ cups dry white wine
2 cups water
Peel of ½ lemon
1½ tsp. lemon juice
1 cup sugar
Sour cream

Save 8 strawberries for garnish and puree the rest in a blender or food processor. Boil wine, water, lemon peel, lemon juice and sugar until sugar is completely dissolved. Pour into strawberries, blend and chill until very cold. Into each of 6 plates, put soup and a tablespoon of sour cream, and garnish with reserved sliced strawberries. *Serves 6.*

cold apple soup

5 apples, peeled, cored and coarsely chopped
2 cups water
½ tsp. cinnamon
½ tsp. grated lemon peel
1 Tbsp. white wine
⅓ cup white bread crumbs
3 cups red wine
Juice of 1 lemon
1 Tbsp. raspberry jam
2 Tbsp. sugar

Boil apples, water, cinnamon, lemon peel and white wine over low heat for 25 minutes. Stir often so that mixture does not burn. Add bread crumbs; simmer 5 minutes. Puree in blender or food processor, add red wine, lemon juice, jam and sugar and blend. Chill until very cold. *Serves 6–8.*

A delicious addition to the soup is:

apple dumplings

3 apples, peeled, cored and grated
    (can be chopped fine in food processor)
1 Tbsp. red wine
½ tsp. cinnamon
½ tsp. grated lemon peel
½ cup sugar
2 cups white bread crumbs
2 eggs

Combine apples, wine, cinnamon, lemon peel, sugar and bread crumbs. Beat eggs well and add. Bake mixture in a greased casserole at 350 degrees for 30 minutes. Allow to cool. Make small round dumplings with a melon baller or with fingers and put 2–3 in each soup plate just before serving.

cherry soup

1 1-lb. jar dark sweet Bing cherries with juice, pitted
3 cups water
¼ tsp. cinnamon
¼ tsp. ground cardamom
Optional: 2 Tbsp. sugar
2 tsp. lemon juice
½ tsp. grated lemon rind
¼ cup red wine
Sour cream

Put all ingredients except sugar and sour cream in a pot, bring to a boil and simmer on low heat for 15 minutes. Puree in blender and strain. Taste for seasoning and add more lemon juice or sugar to taste; soup should be tart. Pour into small cups and garnish with sour cream. If desired soup may be decorated with a few additional cherries. *Serves 4.*

pirogs & pancakes

pirogs and pancakes

Being so fond of bread ("It's a bad dinner with no bread," runs one proverb), Russians are partial to dishes made with batters and doughs. There are stuffed pastries–a large oval pie (*pirog*), smaller individual pastries (*pirozhki*), a square or loaf-shaped pie (*kulebiaka*), a chicken pie (*kurnik*), and cheese pastries (*vatrushki*). (The *kulebiaka* usually has a simple cabbage or fish filling as opposed to the complicated French "coulibiac" with its brioche dough and three or more layers of filling.) There are also dumplings (*pel'meni* or *vareniki*) filled with meat, cheese, potato, or fruit, and pancakes–the yeast-based *bliny, blinchiki* (stuffed with meat or cheese), and *olad'i* (fritters).

A *pirog*, which is quite filling, can be a main dish following a light consommé, or a piece of *pirog* may be served as an accompaniment to a heavier soup. *Pirozhki* can be served as *zakuski* with drinks or with borshch or *shchi*. Small, open *pirozhki* are known as *rasstegai*. An elegant dinner in nineteenth-century St. Petersburg featured salmon soup with "les rasstegais au saumon." All are easy to make, though filling individual *pirozhki* requires more time than stuffing one *pirog*.

Most of the doughs can be made in a food processor or heavy duty mixer. With a yeast dough, which makes a tender, light-textured pastry, there is no need to wait for dough to rise before putting in the filling. The filled *pirog* or *pirozhki* can be left to rise on a baking sheet in a 110-degree oven for about 45 minutes. The heat is then turned up to 350 degrees for the remainder of the baking time. This is quite a risky procedure if you have the least doubt of your oven's accuracy. A safer method is to let the *pirog* rise at room temperature. A sour cream or cream cheese dough must be refrigerated for at least 2 hours (overnight if possible).

Filling a *pirog* requires a bit of patience. It is extremely important not to use too much filling in order to avoid tearing or stretching the dough, and to leave at least a 1½-inch border around the edges of the *pirog* so that there will be sufficient dough for a tight seal between the top and bottom layers.

An easy way to fill a *pirog* is to place the lower sheet of dough on a baking sheet, put the filling on it, drape the top layer of dough over a rolling pin, lower it over the filling, and then turn up the edges of the *pirog* and pinch them together. A bit of cold water or egg white can be used as a sealer. Egg yolk mixed with water brushed across the top will ensure a golden crust. Another method for filling a *pirog* is to roll out one large sheet of dough, put the filling in the center of it, join the edges of both sides over the top of the filling and then invert the *pirog* onto a baking sheet, seam side down. This produces a good-looking *pirog* but there is always a risk that the *pirog* may collapse during the move to the baking sheet. With either method, a greased piece of foil can be placed on the baking sheet to facilitate the removal of the baked *pirog*. Holes should always be pricked in the top of the *pirog* to allow steam to escape. Extra scraps of dough may be cut into attractive shapes and placed around the openings in decorative patterns. Many Russians poke a piece of butter under the top crust or pour a little melted butter in through the opening just before the *pirog* is taken from the oven.

Fillings should be moist but not runny, and should always be cooled before they are spread on the dough. The few minutes spent waiting will make an enormous difference, as a warm filling will result in a very soggy dough. But if the filling has been made ahead of time and refrigerated, be sure that it is at room temperature before using it. Otherwise the dough will not rise properly. The *pirog* can be reheated at a low oven temperature with a piece of butter inserted under the top crust.

There are two schools of thought regarding meat fillings. In one, the raw ground chuck is fried with the onion and other ingredients. In the other, the beef is boiled before being ground (a food processor is excellent for this). Though the two schools are ardently opposed, the difference in the result does not seem very great to me. Fish mixed with chopped egg and a few scallions, rice with butter and scallions, kasha with mushrooms and onions, or potato and onions, are all tasty alternatives to meat fillings.

In making dumplings, care should be taken to pinch the edges of the dough firmly together so that the filling will not spill out. It is most important to avoid getting even a scrap of filling into the seam, for it can spoil the seal and cause leakage. *Pel'meni* are usually shaped in semi-circles, while *vareniki* are larger and more oval. If the *pel'meni* are cut into crescents, they are called *kolduny*, and if in squares, *lazanki*. The *pel'meni* can also be cut into *ushki*, little mushroom-stuffed triangles which are first boiled and then sautéed in butter. Dumplings made only of dough, with no filling, are known as *kletski*, the Russian equivalent of Austrian "nockerl." The basic recipes for *pel'meni* and *vareniki* can be used to make the other shapes as well.

Bliny (pancakes), are traditionally eaten during the last week preceding Lent, the Slavic Mardi Gras. The round *blin*, often made of a mixture of white and buckwheat flours, is a symbol of the spring sun. In former times, pancakes were baked in the oven, and the Russian expression is still to "bake (*pech'*) *bliny*," though they are always fried in butter now. There are literally hundreds of Russian proverbs about *bliny*–round as a *blin*, thin as a *blin*, flat as a *blin* . . .

The saying–"the first *blin* is always lumpy," means that the first attempt at anything is generally unsuccessful. Indeed, the first pancake is usually ragged unless the butter is at the right temperature and the heat is properly distributed over the pan. But in fact, making *bliny* or any other kind of pancake is quite easy. The trick is to use only a very small piece of butter, to keep the pan on quite high heat, and to work quickly, frying the *bliny* for only a minute or two on each side. *Bliny* can be kept warm in the oven between layers of clean, dry kitchen towels. Ideally, the pan used for frying pancakes should never be used for any other purpose, and should not be cleaned with water. It should be wiped off with an oil-soaked paper towel after each use.

Experimentation is the key to successful *pirogs, pirozhki*, and pancakes. The cook should feel free to try out combinations of doughs and fillings other than those suggested here, and to invent new ones. Meat and cabbage stuffings for *pirogs* can be used for *blinchiki*. *Bliny* can be served with jam and confectioners' sugar as well as with smoked fish, caviar, and sour cream.

pirog with yeast dough I
meat or cabbage filling

BAKER

DOUGH:
½ cup lukewarm milk (make sure it is not hot)
1 tsp. sugar
1 envelope dry yeast
¼ lb. unsalted butter (softened)
2 eggs + 1 egg yolk
1 tsp. salt
2½ to 3 cups flour

Dissolve sugar in milk, stir in yeast and let stand in a warm place about 15 minutes. Meanwhile, beat the eggs, and blend in butter and salt. Add 1 cup of flour and yeast mixture and beat till batter is smooth. Add 1 more cup of flour and mix with wooden spoon. Keep adding more flour till dough is thick enough to be turned out onto a board and kneaded by hand. Knead it on a floured board for about 5 minutes till it is smooth and elastic; divide into 2 equal parts. Roll out 1 part into an oval about ½-inch thick and place on a greased 11 x 9-inch baking pan. Spread desired filling evenly over the dough. Roll out second part of the dough and cover the filling. Pinch the edges of the lower and the upper layers of dough together securely. Prick the dough with a fork in about 10 places. Cover with a clean kitchen towel and set aside to rise for about an hour in a warm place, making sure it is not in a draft.

Heat oven to 375 degrees. Just before putting *pirog* into the oven, brush it with a beaten egg yolk. Bake it for 45 minutes.

Remove from oven and place on a wire rack. Cool slightly before cutting. Leftover *pirog* can be served at room temperature, or heated in the oven for a few minutes.

MEAT FILLING:
1 large onion, peeled and finely chopped
1 Tbsp. butter
1½ lbs. lean ground beef
Salt and pepper to taste
4 hardboiled eggs, peeled and chopped
Optional: dill

Sauté chopped onion in 1 Tbsp. butter. Add ground beef and stir to break up all chunks. Season to taste with salt and pepper and cook over medium heat for about 15 minutes, stirring occasionally. Remove from heat and cool to room temperature. Drain off excess liquid, add chopped eggs and minced dill. Taste for seasoning.

CABBAGE FILLING:
1 large cabbage, peeled and finely chopped
1 large onion, peeled and finely chopped
4–6 Tbsp. butter
4 hardboiled eggs, peeled and chopped
Salt and pepper to taste
Optional: dill

Sauté chopped onion in 2 Tbsp. butter until it is soft but not brown. Add remaining butter and when it melts gradually add chopped cabbage. Add salt and pepper to taste and cook over medium heat till cabbage is soft, adding butter as necessary to keep mixture moist. Cool to room temperature. Drain off any excess liquid which forms on bottom. Add chopped eggs and minced dill and taste for seasoning. *Makes 1 pirog (10–12 servings).*

yeast dough II
TRIFUNOVICH

1½ envelopes dry yeast
¼ cup warm water
Pinch salt
1 Tbsp. sugar
About 6 cups flour
3 egg yolks
1 cup warm milk
½ lb. + 1 Tbsp. butter, softened
1 whole egg, beaten

Dissolve yeast in warm water. Add salt and sugar. Stir in ¼ cup flour, place in warm place covered with kitchen towel and let sit for 20 minutes. Combine egg yolks and milk; blend into yeast mixture. Combine ½ lb. butter with yeast mixture and then work in flour gradually (amount will depend on type of flour) until dough is elastic but soft and does not stick to hands. Roll out and fill. Make slit in top and insert 1 Tbsp. butter. Brush with beaten egg. Bake *pirog* for 15 minutes at 200 degrees; then raise the heat to 350 degrees and bake for 45 minutes. *Makes 1 pirog (about 16 servings).*

pirog/kulebiaka with cream cheese dough

MARTIN

This is called a pirog when shaped into an oval, and a kulebiaka when rectangular.

DOUGH:
1½ sticks (12 Tbsp.) sweet butter
2 cups sifted flour
1 small package cream cheese (4 oz.) at room temperature
½–⅔ cup sour cream
2 tsp. sugar
1 tsp. salt
1 egg for brushing top

Cream butter. Sift flour with sugar and salt. Add cream cheese to butter. Then add sour cream and blend until mixture is smooth. Combine with dry ingredients. Divide into 2 equal parts. Wrap in wax paper and chill overnight. Let soften at room temperature before rolling out on a slightly floured board into 2 long rectangles. *Makes 1 pirog or kulebiaka, 10–12 servings.*

MEAT FILLING:
2 medium carrots, peeled and sliced
2 ribs celery, sliced
1 bay leaf
1 tsp. salt
½ tsp. pepper
2 lbs. beef, preferably chuck, not too lean, cut in small cubes
7 cups water
1 medium onion, peeled
2 Tbsp. butter
About 1 cup broth from cooking beef
2 hardboiled eggs, peeled and chopped
2 Tbsp. chopped dill

Put carrots, celery, bay leaf, salt and pepper into 7 cups boiling water. Add beef and boil for 1½ hours on very low heat in water to cover. Strain broth. Allow beef to cool and put through meat grinder or food processor. Chop onion very fine and brown lightly in butter. Combine meat, eggs, onion, dill and about 1 cup broth in which beef was cooked. Meat should be moist. Taste for seasoning. Roll out half of dough to form a rectangle 8 x 5 inches long, and place on lightly greased baking sheet. Place half of filling in center of rectangle and spread over dough, leaving a 1½-inch border. Cover pirog with second rectangle and pinch edges firmly together, overlapping the bottom rectangle over the top. Pinch together firmly and roll the edges up together to ensure a tight seal. Brush top with beaten egg yolk. Prick with a fork in several places on top to allow for escape of steam. Place on a greased baking sheet and brush with beaten egg. Bake at 425 degrees for about 45 minutes.

CABBAGE FILLING:

½ medium cabbage
6–8 Tbsp. chicken fat (or butter if not available)
1½ tsp. salt
¼ tsp. pepper
1 onion, finely chopped
1 bay leaf
1 pinch thyme
1 Tbsp. chopped dill

Cut out hard core and ribs of cabbage. Shred the rest, and cook slowly with onion in chicken fat. Add bay leaf, thyme, salt, pepper and dill. Taste for seasoning. Remove bay leaf. Cool before filling *pirog*.

RICE AND MUSHROOM FILLING:

½ lb. mushrooms
2 Tbsp. butter
1 small onion, peeled and chopped
Salt and pepper to taste
½ tsp. lemon juice
1½ cups cooked rice
1 tsp. chopped dill

Chop mushrooms coarsely and sauté with onion in butter until soft. Add salt, pepper and lemon juice. Mix with rice and dill. Cool before using.

pirog with short pastry dough, meat filling

YAVITZ

DOUGH:
½ cup butter
3 cups flour
½ cup ice water
1 tsp. salt
1 Tbsp. vodka
Optional: 1 egg yolk
1 Tbsp. butter

Crumble butter into flour until mixture is like cornmeal. Add vodka and salt to water, and blend into butter-flour mixture until dough just holds together. Divide into 2 parts, one ⅔ as large as the other. Refrigerate for 1 hour. Roll out larger section on lightly floured board, place filling on top, cover with smaller piece of dough and pinch edges of bottom piece up to meet top. Cut a few slits on top of *pirog*. The top may be brushed with a little egg yolk mixed with water. Bake at 400 degrees for 30 minutes, then reduce heat to 375 degrees and bake for another 10 minutes or until golden brown. Just before serving poke 1 Tbsp. butter through slit in top of *pirog*.

MEAT FILLING:
1 small onion, peeled and chopped
2½ Tbsp. butter
1½ lbs. very lean ground chuck
1 tsp. flour
¼ cup beef broth
Optional: a few drops of Maggi seasoning
    or beef extract
Salt and pepper to taste

Fry onion in 1 Tbsp. butter. In a separate skillet melt remaining butter and sauté chuck until it loses its pink color. Add onion, flour, beef broth, and Maggi seasoning: stir well. Add salt and pepper. Cool slightly and put through meat grinder. Cool before filling *pirog*. *Makes 1 pirog (about 10 servings).*

pirog with veal filling

ODESSER

DOUGH:
½ lb. butter
2 eggs
2 cups flour
Pinch salt

Cream butter; gradually blend in eggs and slowly sprinkle in flour and salt. Knead dough till it sticks together. Divide into 2 parts, wrap in wax paper and chill.

VEAL FILLING:
1 lb. veal for stew (soup meat may be substituted), cubed
1 egg
¼ cup chicken broth
2 Tbsp. sour cream
1 small onion, peeled and chopped
1 Tbsp. butter
Salt and pepper

Simmer veal or soup meat in salted water until very tender (30–40 minutes). Drain and cool. Put meat through grinder or food processor, and combine with egg, chicken broth and sour cream. Fry onion lightly in butter and add to meat; season with salt and pepper to taste. Cool.

Roll out 1 piece of dough to ¼ inch; spread filling on it, leaving plenty of space around edges. Cover with second layer of dough and pinch edges together. Cut a slit in the center. If desired a little egg yolk mixed with water may be brushed on top of *pirog*. Bake on a greased baking sheet for 40 minutes at 375 degrees until *pirog* is golden brown. *Serves 6.*

fish pirog with sour cream dough I

Use sour cream dough made according to *Vatrushki with Sour Cream Dough* (p. 118) but omit vanilla.

Use either of the following fillings:

FISH FILLING I:
6 Tbsp. butter
1 medium onion, peeled and chopped
½ lb. mushrooms, peeled and sliced
1½ lbs. boned white-fleshed fish or salmon, coarsely chopped
Salt and pepper
3 Tbsp. minced parsley
3 Tbsp minced dill
1 cup boiled rice
2 hardboiled eggs, peeled and chopped

Sauté onion and mushrooms in 3 Tbsp. butter. Add fish and sprinkle with salt and pepper; sauté 10–12 minutes. Add parsley, dill, rice and remaining butter and cook 5 minutes on low heat. Remove from heat and when cool, add chopped eggs.

FISH FILLING II:
1 lb. white-fleshed fish (pike, flounder, cod)
1 small onion, peeled and chopped
2 Tbsp. butter
2 pieces white bread, crusts removed, soaked in ½ cup milk
1 egg, separated
2 Tbsp. sour cream
1½ cups boiled rice
Salt

Grind fish. Sauté onion in butter. Add fish and sauté for 6–8 minutes until fish loses raw color. Remove from heat and add bread (with milk squeezed out), egg yolk, sour cream, salt and rice. Beat egg white stiff and fold in.

FISH FILLING III:
Make Fish Filling I but do not add rice or eggs to mixture; use 4 hardboiled eggs instead of 2. On the dough place a layer of fish filling, then a layer of rice, and on top the chopped eggs. Eggs may be seasoned with additional salt and pepper to taste.
Makes 1 pirog. Serves 10.

pirog with sour cream dough II ham and cheese filling

RASKIN

DOUGH:
½ lb. butter
¼ cup sugar
2 egg yolks
2 tsp. rum
1 Tbsp. sour cream
1 tsp. baking powder
2¼ cups flour

Cream butter; add sugar and beat well. Blend in egg yolks, then rum and sour cream. Combine baking powder and flour and blend with butter mixture to form stiff dough. Refrigerate for 1 hour.

FILLING:
½ lb. unsalted farmers cheese
¼ lb. + 1 Tbsp. butter
1 egg yolk
1 Tbsp. sour cream
½ tsp. salt
Pinch sugar
¼ lb. shredded ham
Optional: 1 egg for top of pirog

Divide dough in 2 parts and roll out half into an 11 x 7-inch rectangle. Combine cheese and ¼ lb. butter. Blend egg yolk with sour cream and add to cheese. Mix in salt and sugar, and stir well. Spread on bottom layer of dough. Scatter shredded ham over cheese and cover with top layer of dough, closing tightly. Make slits in top layer and insert 1 Tbsp. butter under slit. If desired, brush top with beaten egg. Bake on greased sheet at 375 degrees for 35–45 minutes, until pirog is golden brown. Serve very hot. *Serves 10.*

cheese pirog

VENGEROVA

This is a sweet pirog that can be served with tea or coffee. It is really a dessert, but made the same way as all other pirogs

DOUGH:
½ lb. unsalted farmer cheese
½ lb. butter
1¾ cups flour

Blend farmer cheese and butter until smooth. Add flour and work with hands until dough is well blended. Refrigerate overnight.

F I L L I N G :
1½ lbs. farmer cheese
½ lb. butter
2 egg yolks
½ cup sour cream
1 tsp. vanilla
1 cup sugar
¼ cup mixed candied fruit
Optional: 1 egg yolk

Blend farmer cheese with butter until smooth. Beat egg yolks well and stir in sour cream and vanilla; add sugar, and beat. Combine egg mixture with farmer cheese mixture and work until very smooth. Add candied fruit. Roll out dough into 2 ovals, about 8 inches long. Put 1 oval on greased baking sheet. Place filling on dough, cover with top layer, and carefully pinch edges together. Brush with beaten egg yolk and prick holes on top. Bake about 30 minutes in 375-degree oven until golden brown. *Serves 6–8.*

potato pirog
BELSKY

A rich, delicious pirog which goes well with an omelet and green salad

D O U G H :
½ cup milk
1 envelope dry yeast
1 tsp. sugar
½ tsp. salt
¼ lb. butter, melted
Juice of ½ lemon
2 cups + 2 Tbsp. flour
3 tsp. potato flour or potato starch
1 Tbsp. grated cheese, preferably Parmesan or Romano
Pinch pepper

Heat milk gently but do not boil. Dissolve yeast in warm milk. Add sugar and salt, and let rest for 10 minutes. Add melted, slightly cooled butter and lemon juice. Combine flour, potato flour, grated cheese and pepper. Slowly combine with liquid ingredients and work with hands until smooth.

FILLING:
1 large potato, peeled
1 8-oz. package cream cheese
1 Tbsp. grated cheese (Parmesan or Romano)
½ tsp. salt
Pinch pepper
¼ tsp. sugar
Optional: 1 egg yolk

Boil potato in water until soft. Peel and blend with softened cream cheese, stirring until smooth. Add grated cheese, salt, pepper and sugar. Divide dough into 2 equal parts and roll out into 2 ovals about 11 inches long. Put filling in center of one oval and spread to sides, leaving a 2-inch border. Place top layer over filling; pinch edges. Brush with a little beaten egg yolk for color, and prick holes in center for escape of steam. Place on lightly greased baking sheet and leave in a 110-degree oven for 45 minutes. Then turn heat up to 350 degrees and bake 30–35 minutes until top is golden brown. *Serves 6–8.*

pirozhki with yeast dough I

NABOKOVA

These pirozhki disappear as soon as they are passed around

DOUGH:
1 envelope dry yeast
½ cup warm water
½ cup warm milk
4 tsp. sugar
1 tsp. salt
½ lb. butter
1 Tbsp. vegetable oil
3½–4 cups flour
2 egg whites, slightly beaten
2 egg yolks, slightly beaten

Dissolve yeast in ½ cup warm water and let stand for 10 minutes. Mix well and add ½ cup warm milk, sugar and salt. Melt butter and add it with oil to yeast mixture, stirring constantly. Add flour and knead for 2 or 3 minutes until dough is malleable and can be rolled out. On a floured board roll out to ¼-inch thickness and cut into circles

2–3 inches in diameter, depending on how large you want the *pirozhki*. Put a teaspoon of filling on each circle, cover with another circle and use the egg white to seal edges, pinching tightly. Cover tops with beaten egg yolk. Place on greased baking sheet in 110-degree oven and leave for 45 minutes or so until *pirozhki* rise. Turn up oven to 350 degrees and bake for 30–35 minutes until golden brown. Serve hot. *Makes 65–70 pirozhki.*

BEEF FILLING:
1½–2 lbs. stewing beef, cut in small cubes
4 Tbsp. vegetable oil
1 tsp. salt
Pinch pepper
2 medium onions, peeled and chopped
1½ cups strong beef broth
½ lb. mushrooms
2 tsp. butter
1 Tbsp. chopped dill
1 Tbsp. chopped parsley
½ tsp. tarragon
½ tsp. basil

Fry meat on all sides in oil. Add salt, pepper and chopped onions. Continue to fry 2–3 minutes, stirring constantly. Pour in beef broth and cook until meat is tender, approximately 25–30 minutes, adding a little water if necessary. Cool and put through meat grinder or food processor. Chop mushrooms and fry in butter; add dill, parsley, tarragon and basil, and mix well with meat. Cool before using.

CABBAGE FILLING:
1 2½–3 lb. head of cabbage
2 large onions, peeled
¼ lb. butter
½ tsp. sugar
1 tsp. salt
Pinch pepper

Shred cabbage finely. Bring 3 quarts of water to a boil and add cabbage. Cook for 1 minute after it returns to a boil. Drain well in a sieve and press out all remaining liquid. Chop onions well and fry in butter till golden. Add cabbage, salt, sugar and pepper, and simmer 15–18 minutes until soft. Cool.

VEAL FILLING:

1½ lbs. boneless breast or neck of veal, cut in small cubes
1 cup water
2 onions, peeled and finely chopped
Salt and pepper to taste
1 pair sweetbreads
1 pair calf brains
2 Tbsp. lemon juice
½ lb. mushrooms
2 Tbsp. butter
2 cups cooked rice
¼ cup chopped fresh dill

Place veal, water, onions, salt and pepper in a heavy saucepan. Bring to a boil, cover and simmer gently until tender, 35–40 minutes. Add more water if necessary, but at end of cooking mixture should be dry. Boil off extra liquid if necessary. Cover sweetbreads with cold water, bring to a boil and simmer 5 minutes. Drain and remove all connective tissue. Soak brains for 2 hours in lemon juice and water to cover; clean off blood and membranes. Drop brains into boiling water. Boil for 5 minutes, drain and remove any remaining membranes. Cut sweetbreads into very small pieces and fry gently in butter; add chopped mushrooms. Continue frying until both are thoroughly cooked and add brains. Cook another 5 minutes to blend well. Grind veal and blend with all other ingredients until smooth. Add rice and dill. Taste for seasoning.

pirozhki yeast dough II
BALAKSHA

1 envelope dry yeast
¼ cup milk
3 eggs, separated
1 egg yolk
½ cup sugar
½ cup sour cream
2 tsp. lemon juice
2 Tbsp. corn oil
¼ lb. butter, softened
3½–4 cups flour

Dissolve yeast in warm milk; let stand in warm place for 10 minutes. Beat 3 egg yolks with sugar and add to yeast mixture; blend in sour cream, lemon juice, and corn oil. Blend in butter and flour alternately until dough is elastic. Beat egg whites stiff and fold in. Roll out dough about ½-inch thick, cut out rough circles and fill; brush with remaining egg yolk diluted with 1 tsp. water. Let filled *pirozhki* stand in warm (110-degree) oven until they rise (30–40 minutes); then turn up heat to 350 degrees and bake for 30–45 minutes. *Makes about 65 pirozhki.*

pirozhki with cream cheese dough and meat filling

B. VINOGRADOVA

DOUGH:
½ lb. cream cheese at room temperature
½ lb. butter at room temperature
2 cups flour
1 scant tsp. baking powder

Cream the cheese with butter until smooth. Add flour and baking powder and knead only until dough holds together. Divide in 2 parts. Roll into the form of 2 long sausages, wrap in wax paper and refrigerate for at least 2 hours. Remove from refrigerator ½ hour before using.

FILLING:
1 large onion, peeled and chopped
2 Tbsp. butter
1½ lbs. ground chuck
½ cup beef broth
1 Tbsp. chopped dill
Salt and pepper to taste
3 hardboiled eggs, peeled and chopped
1 raw egg yolk
1 tsp. water

Sauté onion in butter until golden, and remove from butter. Add meat to pan, stirring till browned. Add broth, salt and pepper, and cook, covered for 15 minutes. Stir in onion and dill and remove from heat. Cool and add chopped eggs.

Cut circles of dough off the "sausage" to form *pirozhki*. Place 1 teaspoon of filling in center of each 2–2½ inch circle, cover with another circle, and pinch edges together, shaping into an oval. Blend egg yolk with a teaspoon of water and brush lightly over tops of *pirozhki*. Bake on lightly greased baking sheet for 15–20 minutes at 350 degrees. *Makes about 3 dozen pirozhki.*

pirozhki with sweet cream cheese dough

TUMARKIN

½ lb. butter at room temperature
½ lb. cream cheese at room temperature
2 cups sifted flour
1 tsp. sugar
1 tsp. salt

Cream butter and cream cheese together, and work in flour, sugar and salt. Work quickly to prevent dough from toughening. If dough seems too soft add a few more tablespoons flour. Wrap in wax paper and leave in refrigerator overnight. Roll out and fill with desired filling. Bake for 20 minutes in 400-degree oven until brown, checking to see that *pirozhki* do not burn. *Makes about 3 dozen pirozhki.*

fried sausage pirozhki

BELSKY

Beer makes an excellent accompaniment to these savory pirozhki

1 cup milk
5 Tbsp. butter
1 cup flour
Pinch salt
3 whole eggs
1 egg yolk
6 frankfurters

FOR FRYING:
½ cup flour
2 eggs, beaten
1 cup fine bread crumbs
1–2 cups vegetable oil

Bring milk and butter to a boil. Remove from heat and add flour and salt, stirring constantly until mixture is thick and smooth. Add eggs and yolk one at a time and beat after each addition until mixture has regained smoothness. Cut frankfurters into 1½-inch lengths. Take a small ball of dough about 3 inches in diameter and roll around sausage piece to cover it completely. Pinch off excess. Roll each *pirozhok* lightly in flour, then dip in beaten eggs and in bread crumbs. Pat coating firmly with edge of a dull knife so that it will adhere. Fry in very hot oil until crisp and brown. These *pirozhki* can be kept warm in a low oven. *Makes about 2 dozen pirozhki.*

potato pirozhki with mushroom filling

8 medium potatoes, peeled, boiled and cooled
4 Tbsp. butter
Pinch salt
½–1 cup flour
2 eggs, separated
Salt and pepper
½ lb. mushrooms
1 large onion, peeled and finely chopped
1 cup bread crumbs
Butter and oil for frying

Mash potatoes, and mix with 2 Tbsp. butter, salt, ½ cup flour and egg yolks. In remaining 2 Tbsp. butter sauté mushrooms and onion until soft; sprinkle with salt and pepper. Roll out flat (2-inch) rounds of potato dough (can be rolled between palms—if too soft, add more flour). Place a teaspoon of filling on each. Cover with another round of dough, or place filling on one end of round and cover with flap, envelope style. Dip each *pirozhok* into slightly beaten egg whites and then into bread crumbs. Fry in mixture of ½ butter and ½ oil until golden and crisp. Drain on paper towels and keep hot in low oven until time to serve. *Makes 12–16 pirozhki.*

ham pirozhki
WOLHEIM

¼ cup butter
1 cup farmer cheese
1 cup + 2 Tbsp. flour
Pinch salt
½ cup chopped, cooked ham
Optional: 1 egg, separated

Blend butter and farmer cheese till smooth: work in flour and salt. Wrap in wax paper and chill for ½ hour. Roll out ¼-inch thick and cut into small 2-inch squares. On ½ of each square put a teaspoon of chopped ham. Cover with adjoining square, and pinch edges together, sealing them with some egg white. Beat egg yolk with a teaspoon of water and brush *pirozhki* tops. Place on a lightly greased baking sheet and bake in 375-degree oven for about 20 minutes until golden. *Makes about 1½ dozen.*

FILLINGS

These fillings are for 1 pirog

m e a t

J. VISSON

The sauce ensures that this filling will remain moist

1 lb. ground chuck
1 Tbsp. finely chopped onion
3 Tbsp. butter
Salt and pepper to taste
1 Tbsp. chopped parsley
1 hardboiled egg, peeled and chopped
1 Tbsp. sifted flour
¾ cup water

Melt 2 Tbsp. butter in skillet and add beef, onion and parsley. Sprinkle with salt and pepper, and stir until well blended and browned. Cool slightly. Place in bowl and add hardboiled egg. Mix well. Melt remaining Tbsp. butter; add flour, and blend well; stir in ³/₄ cup boiling water and whisk until thick. Add sauce to filling and blend. Cool before using to fill *pirog* or *pirozhki*.

m e a t a n d n u t

1 lb. ground chuck
1 small onion, peeled and chopped
½ cup ground walnuts
1 Tbsp. chopped parsley
½ tsp. salt
Pinch pepper
2 Tbsp. butter

Mix meat with salt and pepper; fry all ingredients in butter, breaking up the meat with a wooden fork until the chuck has lost its pink color and the onion is soft. Cool filling before using. Chopped hardboiled eggs can be added if desired.

c a b b a g e a n d b u t t e r

SOSINSKAYA

1 small head of cabbage
2 medium onions, peeled and chopped
3 hardboiled eggs, peeled and chopped
¼ lb. + 4 Tbsp. butter
Salt
Optional: 1 Tbsp. chopped dill

Shred cabbage and place in colander in bowl. Pour a kettle of boiling water over it and allow it to rest several minutes; then cool, drain, and squeeze dry. In a large frying pan lightly sauté onions in 4 Tbsp. butter until golden. Remove from heat and add hardboiled eggs, cabbage, remaining softened butter and dill if desired. Mix well. Be sure mixture is cool before filling *pirog* or *pirozhki*. Add salt to taste.

rice-egg
TRIFUNOVICH

2 cups cooked rice
5 hardboiled eggs, peeled and chopped
¼ lb. + 2 Tbsp. butter
1 medium onion, peeled and chopped
¼ lb. mushrooms, chopped
Salt and pepper to taste

Melt 2 Tbsp. butter and sauté mushrooms and onion until soft. Cool. Combine rice, eggs, softened ¼ lb. butter and the onion and mushroom mixture, and blend thoroughly. Add salt and pepper to taste.

rice-scallion

Make rice filling as above but omit mushrooms, and sauté 6 minced scallions (green and white parts) with onion.

mushroom and sour cream

1 lb. mushrooms, coarsely chopped
2 Tbsp. butter
2 tsp. flour
½ cup sour cream
1 Tbsp. minced dill
1 Tbsp. minced parsley
Salt and pepper to taste

Sauté mushrooms in butter until soft. Sprinkle with flour and stir. Add sour cream and blend until smooth. Stir in dill, parsley, salt and pepper. Be sure mixture is cool before using.

liver

7 Tbsp. butter
1 lb. calf liver, cut in strips
1 medium onion, peeled and finely chopped
1 slice bread, crusts removed, soaked in 1/3 cup milk and squeezed dry
2 Tbsp. cognac
Salt and pepper to taste
Pinch nutmeg

Sauté onion in 1 Tbsp. butter. Remove onion from pan, melt an additional 5 Tbsp. butter, and sauté liver over fairly high heat until cooked through on both sides. Remove liver and put through meat grinder along with soaked bread and onion. Add remaining 1 Tbsp. butter, cognac, salt, pepper and nutmeg. Allow to stand in refrigerator for 2 hours before using.

sauerkraut

2 Tbsp. butter
1 medium onion, peeled and chopped
1 lb. sauerkraut, drained
1 tsp. caraway seeds

Sauté onion in butter. Add sauerkraut and caraway seeds and sauté for 5–6 minutes. Cool and drain off any excess liquid before using.

kasha, mushroom, and onion

1 cup cooked kasha (buckwheat groats), prepared according to package directions
½ lb. mushrooms, coarsely chopped
1 large onion, peeled and coarsely chopped
3 Tbsp. melted butter (more if needed)
Salt and pepper

Sauté onion and mushrooms in butter. Add kasha and add salt and pepper to taste. Stir in enough butter to ensure that mixture is moist.

kasha and liver

Prepare as above but fry ½ lb. coarsely chopped chicken livers together with onion and mushrooms.

carrot

PETIT

6 carrots, peeled and boiled
¼ cup chopped parsley
4 scallions, minced (green and white parts)
5 Tbsp. butter
3 Tbsp. flour
¾ cup milk
Salt and pepper
2 hardboiled eggs, peeled and chopped

Chop carrots and sauté lightly in 3 Tbsp. butter. Add parsley and scallions and simmer for a few minutes. Melt remaining butter; add flour, and stir till golden; whisk in milk and beat till sauce thickens. Add sauce to carrot mixture and stir till thick. Flavor with salt and pepper. Cool slightly and add hardboiled eggs. Taste for seasoning.

salmon filling

1 small onion, peeled and chopped
1 scallion, chopped (green and white parts)
4 oz. mushrooms, coarsely chopped
2 Tbsp. butter
8 oz. canned flaked salmon
½ cup boiled rice
½ tsp. chopped dill
Salt and pepper
2 hardboiled eggs, peeled and chopped

Sauté onion, scallion, and mushrooms in butter. Allow to cool and combine with salmon, rice, dill and salt and pepper to taste. Cool and add chopped eggs.

kurnik (chicken pie)

FRANKFURT

1 recipe *Vatrushki with Sour Cream Dough* (p. 118), omitting vanilla
6 cups water
1 chicken (about 3 lbs.)
1 medium onion, peeled and sliced
1 carrot, peeled and coarsely sliced
1 celery stalk, coarsely chopped
1 bay leaf
3 sprigs parsley
Salt and pepper
1 Tbsp. butter
1 Tbsp. flour
1 tsp. lemon juice
1 Tbsp. minced dill
1 Tbsp. minced parsley
1½ cups cooked rice
2 hardboiled eggs, peeled and chopped
½ lb. sliced mushrooms, stewed for 5–10 minutes

Bring to a boil water, onion, carrot, celery, bay leaf, 3 sprigs parsley, salt and pepper. Simmer for 10 minutes. Add chicken and simmer until meat is tender (40–45 minutes). Remove chicken from pot, and slice all meat off bones. Strain broth and reduce to 3 cups. Melt 1 Tbsp. butter; add flour, and stir. When thick, add 1½ cups chicken broth and continue stirring until very smooth. Add lemon juice, dill and parsley.

Divide sour cream pastry into 2 parts. Roll out one half and place across bottom of 10-inch pie plate. Mix rice with hardboiled eggs, add salt and pepper to taste, and place on pastry. Add a layer of coarsely sliced chicken, and scatter with mushrooms. Cover with more rice and eggs, more chicken, then remaining mushrooms and rice and eggs. Pour thickened chicken broth mixture evenly over pie. Place remaining crust on top and prick a few holes with a fork. Bake for 20 minutes at 400 degrees until top is golden brown. Serve very hot. *Serves 6.*

vatrushki (open cheese pastries with yeast dough)
NABOKOVA

*Though these contain sugar they are not a dessert and should
be served with soup; they are especially good with Green Borshch (p. 74)
The dough should be the same as for Pirozhki with Yeast Dough I (p. 112)*

FILLING:
1 lb. farmer cheese
3 eggs, lightly beaten
2 heaping Tbsp. sugar
2 Tbsp. sour cream
1 Tbsp. flour

Prepare the dough as indicated in the recipe for Pirozhki with Yeast Dough. Blend the farmer cheese with 2 eggs, sugar and sour cream until smooth. Beat in the flour. Roll out the dough on a lightly floured board or cloth to about ¼-inch thickness. It may be easier to divide it into 2 batches. Cut out rounds 3 to 4 inches in diameter. Place 1 heaping tablespoon of filling in the middle and pinch edges to form small tarts with exposed filling. These are open tarts. Place tarts on lightly greased baking sheet. Brush pastry and filling with remaining beaten egg. Bake in a 350-degree oven for about 25 minutes or until lightly browned. Cool on a rack or serve hot with Green Borshch. *Makes about 4 dozen.*

vatrushki with sour cream dough
B. VINOGRADOVA

DOUGH:
2 cups flour
½ lb. butter

½ cup sour cream
1 tsp. vanilla extract

Cut butter into flour with pastry blender or mix with 2 forks until mixture is like corn-meal. Add sour cream and vanilla and mix well. Refrigerate for 1 hour.

FILLING:
1 lb. farmer cheese
2 eggs, slightly beaten
2 Tbsp. sugar
2 Tbsp. sour cream
1 Tbsp. flour
1 cup raisins

Combine all ingredients and blend thoroughly. Roll out dough into 3-inch rounds about ½-inch thick. Place a heaping tablespoonful of filling in center of round and crimp edges, leaving the filling exposed. Bake on lightly greased sheet 25–30 minutes in a 350-degree oven until pale golden. *Makes about 3½ dozen.*

pel'meni

DOUGH:
2 cups flour
½ tsp. salt
2 eggs
4–5 Tbsp. water

Mix flour and salt. Combine eggs and water, stir in dry ingredients and knead dough until elastic. Let it rest for 1 hour. Roll out into small rounds (no more than 1½-inch diameter). In center of each place ½ teaspoon of filling.

FILLING
1 lb. ground chuck (not too lean)
1 small onion, peeled and chopped
1 tsp. butter
Salt and pepper

Combine all ingredients and mix well. Place ½ teaspoon of filling in center of dough round; cover with another dough round and pinch edges together tightly. Drop into boiling salted water or into soup broth, and simmer for 10–15 minutes until *pel'meni* rise to surface. Either serve with broth, or remove with slotted spoon and serve with sour cream and melted butter or with white vinegar. *Serves 4.*

ushki

1 recipe *pel'meni* dough
2 large onions, peeled and chopped
½ lb. mushrooms, chopped
2–3 Tbsp. butter
Salt and pepper

Sauté mushrooms and onions in butter till soft. Sprinkle with salt and pepper to taste. Cut dough into triangles instead of small circles, fill and pinch edges together. Drop into boiling salted water for 5 minutes, drain well, and fry in butter for another 5 minutes. Serve with sour cream. *Serves 4.*

vareniki

MARTIN

These boiled dumplings with cheese or cherries could be a meal in themselves

DOUGH:
2 whole eggs, beaten
2 Tbsp. cold water
2 cups flour
½ tsp. salt

Mix eggs with water, and combine flour with salt. Blend together to form an elastic dough. Form into 2-inch balls and press your thumb into center to form an indentation. Fill the hollow with a filling (below) and close ball on top to form an oval. Simmer in lightly salted boiling water for 10–12 minutes until *vareniki* rise to surface; remove with slotted spoon and serve with sour cream. *Serves 5.*

COTTAGE CHEESE FILLING
MARTIN

½ lb. cottage cheese, sieved
¾ cup sugar
1 egg, beaten
1 Tbsp. melted butter
½ tsp. vanilla extract
¼ cup raisins, chopped

Combine all ingredients and mix well. If mixture is thin, a tablespoon of flour may be added to make filling thick enough to hold together.

CHERRY FILLING

Fill each *varenik* with 2 or 3 pitted cherries which have been rolled in granulated sugar.

COTTAGE CHEESE–POTATO FILLING

KUJBIDA

2 large potatoes, peeled, boiled and cooled
½ cup farmer cheese
2 Tbsp. butter
1 small onion, peeled and chopped
Salt and pepper

Fry onion in 1 Tbsp. butter. Mash potatoes with cheese and remaining Tbsp. butter; add onion and salt and pepper to taste.

kletski (dumplings)

2 eggs, separated
2 tsp. butter
7 Tbsp. flour
2 Tbsp. cold water
¼ tsp. salt
5 cups chicken or beef broth

Cream butter and beat in egg yolks. Gradually sprinkle in flour and salt, alternating with water (mixture will be fairly thin). Beat whites stiff and fold in. Drop by teaspoonfuls into boiling chicken or beef broth. Simmer for 6–8 minutes, until *kletski* are firm–they will be rounded but ragged in shape. May be served in broth as a soup course or drained with sour cream. *Serves 4.*

bliny I

3 cups milk
1 envelope dry yeast
2 eggs, separated
3 cups white flour
1 cup buckwheat flour
1 tsp. salt

Scald milk and let cool. Dissolve yeast in milk and let sit 10 minutes. Add beaten egg yolks. Sift flours with salt, whisk into mixture and allow to rise for 2 hours in a warm place, in a bowl covered with a kitchen towel. Beat egg whites stiff and fold into mixture. Drop onto a hot buttered griddle and fry on both sides. *Makes about 3½ dozen, depending on size.*

bliny II

2½ cups lukewarm milk
1 Tbsp. (1 envelope) dry yeast
1 cup sifted white flour
1 cup sifted buckwheat flour
3 Tbsp. sugar
½ tsp. salt
6 Tbsp. unsalted butter, melted and cooled
3 eggs, lightly beaten
Melted butter for frying

In a small bowl combine the warm milk and yeast and whisk to dissolve. In a large bowl, combine both flours, sugar and salt. Beat in each addition with a wire whisk; add milk and yeast mixture, 6 Tbsp. melted butter and the eggs. Beat until smooth. Cover bowl with cloth or plastic wrap and set in a larger bowl containing warm water. Put in a warm, draft-free place and let rise for 1 to 1½ hours or until double in bulk. Heat oven to 200 degrees to keep finished *bliny* warm while remainder are being fried. Put prepared *bliny* in pan covered by kitchen towels. *Yield: 2 to 3 dozen bliny, depending on size.*

FOR BOTH RECIPES:
Preheat crêpe pan or griddle over medium heat and brush very lightly with melted butter. Pour about 3 Tbsp. of the batter onto a griddle or crêpe pan and fry until golden brown on both sides. Brush pan with butter as needed. Serve with melted butter, sour cream, caviar or smoked fish.

blinchiki with meat

B. VINOGRADOVA

These rolled stuffed pancakes freeze well. Reheat in a moderate oven

BATTER:
4 eggs
1 cup flour
½ tsp. salt

½ tsp. baking soda
1 cup milk
2 tsp. butter

Beat eggs; add flour, salt and baking soda and mix. Gradually add milk and 1 tsp. butter, melted. Melt remaining 1 tsp. butter in a small (6-inch) skillet. Heat till foam has subsided and skillet is very hot. Pour in ½ soup ladle of batter; cook a few minutes until light brown on bottom. Remove to clean towel. Do not fry on other side. Continue until all batter is used; use wax paper between layers of pancakes. Cover with towel to keep warm.

FILLING:
1 medium onion, peeled and chopped
1 lb. ground chuck
¼ cup beef broth
2 Tbsp. butter
½ raw potato, peeled and grated
Salt and pepper to taste

Fry onion in butter until golden. Add all other ingredients and stir well until meat is browned and has lost pink color. Place 1 heaping tablespoon on each pancake and roll up into a long tube. Bake filled pancakes in lightly greased baking dish at 325 degrees for 10 minutes. Serve with sour cream. *Makes 16–20 blinchiki.*

blinchiki with cheese
ODESSER

Stuffed with meat these could be a main course; with this cheese filling they could be a dessert

BATTER:
1 cup milk
2 eggs
1 cup flour
Pinch salt
Butter for frying

Beat milk and eggs together and gradually whisk in flour and salt. Drop ½ soup ladle of batter onto buttered griddle, turning *blinchiki* to fry on other side for a few seconds. Keep on kitchen towels until ready to fill.

FILLING:
½ lb. cottage cheese, sieved
1 egg yolk
2 tsp. sour cream
2 Tbsp. sugar
½ tsp. vanilla extract
1 Tbsp. butter
½ tsp. cinnamon

Blend all ingredients until smooth. Serve *blinchiki* with additional sugar and sour cream on top. *Makes approximately 10–15 blinchiki, depending on size.*

sour cream blinchiki

MRS. YU.

4 eggs, separated
½ cup sugar
1½ cups sour cream
1¼ cups flour
Butter

Beat egg yolks with sugar until white; blend in sour cream and slowly sprinkle in flour. Beat whites stiff and carefully fold in. Drop from ladle onto hot buttered skillet; *blinchiki* should be about 4 inches across. These are delicious served with a teaspoon of strawberry jam topped with sour cream. *Makes about 15 blinchiki.*

cheese olad'i

WEINSCHENKER

½ cup yogurt
½ lb. farmer cheese
2 eggs, beaten
½ cup sugar
1¾ cups flour
2 Tbsp. butter
Vegetable oil for frying

Put farmer cheese through sieve; combine with yogurt, eggs, sugar and flour. Wet hands in warm water and form into 2-inch round, flat cakes. Dot with tiny bits of butter and fry quickly on both sides in hot oil. Insides will be soft. Drain on paper towels. Serve with cherry jam. *Makes 12.*

russian crêpes

J. VISSON

2 eggs, separated
1 cup milk
4 Tbsp. flour
Butter for frying

Beat egg yolks and whisk in milk; stir in flour. Beat egg whites stiff and fold in carefully. Fry on a small (5–6 inch) griddle in a little butter, turning crêpes so that both sides are lightly browned. May be kept warm in oven. Can be served with red caviar or smoked fish. *Makes 5–6 crêpes.*

dessert crêpes

MILLER

1 recipe for J. Visson crêpes
1 cup grated Munster cheese
4 Tbsp. butter
½ cup orange marmalade
3 Tbsp. Triple Sec liqueur

Make crêpes according to recipe instructions; fill with cheese, roll up, and keep warm in a 250-degree oven. Combine butter, marmalade, and Triple Sec in a small saucepan and heat until butter melts. Pour over crêpes and serve. Serves 4.

apple olad'i (fritters)

GEOFFREY

This is an excellent brunch dish as well as a light dessert

3 eggs
2 Tbsp. sugar
⅓ cup flour
2 large apples
2 tsp. butter

Mix eggs and sugar until well blended. Add flour and beat until smooth. Peel and core apples; slice into very thin rounds. Mix into batter. Heat 2 tsp. butter in a small (4–6 inch) skillet until very hot. Drop in batter (about 2 tablespoons per pancake). Be sure that each contains apple slices. Fry on both sides till golden. Serve hot sprinkled with sugar, jam or sour cream. *Makes about 12–15 fritters.*

buttermilk apple fritters

MRS. YU.

A dessert or an unusual brunch dish

1 egg
½ cup buttermilk
1 cup flour
Pinch salt
3 medium apples, peeled, cored and cut into ¼-inch rings
4 Tbsp. butter
4 Tbsp. vegetable oil
Confectioners' sugar

Combine egg and buttermilk and beat well; gradually stir in flour and salt. Mixture will be thick and slightly lumpy. Melt butter and oil and have mixture very hot. Dip apple slices in buttermilk mixture and fry in butter and oil on both sides until puffy and golden brown. Drain immediately on paper towels and sprinkle with confectioners' sugar. Serve warm with sour cream on the side. *Makes 12–15 fritters.*

squash olad'i (fritters)

It is very difficult to guess that these sweet pancakes are made with squash

1 lb. zucchini
2 Tbsp. + 1 tsp. butter
1 egg, beaten
Pinch salt
1½ Tbsp. sugar
1 cup + 2 Tbsp. flour
½ tsp. baking soda

Clean, peel and cut zucchini into ½-inch slices. Boil in water until quite soft, about 20 minutes. Drain, mash to a puree and cool slightly. Add 2 Tbsp. butter, egg, salt and sugar, and beat well. Beat in flour and baking soda and mix until bubbly. Melt 1 tsp. butter in a small 4–6 inch skillet, and when the skillet is very hot, drop in the batter from a soup ladle. Fry *olad'i* quickly on both sides until firm and golden. Serve with sour cream. *Makes about 18–20 olad'i.*

fish

fish

A great variety of fish and shellfish live in Russia's brooks, lakes and rivers. Some of those native to Russia are not found in the United States, but substitutions do not pose a problem. Sole, flounder, halibut and other whitefleshed fish can be used in most of the recipes. Fish are poached in bouillon or wine, fried and served with mushrooms or mustard sauce, baked with sour cream, or served with lemon butter, hardboiled eggs and boiled potatoes. There are also recipes for fish pudding with whipped cream, fish dumplings, and an unusual combination of smoked salmon and macaroni. Care should be taken in all the recipes to avoid overcooking fish, which can easily toughen and lose its flavor.

Russians often prefer nibbling on cold smoked fish or an *hors d'oeuvre* such as lox, smoked whitefish, or sturgeon on a piece of black bread rather than having a main course of fish. Some Russians think fish is not really a "man's dish," and many a Russian man feels—or says he feels—downright hungry after a huge fish dinner.

cold salmon

WEINSCHENKER

4 small salmon steaks
4 cups water
1 stalk celery, sliced
1 medium onion, peeled and sliced
Salt and pepper
2 tsp. white vinegar
Pinch sugar
1 envelope gelatin
¼ cup warm water
½ cup heavy cream
⅓ cup sour cream
2 Tbsp. mayonnaise
1½ Tbsp. chopped dill
1 tsp. Dijon-style mustard
¼ tsp. pepper
Pinch salt

Bring water to a boil with celery, onion, salt, and pepper. Carefully drop in salmon steaks and simmer until just cooked, 5–8 minutes. Remove salmon steaks to a platter. Reduce broth to 2 cups; add vinegar and pinch of sugar, and simmer for a few minutes. Dissolve gelatin in ¼ cup warm water and add to broth. Place fish in shallow dish and pour broth over it. Chill for at least 6–8 hours. Beat heavy cream until stiff; add sour cream, mayonnaise, dill, mustard, pepper, and salt to taste. Serve separately. *Serves 4.*

Note: If desired, fish may be served cold without aspic; chill steaks when they are removed from broth and serve with sauce on the side.

cold fish in tomato sauce

B. VINOGRADOVA

A touch of sour salt gives this dish a tangy, sweet-sour taste

4 fish fillets (such as scrod or flounder)
⅓ cup flour
3–4 Tbsp. vegetable oil
3 Tbsp. butter
1 medium onion, peeled and sliced into rings
1 medium carrot, peeled and sliced
1 Italian green bell pepper, deribbed, seeded and minced
3 Tbsp. tomato paste
⅓ cup water
1 8-oz. can tomato sauce
⅛ tsp. pepper
¼ tsp. salt
1 tsp. sugar
¼ tsp. sour salt

Dip fish fillets in flour and fry 1–2 minutes in hot oil. Sauté onion rings separately in 3 Tbsp. butter. Remove fish to plate and cover loosely with foil. Add carrot, green bell pepper, tomato paste mixed with water and tomato sauce to the onion. Stir until smooth. Blend in salt, pepper, sour salt, and sugar and taste for seasoning. Simmer over low heat for 30 minutes. Place fish fillets in lightly greased baking dish and pour sauce over them. Bake in 350-degree oven for 15 minutes. Refrigerate and serve cold. *Serves 4.*

Note: If fish fillets are very large or you wish a greater quantity of sauce, proportions for tomato paste and tomato sauce may be doubled.

cold stuffed pike

PENDILL

1 pike (or carp) head
1 whole 3-lb. pike (or carp)
½ lb. whitefish
1 white roll
⅓ cup milk
¼ lb. sweet butter
2 large onions, peeled and chopped
Salt and pepper
2 egg yolks
1 Tbsp. fresh chopped dill
½ tsp. nutmeg
2–5 Tbsp. water
1 medium carrot, peeled and sliced
1 bay leaf
1 stalk celery, sliced
2 sprigs parsley
1 envelope gelatin
4¼ cups water

Have fish cleaned, removing bones and innards, but leaving skin intact. Soak roll in milk and squeeze dry. Grind pike flesh and whitefish, onions, butter and roll, blending well. Add salt, pepper, egg yolks, dill and nutmeg. Add water slowly by tablespoonfuls, mixing only as much as the mass will absorb while not losing a firm consistency. Place stuffing carefully inside skin and sew up edge with needle and fine thread. Combine fish heads, bones, fish trimmings, carrot, bay leaf, celery, parsley, salt and pepper with 4 cups water, and simmer for 40 minutes. Strain. Place fish in deep pan, cover with broth, and cook on low heat for 50–60 minutes, periodically basting with broth. Remove fish to serving dish; dissolve gelatin in ¼ cup warm water, and add to strained bouillon. Adjust seasoning and pour over fish. Chill overnight. Serve with lemon wedges and sprigs of fresh parsley. *Serves 6–8.*

baked fish with sour cream

GREY

An extremely simple but elegant dish

4 fish fillets (carp, sole, or flounder)
1 tsp. salt
Pinch pepper
6 Tbsp. butter
½ cup sour cream
1 Tbsp. fresh chopped dill

Grease baking dish well. Place fillets in dish and sprinkle with salt and pepper; place 1 Tbsp. butter on each fillet. Bake in 375-degree oven for 15 minutes. Melt remaining 2 Tbsp. butter. Remove dish from oven and spread sour cream equally over the 4 pieces. Drizzle melted butter on top. Sprinkle with dill. Return to oven and bake 6–8 minutes. Serve immediately with boiled potatoes. *Serves 4.*

small fish in sour cream

10–12 small fish (such as smelts)
Salt
1 egg
⅔ cup fresh bread crumbs
⅔ cup sour cream
1 Tbsp. fresh chopped dill
1 Tbsp. fresh chopped parsley
4 Tbsp. butter

Sprinkle fish with salt and allow to rest for 30 minutes. Beat egg. Dip each fish first into egg and then into bread crumbs, patting gently with dull knife to make bread crumbs adhere. Fry in 3 Tbsp. hot butter, adding more if necessary. Carefully remove fish to casserole. Cover with sour cream and dot with remaining butter. Bake 15 minutes in 350-degree oven. Sprinkle with dill and parsley. *Serves 2–3.*

fish with eggs and lemon butter

ODESSER

There are many variations on this dish (also known as Sudak po-pol'ski or Polish zander) in Russian cooking

2 lbs. white-fleshed fish, cut into serving pieces
4 cups water
1 medium carrot, peeled and sliced
3 sprigs parsley
1 medium onion, peeled and sliced
Salt and pepper
2 tsp. lemon juice
3 hardboiled eggs, peeled and chopped
1 Tbsp. fresh chopped parsley
5 Tbsp. melted butter

Boil 4 cups water with carrot, parsley, onion, salt and pepper; simmer 15 minutes. Carefully lower fish into broth and cook until just tender, 6–8 minutes. Remove fish to a platter and keep warm. Combine lemon juice, hardboiled eggs, parsley and melted butter and pour over fish. This dish is delicious served with hot boiled potatoes. *Serves 4.*

poached cod

MRS. YU.

2 lbs. cod fillets
6 cups water
1 medium carrot, peeled and sliced
1 large onion, quartered
2 bay leaves
8 peppercorns
½ tsp. salt
3 hardboiled eggs, peeled and chopped
½ cup (8 Tbsp.) butter, melted
1 Tbsp. chopped dill
1 Tbsp. chopped parsley
8 medium potatoes, peeled and boiled

Cut cod fillets into serving pieces. Combine water, carrot, onion, bay leaves, peppercorns and salt, and bring to a boil; simmer 20 minutes. Place fish in simmering broth and poach on low heat for 10 minutes. Remove fish and place on platter surrounded by hot boiled potatoes. Combine hardboiled eggs, melted butter, dill, parsley and 1/2 cup of the strained fish bouillon, and pour over fish and potatoes. *Serves 4.*

dorpat perches

PETIT

Though this dish was originally made with perch, it is just as good with smelts or whiting

16 small fish (smelts, whiting, etc.); number will depend on size of fish
Salt and pepper
Butter
2 Tbsp. chopped parsley
3 Tbsp. bread crumbs
3 hardboiled eggs, peeled and chopped

Sprinkle fish with salt and pepper and fry quickly in hot butter. Remove to platter and keep warm. Melt 3 Tbsp. hot butter and quickly sauté parsley and bread crumbs in it. Swirl in an additional tablespoon butter, pour over fish, scatter eggs on top, and serve immediately. *Serves 4.*

fish in wine

2 lbs. fish, cut into serving-size pieces (flounder, turbot, sole)
¼ cup pickle juice
2 cups water
1 cup dry white wine
3 small dill pickles, quartered
1 stalk celery, sliced
3 sprigs parsley
1 bay leaf
5 peppercorns
Pinch nutmeg
1 Tbsp. butter
1 Tbsp. flour

Arrange fish in serving portions in shallow pan with pickle juice, water, wine, pickles, celery, parsley, bay leaf, pepper and nutmeg. Liquid should just cover fish. Simmer gently for 12 minutes. Remove fish and strain liquid. Melt butter; add flour, and add 1 cup liquid. Stir till mixture thickens, pour over fish and serve. *Serves 4.*

flounder or sole in white wine

4 fish fillets (sole or flounder)
1 medium onion, peeled and sliced
1 Tbsp. chopped parsley
3 Tbsp. butter
1 tsp. lemon juice
Salt and pepper
1 cup dry white wine
1 Tbsp. flour
½ cup heavy cream
2 egg yolks, well beaten

Sauté onion and parsley in 2 Tbsp. butter. Rub fish with lemon juice, salt and pepper; add fish to pan and pour in wine. Simmer for 10–12 minutes on low heat until fish is just tender. Carefully remove fish to platter and keep warm. Strain broth. Melt remaining Tbsp. butter; add flour, and blend. Whisk in ½ cup broth and ½ cup cream. Turn off heat and add egg yolks; do not boil. Taste for seasoning, and add salt or lemon juice as necessary. Pour over fish and serve at once. *Serves 4.*

fish with horseradish and apples

2 lbs. white-fleshed fish
1 celery stalk, peeled and sliced
2 scallions, minced (white part only)
1 medium onion, peeled and chopped
2 tsp. sugar
3 Tbsp. white vinegar
1 bay leaf
Pinch thyme
Pinch pepper
1 tsp. salt
5 cups water
3 Tbsp. commercially prepared white horseradish
3 apples, peeled, cored and grated or put through food processor

Place celery, scallions, onion, ½ tsp. sugar, 1 tsp. vinegar, bay leaf, thyme, pepper and salt in pan with 5 cups water. Bring to a boil and simmer 5 minutes. Add fish, cut in serving-size pieces, and cook about 10 minutes until fish is done. Remove fish. Combine horseradish, apples, remaining sugar and vinegar, and blend well. Heat gently, taking care that mixture does not burn. Pour over fish and serve with lemon wedges. *Serves 4.*

fish with cranberries

1¾ lbs. fish fillets (such as cod, halibut, flounder)
1¾ cups cranberries
1 cup water
⅓ cup sugar
¼ tsp. red prepared horseradish
Salt and pepper

Boil cranberries in 1 cup water until they pop, and puree with their liquid and sugar in blender. Puree in small batches to keep the hot puree from overflowing. Return to pot and simmer on very low heat for 10 minutes. Add horseradish just before removing from heat. Place fish fillets, cut in serving pieces, in a single layer in lightly buttered casserole. Sprinkle with salt and pepper to taste. Pour sauce over fish and bake in a 350-degree oven until fish is cooked through, 8–12 minutes depending on thickness of fillets, until fish flakes and is no longer translucent. Do not overcook. This dish is good with boiled potatoes sprinkled with parsley. *Serves 4.*

baked fish with mustard sauce

4 fish fillets (sole, flounder, turbot)
7 Tbsp. butter
1 medium carrot, peeled and sliced
1 Tbsp. fresh chopped parsley
1 medium onion, peeled and chopped
Salt and pepper
¼ cup bread crumbs
2 eggs
1 cup sour cream
1 Tbsp. milk
1 Tbsp. flour
1 tsp. Dijon-style mustard

In 4 Tbsp. butter, sauté carrot, parsley and onion. Salt and pepper fish fillets and add to vegetables, frying for 2–3 minutes on each side. Remove to baking dish. Melt remaining 3 Tbsp. butter. Pour beaten eggs over fish; scatter bread crumbs on top, pour melted butter over all and bake at 325 degrees for 10–12 minutes until eggs are set. Blend sour cream, milk, flour and mustard, and bring to a boil. Simmer 3–4 minutes. Pour over fish and serve. Serves 4.

fish with mushrooms and tomato sauce

4 flounder fillets (sole or turbot is also fine)
Salt and pepper to taste
½ lb. mushrooms, peeled and sliced
2 Tbsp. butter
1 Tbsp. flour
3 tomatoes, pureed in blender or food processor
¼ tsp. sugar
¼ cup dry white wine

Salt and pepper fish fillets. Put in shallow pan with water just to cover, and bring to a boil. Add mushrooms, and simmer 10 minutes. Remove from heat, and with slotted spoon or pancake turner remove fish and mushrooms. Reserve broth. Put fish in casserole. Melt 1 Tbsp. butter, add flour, pureed tomatoes, sugar, mushrooms, ⅔ cup reserved broth and salt and pepper. Blend well and simmer sauce 5 minutes. Add wine and remaining Tbsp. butter, and simmer another 5 minutes. Taste for seasoning. Pour over fish in baking dish and bake for 5–8 minutes at 375 degrees. Serve with boiled potatoes. *Serves 4.*

fish with mushrooms and cheese

4 fish fillets (carp, sole, flounder)
Salt and pepper
4 Tbsp. butter
½ lb. mushrooms
¼ cup water
1 large onion, peeled and chopped
1 cup sour cream
1 Tbsp. flour
2 Tbsp. grated Parmesan cheese
2 Tbsp. bread crumbs

Rub fish fillets with salt and pepper. Place in greased baking dish and dot with 2 Tbsp. butter; bake in 375-degree oven for 10–12 minutes. Meanwhile, chop mushrooms. In a small pot place ¼ cup water, mushrooms, onion, and salt and pepper to taste. Cook on low heat until vegetables are tender, about 5–7 minutes. Drain off any excess liquid. Scatter vegetables over fish. Combine sour cream with flour and salt to taste. Spread over fish. Mix cheese and breadcrumbs, and sprinkle evenly over fillets. Melt remaining butter and drizzle over fish. Bake at 375 degrees for 10–15 minutes, until golden crust has formed. Serve very hot. *Serves 4.*

fish solianka

RASKIN

2 lbs. fish fillets
1 medium onion, peeled and chopped
6 Tbsp. butter
1 lb. sauerkraut, drained
1 Tbsp. tomato puree
2 tsp. red wine vinegar
1 tsp. sugar
4 cups water
1 small dill pickle, chopped
1 bay leaf
Salt and pepper
4 Tbsp. bread crumbs
1 tsp. chopped dill

Sauté onion in 1 Tbsp. butter. Add sauerkraut, tomato puree, vinegar, sugar and 2 more Tbsp. butter and cook gently 10 minutes. Bring 4 cups water to a boil with pickle, bay leaf, salt and pepper; add fish and simmer 10 minutes. Drain. Grease casserole and line with 2 Tbsp. bread crumbs; place half of sauerkraut mixture in dish; top with fish, and then spread remaining sauerkraut on top. Sprinkle with remaining 2 Tbsp. bread crumbs and dot with remaining butter. Bake at 350 degrees for 10 minutes. Sprinkle with dill before serving. *Serves 4–5.*

fish with cheese

PENDILL

Cheddar and oregano make for a flavorful dish

1½ lbs. fish fillets (sole, flounder) cut into serving-size pieces
4 oz. sharp Cheddar cheese, preferably in brick form

4 scallions
½ tsp. oregano
¼ tsp. salt
Pinch pepper
1 1-lb. can tomato sauce
2 Tbsp. butter

Cut thin slices from Cheddar brick in neat squares and arrange on fish fillets. On each fillet put equal portions of the chopped scallions, oregano, salt and pepper. Roll up fillet and close with toothpick. Put fillets in ovenproof greased casserole and cover with tomato sauce. Dot top with butter. Bake in 350-degree oven for 20 minutes. *Serves 4.*

puffy fried fish

A. VINOGRADOVA

1¼ lbs. white-fleshed fish (such as flounder, turbot, hake, cod)
¾ cup flour
3 eggs, well beaten
½ tsp. salt
Optional: pinch cayenne pepper
Oil for frying (corn or safflower oil; do not use olive oil)
Mayonnaise, tartar sauce or cocktail sauce

For appetizer-sized portions cut fish fillets into 1½-2 inch long pieces; as a main course fillets should be 5 to 6 inches long. Place flour in a bowl, add salt and pepper and mix well. Make a well in center of flour and pour in eggs. Stir until mixture has consistency of very thick cream. Heat half an inch of oil in frying pan at medium high heat until it is nearly smoking or until a drop of water sizzles when it hits the surface. Spear the end of a piece of fish with a fork (a two-pronged fork is best), dip into egg mixture to coat thoroughly, and allow excess coating to drip back into bowl. Lower carefully into hot oil and fry until pale gold on one side. Turn fish and fry till pale gold on other side. Then turn again and fry until fish turns deep golden brown. Continue adding pieces of fish to pan, turning each piece twice. Do not crowd pieces; they should not touch. Fish will puff up as it cooks. Dry on paper towels and keep hot in warm oven.

In Russia the dish is often served with mayonnaise on the side, but you may prefer tartar sauce or any cocktail sauce. *Makes 8 appetizer or 4 main course servings.*

baked carp with mushrooms

2 lbs. carp, cut in fillets
Salt and pepper
½ lb. mushrooms
¼ cup water
1 medium onion, peeled and sliced into rings
1½ cups sour cream
1 Tbsp. flour
2 Tbsp. grated Parmesan cheese
2 Tbsp. bread crumbs, fried in 1 Tbsp. butter

Lightly salt and pepper fish fillets; place in well-greased casserole and bake for 8–10 minutes at 350 degrees. Wash mushrooms and chop fairly coarsely. Place in pot with onion, salt, pepper, and ¼ cup water. Simmer 7–8 minutes. Scatter mushroom mixture (and any remaining liquid) over fish. Combine sour cream with flour and a pinch of salt; spread over fish. Sprinkle with cheese mixed with bread crumbs. Return to oven and bake for 10 minutes, until top is nicely browned. *Serves 4.*

carp à la russe
PETIT

1 carp (3–4 lbs.) cut into serving pieces
Pinch salt and pepper
1 cup dry white wine
1 cup water
½ tsp. lemon juice
2 Tbsp. butter
1 cup sauerkraut, drained
1 scallion, minced (green and white parts)
1 Tbsp. chopped parsley
¼ lb. mushrooms, chopped
1 small dill pickle, chopped
½ cup sour cream
1 Tbsp. horseradish
1 Tbsp. milk
1 Tbsp. flour

Rub fish with salt and pepper. Place wine and water in baking dish; add fish and lemon juice and bake in 375-degree oven for 20–25 minutes until fish is just tender, and drain. Melt butter. Add sauerkraut, scallion, parsley, mushrooms and pickle and simmer 10 minutes until tender. Place sauerkraut on serving platter. Arrange fish fillets on top and keep warm. Combine sour cream, horseradish, milk and flour; simmer 5 minutes. Pour over fish. *Serves 6.*

stuffed pike

1 pike (about 3 lbs.)
1 small onion, peeled and chopped
5 Tbsp. butter
1 hard white roll
½ cup warm water
⅔ cup sour cream
1 egg (raw)
1 tsp. chopped fresh dill
1 tsp. chopped fresh parsley
Salt and pepper
2 scallions, minced (white part only)
2 hardboiled eggs, peeled and chopped
Flour

Have fish cleaned and boned, leaving skin whole. Sauté onion in 1 Tbsp. butter. Soak roll in warm water and squeeze dry. Combine onion, roll, 1 Tbsp. sour cream, raw egg, dill, parsley, salt, pepper and scallions. Put this together with pike fillets through grinder or food processor. Add hardboiled eggs. Stuff back into fish skin and sew up. Roll lightly in flour, and sauté for a few minutes in remaining hot butter. Place in greased baking dish and bake for 45 minutes in 350-degree oven. Ten minutes before end of cooking baste with remaining sour cream. Add butter to keep from burning. *Serves 6.*

stuffed trout

2 trout
6 Tbsp. butter
2 scallions, chopped (green and white parts)
½ cup cooked kasha (buckwheat groats)
Salt and pepper
2 Tbsp. fresh chopped dill
2 Tbsp. fresh chopped parsley
½ cup sour cream

Clean trout. Sauté scallions in 2 Tbsp. butter. Add kasha, salt and pepper, and mix well. Add 1 Tbsp. dill and 1 Tbsp. parsley. Stuff fish with kasha mixture, close loosely with toothpicks, and put in greased casserole. Pour remaining 4 Tbsp. of butter, melted, over fish and bake for 15 minutes in 375-degree oven. Cover with sour cream and sprinkle remaining parsley and dill over fish and return to oven for another 10 minutes. *Serves 2.*

salmon with fresh vegetable sauce

4 salmon steaks
3 Tbsp. butter
1 Tbsp. flour
⅔ cup chicken broth
¼ cup white wine
3 Tbsp. sour cream
4 large radishes, tops removed, washed and minced
2 scallions, green and white parts, minced
1 Tbsp. fresh chopped parsley
1 tsp. fresh chopped dill
Salt and pepper
Lemon wedges

Melt 1 Tbsp. butter in small saucepan, add flour and blend well with a whisk. Add chicken broth and wine, stirring constantly until mixture comes to a boil. Remove from heat and stir in sour cream, radishes, scallions, parsley and dill. Taste for salt and pepper; because of the sharpness of the radishes the dish will need very little if any salt. Cover and keep warm on very low heat.

Lightly salt and pepper salmon steaks. Melt remaining 2 Tbsp. butter and brush steaks lightly. Broil fish 3–5 minutes on each side depending on thickness, turning once. Do not overcook; fish should lose deep orange color and flake easily. Pour sauce over fish and serve immediately with lemon wedges on the side. *Serves 4.*

macaroni and smoked salmon
PETIT

1½ cups elbow macaroni
1 tsp. salt
Pinch pepper

⅛ tsp. nutmeg
3 Tbsp. butter
1 Tbsp. grated Parmesan cheese
⅓ cup fresh bread crumbs
¼ lb. smoked salmon
1½ cups tomato sauce

Boil macaroni in salted water; drain, splash with cold water. Season with pepper and nutmeg; add 2 Tbsp. butter and grated cheese. Grease casserole with remaining butter and sprinkle with bread crumbs. Place half of macaroni in casserole; cover with thin slices of smoked salmon, and place remaining macaroni on top. Pour tomato sauce over all. Bake in 350-degree oven for 25 minutes. *Serves 4–6.*

smelts à la Ladoga

PETIT

This rich and elegant dish would make a pretty centerpiece for a dinner table.

1½ lbs. boned smelts, heads and tails removed
5 medium potatoes
1 Tbsp. potato flour or potato starch
1¼ cups heavy cream
3 Tbsp. butter
3 eggs, separated
Salt to taste
Pinch pepper
Pinch nutmeg
1 tsp. lemon juice
Butter and oil for frying, about 4–5 Tbsp.

S A U C E :
1 Tbsp. butter
1 Tbsp flour
1 cup chicken broth
½ tsp. fresh chopped parsley
½ tsp. chopped chervil
½ tsp. chopped chives
1 tsp. lemon juice
¼ tsp. salt
Pinch pepper

Boil, peel and mash potatoes. In a saucepan dissolve potato flour in 1 cup heavy cream, then heat till boiling and very thick. Add 3 Tbsp. butter and continue stirring until butter is absorbed. Remove from heat. Season mashed potatoes with salt, pepper and nutmeg, and add to cream mixture. Beat until smooth. Add remaining heavy cream. Beat yolks well and add slowly to mixture, beating well. Beat whites stiff and fold in. Pour into ovenproof casserole and bake at 350 degrees for 25 minutes, until puffed and lightly browned.

While potato mixture is baking, fry smelts in equal quantities of butter and oil, sprinkling with salt, pepper and lemon juice. Turn once. When smelts are done (5–6 minutes) remove from heat. Five minutes before potatoes are done, place smelts in center of potato mixture and allow it to finish baking. Serve with the following sauce: Melt 1 Tbsp. butter, add flour and stir. Blend in chicken broth and cook until thick, stirring constantly. Add parsley, chervil, chives, lemon juice, salt and pepper to taste. Serve very hot. *Serves 4–6.*

fish dumplings
RASKIN

1 lb. fish trimmings (heads, bones, etc.)
2 small onions, peeled
1 medium carrot, peeled and sliced
Salt and pepper
7 cups water
1 lb. mackerel or flounder fillets
3 pieces white bread, crusts removed
1 cup warm water
1 egg, beaten

Place fish skin, bones and head in a pot with 1 onion, quartered, carrot, salt and pepper, and 7 cups water. Simmer gently for 50 minutes. (A mixture of ½ water ½ bottled clam juice may be substituted for fish trimmings and water. In that case, simmer with onion, carrot, salt and pepper for 10 minutes.) Strain. Combine fish fillets, 1 onion (chopped), bread soaked in warm water and squeezed dry, egg, salt and pepper to taste, and grind. Form into small dumplings and lower on a spoon into simmering broth. Simmer on very low heat for 40 minutes, adding water if needed. Remove with slotted spoon. Good served with boiled potatoes and horseradish. *Serves 4.*

fish pudding
BELSKY

Broccoli or sautéed potatoes go nicely with this dish

2 lbs. fish fillets (cod, scrod, sole)
½ of the white part of a day-old French bread
    (or 1½ cups white bread crumbs)
1 cup heavy cream
5 Tbsp. butter
1 small onion, peeled and finely chopped
3 eggs, separated
Salt and pepper to taste

Soak bread or crumbs in ½ cup cream for 10 minutes. Put fish through grinder with 4 Tbsp. butter and onion. Squeeze bread dry and add to fish. Add yolks and mix well, Sprinkle with salt and pepper to taste. Whip remaining ½ cup cream and add. Beat whites stiffly and fold into mixture. Turn into lightly buttered casserole set in a pan of hot water and dot with 1 Tbsp. butter. Bake in a 350-degree oven for about 35–40 minutes, until firm and slightly browned. This can be served with a hollandaise sauce. *Serves 6.*

very rich soufflé
PETIT

1 lb. pike, flounder, sole or turbot
¼ lb. butter
1 tsp. salt
¼ tsp. pepper
⅛ tsp. nutmeg
3 eggs, beaten
1½ cups heavy cream, whipped

SAUCE:
2 Tbsp. butter
1½ Tbsp. flour
1 cup chicken stock
1 egg yolk
¼ cup heavy cream
Salt and pepper

Grind fish with ¼ lb. butter or put through food processor. Season with salt, pepper and nutmeg. Add eggs and process or grind again. Refrigerate for 1 hour. Whip 1½ cups cream and fold into fish mixture. Place in buttered mold and set in boiling water bath; bake at 350 degrees for about 50 minutes.

Melt 1 Tbsp. butter. Add flour, and stir in chicken stock. Whisk until thick. Cool slightly. Combine egg yolk and ¼ cup cream and beat into sauce. Beat in remaining Tbsp. of butter. Taste for seasoning and add salt and pepper as needed. Do not boil. Serve in a sauceboat with soufflé. *Serves 6.*

meat & poultry

meat and poultry

Game and poultry were often found on Russian tables, since hunting has always been a popular sport. The people of Kievan Rus' ate chicken, duck, and goose, as well as bear and wild boar. Twelfth-century chronicles mention black and hazel grouse, wild duck, geese and hare.

Chicken has always been popular, but because of its cost it is primarily served only on special occasions. There are recipes in this section for ground chicken cutlets, chicken and veal loaves, chicken stuffed with grapes, and chicken breast with truffles. The recipe for ground turkey cutlets with cherry sauce is a tasty way of using leftover turkey.

Meat has always been scarce and expensive in Russia, and the peasants sometimes went without it for months. To make meat go farther Russians invented a number of dishes that today's cooks will find delicious and inexpensive. One of the best and most common is *kotlety*. Though made of ground beef shaped into patties and fried, these bear no resemblance to hamburger. In the old days the meat was hacked, not ground, with superior results, as Mrs. Sofia Nabokova, one of the contributors to this book, recalls: "I remember very well that when I was a child of about seven or eight, even in our kitchen, meat was always hacked with two huge knives which the cook held in both hands as he pounded the meat on a wooden board. I could always hear that specific noise coming from the kitchen. In those days no grinder was used, and I must admit that the croquettes or whatever was hacked (and not ground) did taste better than nowadays!"

Few Russians enjoy rare meat, and they have not really acquired a taste for Western-style steak. A well braised pot roast or a stew with potatoes and vegetables is often far more appealing to the Russian palate than a large, bloody Porterhouse. Stews are made with mixtures of different kinds of meat, and there is a variety of pot roasts, usually marinated, browned, and slowly braised with vegetables. For fried and sautéed meats it is best to use a mixture of butter and oil.

Veal is ground into patties, braised in cream, stewed with squash, or roasted with garlic and paprika. Leg of lamb is made into *shashlyk*, a dish that has become well-known in the West where it often appears in strange guises (Russians would never skewer such oddities as pineapple or eggplant chunks with their lamb). Leg of lamb is sometimes combined with plums or mushrooms, and organ meats such as kidneys may be flavored with whiskey, juniper sauce, and sour cream.

Russians do not make elaborate sauces for meats. Leftover soup meat is served hot or cold with horseradish sauce or sour cream sauce, somewhat like boiled beef. Hot dishes are often accompanied by a few spoonfuls of natural meat juice, sharp mustard, or a simple sour cream sauce with crisp fried or boiled potatoes sprinkled with parsley, or buttered noodles on the side. The more elaborate meat dishes such as breast of veal with mushrooms or cutlets Maréchal reflect French influence.

BEEF

kotlety I

YAVITZ

The cold water and ice make these kotlety light and fluffy

1 lb. ground beef
1½ cups bread crumbs
1 small onion, peeled and chopped
1 Tbsp. butter
½ tsp. salt
Pinch pepper
1 Tbsp. chopped dill
1 egg
¾ cup very cold water
½ cup small chips of ice
Butter for frying

Fry onion in butter until golden. Combine beef, ¾ cup bread crumbs, fried onion, salt, pepper, dill and slightly beaten egg. Work in the cold water by the tablespoon until it is all absorbed and mixture is light and fluffy. Form into small oval-shaped patties (about 2 inches across.) In the center of each put a small chip or two of ice and fold meat around it to squeeze *kotlety* back into oval shape. Roll in the remaining breadcrumbs and fry in hot butter until browned (about 12–15 minutes.) Serve with sour cream. Boiled potatoes, peas or creamed mushrooms all go well with *kotlety. Makes about 12–14 kotlety.*

kotlety II

ODESSER

1 lb. ground chuck
1 Tbsp. ketchup
1 tsp. Dijon-style mustard

1 egg
½ cup bread crumbs
½ tsp. salt
¼ tsp. pepper
Butter for frying

Combine all ingredients and blend well. Form into small oval patties about 2 inches in diameter, and fry in butter until golden. *Makes about 12 kotlety.*

kotlety III

MARTIN

These kotlety have a fairly heavy consistency

1 lb. ground beef
2 slices white bread, crusts removed
½ cup cold water
1 egg
1 small onion, peeled and chopped
1 Tbsp. butter
1 tsp. salt, pepper to taste
1 Tbsp. chopped dill
Butter for frying

Soak bread in water and squeeze dry. Combine with meat and blend well. Add egg and mix. Fry onion lightly in butter. Add to meat. Season with dill, salt and pepper. Form into small oval patties and fry on both sides in butter until brown. *Makes 12–14 kotlety.*

light kotlety

The beaten whites give these kotlety an airy texture

1½ lbs. ground beef
1 large roll
1 cup beef broth
½ tsp. salt
Pinch pepper
1 Tbsp. butter + butter for frying
2 eggs, separated
⅔ cup sour cream
Flour

Soak roll in ½ cup beef broth. Squeeze dry and combine with meat. Add salt, pepper, 1 Tbsp. butter, and egg yolks. Beat egg whites and carefully fold into mixture. Form into small oval patties. Dredge lightly with flour and fry on both sides in butter. When almost done add remaining ½ cup broth and sour cream, and simmer 10 minutes. *Makes about 14–16 kotlety.*

❖ kotlety with potato filling

CHERNYAKHOVSKAYA

The potatoes acquire a great flavor from being cooked inside the beef

1 recipe kotlety III (Martin) (p. 155)
2 medium potatoes, peeled and boiled
3 Tbsp. heavy cream (approximately)
Salt and pepper
1 small onion, peeled and finely chopped
1 Tbsp. oil
2 tsp. butter

Prepare *kotlety* as in the *kotlety* III recipe, but do not add the onion to the meat; fry it in butter until it turns a dark golden color. Mash potatoes well with heavy cream, adding the cream by teaspoonfuls to ensure that the potatoes are very thick. Sprinkle in salt and pepper to taste and blend in the onion, stirring well.

Form oval *kotlety*, making a dent with your thumb in the middle of each patty. Place a teaspoon of the mashed potato mixture in the center of the patty, and pinch the edges of the patty together on all sides to form a tight seal. Fry in butter until golden brown, turning once. Serve any extra mashed potatoes on the side. *Makes 10-12 kotlety*

❖ walnut and prune kotlety

CHERNYAKHOVSKAYA

The sweetness of the prunes creates a nice balance to the meat

1 recipe kotlety III (Martin) (p. 155)
½ cup shelled walnuts (whole or halved)
12-14 prunes, pitted
1 cup prune juice
½ cup sour cream

Prepare *kotlety* as in the *kotlety* III recipe, but omit the onion and the dill. Warm prune juice over low heat for 3-4 minutes and remove from heat. Allow prunes to steep in the juice for 30 minutes. Drain the prunes well, reserving the juice. Stuff a whole or half walnut (this will depend on the size of your walnuts) into each prune. As you form the meat into patties, make an indentation with your thumb in the middle of the oval, and insert a prune, rolling the meat around to completely cover the prune and pinching the edges tightly so that no juice escapes.

   Combine the reserved prune juice with the sour cream, and mix well. Fry on both sides in butter until almost done (meat will be turning golden brown), turning once. Drain off excess butter. Pour the prune juice and sour cream mixture over the patties, and allow to simmer for five minutes. *Makes 10-12 kotlety*

a p p l e   k o t l e t y

*The potatoes and apples in these big kotlety give them
a different consistency and flavor*

1½ lbs. ground beef
4 small potatoes, peeled, boiled and mashed
1 egg yolk + 1 whole egg
2 Tbsp. chopped parsley
½ tsp. salt
¼ tsp. pepper
1 large apple, peeled, cored, and cut into ½-inch thick slices about 1 inch long
1 cup white bread crumbs
Butter for frying (about 6–8 Tbsp.)

Combine ground beef, mashed potatoes, egg yolk, parsley, salt and pepper. Form into patties 3 inches in diameter. Place a piece of apple in the center of half of the patties, and cover each piece well with another half patty. Pinch the edges together tightly. Dip patties in egg and roll in bread crumbs. Fry patties on both sides in butter until golden, about 10–15 minutes. Then place in a lightly buttered casserole and bake at 350 degrees for about 20–25 minutes. (These patties are so thick that when the outside is gold and crusty the inside is still raw, and they will burn if you keep on frying; the baking process will cook the inside and keep the outside crisp.) *Serves 6.*

bitki (little meatballs) in sour cream

NABOKOVA

1 lb. ground, lean beef (round or sirloin)
2 small rolls or 2 slices white bread, crusts removed
¾ cup water
1 small onion, peeled and chopped
2 tsp. chopped dill
Pinch pepper
½ tsp. salt
1 cup fresh bread crumbs
1 cup sour cream
2 tsp. flour
2 Tbsp. milk
4 Tbsp. butter

Soak rolls or bread in water for about 10 minutes. Squeeze dry and add to meat. Sauté onion in 1 Tbsp. butter until lightly browned, and add to mixture along with salt, pepper and dill. Blend mixture until smooth. Shape into 1-inch thick patties about 2½ inches in diameter. Roll in bread crumbs, and fry in remaining butter until brown on both sides. Place in an ovenproof casserole. Combine sour cream, flour and milk. Pour over *bitki* and bake at 300 degrees for 15 minutes. *Makes 12–14 bitki.*

zraza

MARTIN

2½ lbs. ground chuck
6 medium or 8 small potatoes, peeled and quartered
2 tsp. salt (or to taste), pepper to taste
⅛ tsp. nutmeg
1 large onion, peeled and chopped
5 Tbsp. butter
2½ Tbsp. milk
2 pieces white bread, crusts removed
1 cup water
2 Tbsp. chopped parsley
1 Tbsp. chopped dill

Cook potatoes with 1 tsp. salt in boiling water until well done (about 25 minutes). Fry onion lightly in 2 Tbsp. butter. Drain potatoes and mash with 1 tsp. salt, ¼ tsp. pepper and ⅛ tsp. nutmeg. Add remaining butter and milk. Beat with wooden spoon until smooth and firm. Soak bread in water and squeeze dry. Combine meat, bread, fried onion, pinch salt, pepper, parsley and dill, and mix until very smooth. Divide meat mixture into 2 parts. Pat one half into an oval about 10 inches long in a greased and floured casserole. Place potato mixture on top to within 1½ inches of border. Pat top layer of meat over filling and pinch edges very firmly shut. Bake at 350 degrees for 50 minutes to 1 hour until nicely browned. *Serves 6–8.*

May be served with:

MUSHROOM SAUCE
½ lb. mushrooms
2 Tbsp. + 1½ Tbsp. butter
½ tsp. lemon juice
½ tsp. salt
¼ tsp. pepper
1 Tbsp. flour
1 cup beef broth
¾ cup sour cream

Fry mushrooms in 2 Tbsp. butter until liquid has almost evaporated. Add lemon juice, salt and pepper. In a small pan, separately melt 1½ Tbsp. butter. Add flour and stir. Blend in beef broth, whisking until smooth. Put in mushrooms and heat through. Stir in sour cream. Check seasoning and sprinkle with salt, pepper or lemon juice as needed.

z r a z y
NABOKOVA

Inexpensive and easy to make, but very elegant on the table

MEAT:
2 lbs. ground lean beef
¾ cup water
2½ slices dry white bread
1 onion, peeled and finely chopped
1 Tbsp. butter
¼ tsp. garlic powder
½ tsp. salt

FILLING:
½ lb. mushrooms, peeled and sliced thin
4 hardboiled eggs, peeled and chopped
2 cups cooked buckwheat groats (kasha)
1 Tbsp. chopped dill
Salt
1 cup bread crumbs
¼ lb. butter

Soak bread in water for about 10 minutes. Squeeze dry and add to meat. Sauté onion in 1 Tbsp. butter until lightly browned and add to meat. Add garlic and salt. Mix until mixture is very smooth. Set aside. Sauté mushrooms in 2 Tbsp. butter until soft. Mix mushrooms, chopped eggs, kasha (cooked according to package directions) and dill. Add salt to taste. On a wooden board sprinkled with crumbs, form meat mixture into ½-inch thick rounds 4 inches in diameter. Put 1 tablespoon of filling on each round. Draw up edges on both sides of meat and pat together with fingers, firmly closing edges and forming even stick-shaped patties. Roll in crumbs and fry in remaining butter. These can be served with tomato or meat sauce. *Makes about 16–18 sticks.*

golubtsy I (stuffed cabbage)

1½ lbs. ground beef
½ cup cooked rice
1 Tbsp. minced parsley
1 egg
1 small onion, peeled and chopped
6 Tbsp. butter
1 Tbsp. flour
12–14 large cabbage leaves
3 Tbsp. tomato sauce
¾ cup sour cream
½ cup beef broth
1 tsp. salt
½ tsp. pepper

Wash cabbage leaves in cold water and cut off tough bottoms. Boil 5–7 minutes in salted water. Mix beef, rice, parsley, egg, salt, and pepper. Fry onion in 1 Tbsp. butter and add to meat mixture. Put about 2–3 Tbsp. of meat filling into each cabbage leaf and roll up carefully, closing with a long wooden toothpick. Brown in 4 Tbsp. butter for 10–15 minutes, be careful not to let *golubtsy* burn—it is not necessary to turn them. Remove from pan and let remaining juices boil until reduced to about 3 Tbsp. Combine tomato sauce, sour cream, and broth. Add pan juices and season to taste with additional salt and pepper. Melt remaining Tbsp. butter; add flour, and blend. Whisk in sour cream mixture and simmer until smooth. Pour sauce over *golubtsy* and simmer 40 minutes. *Serves 6.*

golubtsy II
WEINSCHENKER

1 lb. ground chuck
6 large cabbage leaves
1 8-oz. can tomato sauce
¼ cup ketchup
2 bay leaves
Pepper to taste
½ tsp. brown sugar
½ tsp. white sugar
1 medium onion, peeled and chopped
½ cup cooked rice
1 Tbsp. butter
1 egg
1 Tbsp. chopped dill
¼ cup cold water
½ tsp. salt

Boil cabbage leaves for 5 minutes in salted water. Drain, reserving 2 cups of water in which cabbage was cooked. Combine water from cabbage with tomato sauce, ketchup, bay leaves, pepper, and brown and white sugars. Sauté onion in 1 Tbsp. butter. Combine onion, meat, rice, egg, dill, ¼ cup cold water, ½ tsp. salt, and pepper and mix well. Place 2–3 Tbsp. meat on each cabbage leaf and roll up, securing with wooden toothpick. Place in flameproof casserole and pour sauce over. Simmer on low heat for 45 minutes. Remove toothpicks. Bake at 325 degrees for 25 minutes. *Serves 6.*

golubtsy III
GEOFFREY

Prepare meat filling as above. Fill cabbage leaves. Fry rolls lightly in butter. Place in casserole and cover with 2 cups milk. Bake at 325 degrees for 1 hour. Remove from oven and add 2/3 cup sour cream. Return to oven and bake 20 minutes. *Serves 6.*

lazy golubtsy

This dish is "lazy" because the meat mixture is not wrapped in cabbage leaves

1¼ lbs. lean ground beef
1 small onion, peeled and chopped
2 Tbsp. butter
½ small cabbage, shredded
2 medium carrots, peeled and shredded
1 parsnip, peeled and shredded
1 Tbsp. chopped parsley
2 cups beef broth
Salt and pepper
Sour cream

In a large Dutch oven or ovenproof casserole sauté onion in 1 Tbsp. butter until soft. Add remaining butter, and when melted add meat, cabbage, carrots, parsnip and parsley. Cook on medium heat, stirring constantly, breaking up ground beef, until meat is lightly browned. If necessary, add a little more butter to keep mixture from burning. Sprinkle lightly with salt and pepper, and pour in beef broth. Bake casserole in 350-degree oven for 45–50 minutes until cabbage is soft; check to be sure mixture remains moist and add a little more beef broth if needed. Taste for salt, and serve with sour cream on the side. *Serves 6.*

beef steaks with pickles and sour cream

4 thin steaks, such as round steak
Salt and pepper
Flour
2 Tbsp. butter

2 strips bacon, minced
1 large onion, peeled and chopped
1 dill pickle, minced
⅔ cup beef broth
1 cup sour cream

Season steaks with salt and pepper. Dredge lightly with flour. Sauté bacon, onion and pickle in 2 Tbsp. butter on medium heat for 5–8 minutes until bacon is crisp. Divide mixture evenly on top of steaks. Pour broth over meat, cover casserole and simmer 30 minutes. Add sour cream, simmer an additional 5 minutes, and serve. Fried potatoes make an excellent accompaniment to this dish. *Serves 4.*

russian steak

4 thin steaks
Salt
1 Tbsp. oil
1 Tbsp. butter
4 tsp. prepared red horseradish

Lightly salt steaks. Fry quickly in oil and butter. Just before each steak is done, spread ½ tsp. horseradish on one side. Cook 2 minutes, turn and spread horseradish on other side. Serve with boiled potatoes sprinkled with fresh parsley. *Serves 4.*

beef stroganoff I

MARTIN

2 lbs. sirloin, cut into thin strips
½ cup flour
½ tsp. salt
Pepper
9 Tbsp. butter
1 medium onion, peeled and chopped
½ lb. mushrooms, peeled and sliced
1½ cups sour cream
3 Tbsp. Dijon-style mustard
    (or less, depending on strength of mustard)

Combine flour, ½ tsp. salt and a pinch of pepper. Dredge meat in flour and sauté quickly in 6 Tbsp. butter until meat loses pink color and is well browned. Remove from heat. Fry onion in remaining butter for 2–3 minutes. Add mushrooms and continue to sauté on fairly high heat until mushrooms are soft and liquid is thickened and reduced (about 6–8 minutes.) Add the meat and simmer 5 minutes. Have sour cream at room temperature, and combine with mustard. Add to meat mixture and simmer on low heat for a few minutes until sour cream is heated through and blended. Do not boil. Add salt and pepper and taste for seasoning. If sauce is very thick, thin with a few drops of milk. Serve at once with noodles or boiled rice. *Serves 4–6.*

beef stroganoff II

M. VISSON

2 lbs. sirloin, cut into strips
½ cup flour
1 tsp. salt
¼ tsp. pepper
¼ lb. butter
2 6-oz. cans tomato paste
2 cups water
2 cups sour cream

Combine flour, salt and pepper. Dredge beef in flour and fry quickly in butter until brown on all sides. Place in a large pot and add tomato paste and water. Simmer on low heat until tender, about 1 hour. Just before serving add sour cream and stir thoroughly to heat through. Taste for seasoning, and add salt and pepper as needed. *Serves 4.*

beef and kasha

4 thin steaks
½ cup kasha (buckwheat groats)
Salt and pepper
½ medium onion, peeled and chopped
¼ lb. mushrooms, peeled and sliced
4 Tbsp. butter
¼ cup beef bouillon
1 cup sour cream

Cook kasha according to package directions. Season with salt and pepper. Fry onion and mushrooms in 2 Tbsp. butter and add to kasha. Sprinkle beef with salt and pepper and fry quickly in remaining butter until browned on both sides. Divide kasha mixture equally between 4 steaks. Place in center and roll up, securing with toothpicks. Place in casserole. Combine pan drippings, bouillon, and sour cream; season to taste with salt and pepper. Pour over meat and bake in 350-degree oven for 25 minutes. Cucumber salad makes a good side dish. *Serves 4.*

russian pot roast in sour cream

1½ to 2½ lbs. pot roast (chuck)
5 large potatoes, peeled and cubed
2 medium onions, peeled and cut into rings
6 Tbsp. butter
¾ cup beef broth
1 cup sour cream
1 bay leaf
Salt and pepper
½ tsp. lemon juice
1 Tbsp. chopped dill
1½ Tbsp. chopped parsley

Fry potatoes and onions in butter until onions are golden. Remove with a slotted spoon, and lightly fry pot roast on all sides in the same pan until browned. Sprinkle potato-onion mixture with salt and pepper. Place in covered casserole, add meat, beef broth, sour cream and bay leaf and bake in 325-degree oven for 1 hour, basting occasionally and adding more beef broth if necessary. Remove from oven; add lemon juice and sprinkle with dill and parsley. Return to oven and bake another 30 minutes, until meat is very tender; taste sauce for seasoning. *Serves 4.*

russian pot roast in red wine

Make the above recipe, but omit the sour cream. Along with onions and potatoes fry 1 sliced carrot, 1 sliced stalk celery, and ½ lb. sliced mushrooms. Add 1½ cups dry red wine to beef broth before pouring over meat. Bake as in previous recipe, adding broth if necessary to keep meat from burning. *Serves 4.*

pot roast with mushrooms, eggplant, and tomatoes

3 lbs. pot roast
1 medium eggplant, peeled and diced
Salt and pepper
1½ lbs. mushrooms, peeled and sliced
1 large onion, peeled and chopped
¼ lb. butter (approximately)
2 tomatoes, chopped
2 Tbsp. tomato paste
2½ cups water
1 bay leaf
1 small green bell pepper, deribbed, seeded and chopped
1 Tbsp. chopped parsley

Sprinkle eggplant with salt and allow to stand for 20 minutes. Pat dry with paper towels. Fry mushrooms and onion in 2 Tbsp. butter until onion is golden. In a separate pan in 2 Tbsp. butter, fry eggplant and tomatoes until soft, adding butter if needed to keep eggplant from burning. Sprinkle meat with salt and pepper. Fry meat lightly on all sides in remaining butter until just browned. Place in a large pot and add tomato paste, water and bay leaf. Cover and cook on low heat for about 1½ hours, until meat is tender. Add mushroom and onion mixture, green bell pepper, and eggplant and tomato mixture. Cook 15 minutes. Taste for seasoning and sprinkle with parsley. *Serves 6.*

pot roast in beer

3–4 lbs. pot roast (chuck)
1 tsp. salt
Pinch pepper
2 Tbsp. butter
2 large carrots, peeled and sliced
1 medium onion, cut into rings
1 stalk celery, sliced
2 Tbsp. chopped parsley
1 bay leaf
1 8-oz. can beer

Sprinkle meat with salt. In a large casserole melt butter. Add carrots, onion, celery, parsley, bay leaf and pepper and sauté for 2–3 minutes; add meat and brown lightly on all sides. Pour beer over meat, and prick meat in several places with fork. Bake in

325-degree oven for 1–1½ hours, until meat is tender. Skim fat, and strain gravy. Taste for seasoning. Serve with boiled potatoes. *Serves 6–8.*

sweet and sour pot roast

3 lbs. pot roast
1 medium onion, peeled
1 large carrot, peeled
3 Tbsp. butter
½ cup water
1 bay leaf
¼ cup red wine vinegar
2 Tbsp. tomato paste
1–2 Tbsp. brown sugar
¼ cup raisins
Salt and pepper to taste

Chop onion and carrot well. Sauté in butter in Dutch oven until soft. Rub meat with salt and pepper to taste. Push vegetables to side of pot and brown meat well on all sides, taking care that it does not burn. Add water and bay leaf, cover, and simmer 1 hour, turning meat occasionally. Keep heat low. Add vinegar, tomato paste, sugar and raisins, adjusting sugar to taste. The dish should be slightly tart. Cover and cook for 40 minutes, or until meat is tender. Taste sauce and correct seasoning. Skim fat if desired. Serve with boiled potatoes or noodles. *Serves 4–6.*

beef and vegetable stew

1½ lbs. lean beef for stew, cut in 1-inch cubes
4 Tbsp. butter
1 medium onion, peeled and chopped
1 bay leaf
1½ cups pumpernickel or dark rye bread crumbs
2 medium turnips, peeled and coarsely chopped
5 small potatoes, peeled and quartered
3 medium carrots, peeled and diced
1½ cups beef broth
½ cup sour cream
1 clove garlic, peeled and minced
Salt and pepper

Pound meat with mallet and wipe dry. In a small frying pan sauté onion in 1 Tbsp. butter until soft but not brown and set aside. In a large Dutch oven melt remaining 3 Tbsp.

butter, add bay leaf and sprinkle in pepper. Add meat and brown lightly on all sides. Sprinkle with chopped onion and bread crumbs, then add a layer of the turnips, then a layer of the potatoes, and then the carrots. Do not stir. Pour in beef broth, sprinkle with salt, cover, and bake in 350-degree oven for 1½ hours. Stir in sour cream and garlic; taste for salt, and bake for another 15 minutes. *Serves 4–5.*

beef with mushroom sauce

2 lbs. beef for stew, cubed
4 cups water
1 tsp. salt
¼ tsp. pepper
6 Tbsp. butter
1 medium onion, peeled and chopped
2 Tbsp. flour
1½ cups broth in which beef was cooked
½ cup sour cream
3 Tbsp. grated Parmesan cheese
½ lb. mushrooms, peeled and sliced
½ tsp. lemon juice
1 egg yolk

Bring salt, pepper and water to a boil. Add beef and simmer, covered, for 35 minutes. Melt 4 Tbsp. butter and fry onion till golden. Add flour and stir until flour is absorbed. Strain broth and add 1½ cups to onion mixture. Stir until thick, add sour cream and Parmesan cheese and stir until cheese is melted. Sauté mushrooms in 2 Tbsp. butter over fairly high heat until liquid has almost entirely evaporated. Add lemon juice, and, when very little liquid is left, add to sauce. Add meat, and keep warm. Beat egg yolk and just before serving beat into ½ cup of sauce. Stir back into meat but do not allow to boil or the egg will curdle. *Serves 4.*

beef with prunes

BOGRASH

2½ lbs. lean beef, cut in 1-inch cubes
4 Tbsp. butter
1 Tbsp. flour
1½ cups beef broth
18 oz. bite-size pitted prunes
½ tsp. sugar
¼ tsp. salt

Pat beef cubes dry with paper towels. Melt butter in a large casserole or Dutch oven, and brown on all sides over medium high heat. Sprinkle with flour. Add beef broth and stir, scraping up brown bits on bottom of pan. Add prunes, sugar and salt. Reduce heat, cover, and simmer on *very low heat* for 2–2½ hours, until meat is very tender. Stir occasionally to keep bottom from burning, and add a little broth as needed. Taste for seasoning; the dish should be sweet rather than sour, so do not oversalt. *Serves 8.*

meat pudding

1½ lbs. leftover cooked meat, diced
1 medium onion, peeled and chopped
2 Tbsp. butter
Salt and pepper
1 cup sour cream
2 eggs
¾ cup fresh bread crumbs

Fry onion in 1 Tbsp. butter. Add meat, and cook for 2–3 minutes. Sprinkle with salt and pepper. Combine sour cream with eggs, salt, pepper and ½ cup of bread crumbs. Mix with meat. Place mixture in lightly greased casserole; sprinkle with remaining crumbs and dot with remaining butter. Bake for 25 minutes at 350 degrees. May be served with Mushroom Sauce (p. 159). *Serves 4.*

meat and potato layered pudding (pashtet)

3 medium potatoes, peeled and quartered
Water
Salt
Pepper
¼ lb. butter
½ cup bread crumbs
3 whole cloves, crushed
2 slices white bread, crusts removed
½ cup + 2 Tbsp. milk
2 medium onions, peeled and chopped
1½ lbs. ground chuck
2 eggs
1 Tbsp. grated Parmesan cheese

Boil potatoes in salted water. Drain and mash with 3 Tbsp. butter and ¼ cup bread crumbs. Add salt to taste. Fry onions in 2 Tbsp. butter; remove from heat. Combine meat, salt, pepper and cloves. Soak bread in milk, squeeze dry and add to meat. Butter casserole and sprinkle with bread crumbs. Place half of onions in casserole; top with half of meat, then remaining onions, half of potatoes, remaining meat, and remaining potatoes. Beat eggs with 2 Tbsp. milk, salt and pepper and pour over casserole. Dot with remaining butter. Sprinkle with 1 Tbsp. bread crumbs and with grated cheese. Bake at 350 degrees for about 50–55 minutes. *Serves 4–5.*

fake "rabbit" loaf

TRIFUNOVICH

2 lbs. ground chuck
1½ cups bread crumbs
1 slice white bread, crusts removed,
    soaked in ⅓ cup milk and squeezed dry
2 eggs
2 Tbsp. sour cream
½ tsp. salt
Pepper
2 tsp. chopped dill
1 clove garlic, crushed
3 Tbsp. butter
1 8-oz. can tomato sauce
¼ lb. mushrooms
1 large onion, peeled and chopped
1 Tbsp. flour
½ cup warm milk
½ cup sour cream

Combine meat, bread crumbs, bread soaked in milk and squeezed dry, eggs, 2 Tbsp. sour cream, salt, pepper, dill and garlic. Place in lightly greased loaf pan. Poke holes in top and insert 1 Tbsp. butter, cut into bits. Pour tomato sauce over all. Bake at 350 degrees for 1 hour. Fry mushrooms and onion in 2 Tbsp. butter and sprinkle with flour. Stir in warm milk, blending until smooth. Season to taste with salt and pepper. Before serving add sour cream and pour over meat loaf. *Serves 4–6.*

LAMB

marinated leg of lamb

NABOKOVA

This dish requires some advance planning, but is well worth it

1 5-lb. leg of lamb
1 clove garlic, peeled and slivered
Salt and pepper to taste
8–10 marinated plums and 4 Tbsp. of their marinade
    or ½ lb. marinated mushrooms (see below)

MARINADE FOR LAMB:
2 cloves garlic, quartered
1 large onion, peeled and sliced in rounds
8 black peppercorns
2 bay leaves
¾ cup red wine vinegar
1½ cups water
2 Tbsp. sugar
1 tsp. salt

If using mushrooms, use Baker's recipe for Marinated Mushrooms in *Zakuski* section (p. 31), reserving 2 tablespoons of marinade. For plums use recipe below:

MARINATED PLUMS:
5 lbs. ripe plums
5 cups red wine vinegar
4 cups sugar
1 stick cinnamon, cut in 2 lengthwise
4 cloves

Wash and thoroughly dry plums. Prick all over with a sharp needle and place in a deep enamel or glass dish. Blend vinegar, sugar and spices in another enamel saucepan and bring to the boil. Then pour this mixture evenly over the plums and leave them in it, loosely covered, overnight. The next day drain off the marinade, bring it to a boil in saucepan and again pour it over the plums. Let stand another day and the next day repeat this procedure. On the following day, pour plums and marinade into glass jars so that plums are completely covered by liquid.

LAMB:

Cut off as much fat as possible from leg. Put onion, garlic, bay leaves, peppercorns, sugar and salt into saucepan, pour vinegar and water over them and bring to the boil. Let simmer 1 minute and set aside to cool. Put lamb into saucepan or pot into which it fits snugly, and pour lukewarm marinade over it. When cool refrigerate and turn the leg several times during the next 24 hours.

The next day, remove leg from marinade and insert slivered garlic into the meat. Rub with salt and pepper, place in roasting pan and roast at 400 degrees until lamb is just browned (about 10–15 minutes.) Add marinade ingredients, baste with marinade and reduce heat to 350 degrees. Roast for 1½ to 2 hours, continuing to baste, until leg is done. A half an hour before roasting is finished, add the pitted, marinated plums or mushrooms with a few Tbsp. of their liquid and baste. Serve with the sauce from the pan and white rice. *Approximately 6 servings.*

lamb and beef stew

WEINSCHENKER

1 lb. stewing beef, cubed
1 lb. lamb, cubed
4 Tbsp. vegetable oil
2 medium onions, peeled and chopped
1 clove garlic, peeled and minced
1 green bell pepper, deribbed, seeded and minced
2 large carrots, peeled and sliced
2½ cups beef stock
1 stalk celery, chopped
3 medium potatoes, peeled and diced
1 cup string beans, trimmed
1 cup peas, fresh or frozen
2 tsp. minced dill
Salt and pepper

Sauté onions, garlic, green bell pepper, 1 carrot and celery in 2 Tbsp. oil until soft. In a separate pan, sauté meat in remaining oil, adding oil if necessary. When meat is lightly browned drain off excess fat and add to garlic and onion mixture. Add beef broth. Stir, partially cover, and simmer on low heat for about 1 hour, until meat is soft. Add potatoes, beans, peas, remaining carrot and salt and pepper to taste, and cook for 20–25 minutes. Taste for seasoning and add dill. Heat for 5 minutes. Serve with buttered noodles. *Serves 4–6.*

lamb in wine sauce

2 lbs. lamb, cut from shoulder, cubed
6 cups water
½ tsp. salt
Pinch pepper
1 bay leaf
1 small onion, peeled and quartered
1½ Tbsp. butter
2 Tbsp. flour
½ tsp. lemon juice
¼ cup dry red wine
1 egg yolk, well beaten
Pinch sugar

Boil water with salt, pepper, bay leaf and onion. Add lamb and simmer 30 minutes. Strain and reserve broth. Melt butter; whisk in flour and stir in 1½ cups strained lamb broth, adding water if necessary to make up 1½ cups. Whisk till smooth. Add lamb, lemon juice, red wine and sugar. Check seasoning and add salt and pepper to taste; simmer 10 minutes. Beat egg yolk well. Remove lamb from heat and add ½ cup of slightly cooled sauce from lamb to egg yolk. Beat back into lamb mixture. Do not boil. *Serves 4.*

lamb with tomato sauce and apples

2 lbs. lamb for stew, cubed
3 Tbsp. butter
1½ cups water
2 Tbsp. tomato paste
2 apples, peeled, cored and diced
1 Tbsp. flour
½ tsp. salt
Pepper
2 tsp. red wine vinegar
2 tsp. sugar
1 Tbsp. chopped parsley

Sauté lamb in 2 Tbsp. butter until lightly browned. Add 1 cup water and simmer until lamb is soft. Add tomato paste and apples; cook 20 minutes. Melt remaining Tbsp. butter. Add flour, and blend. Whisk in ½ cup sauce from meat and ½ cup water and stir till smooth. Combine with lamb. Add salt, pepper, vinegar and sugar and taste for seasoning. Simmer 30 minutes. Serve sprinkled with chopped parsley, with hot boiled potatoes on the side. *Serves 4.*

lamb and prunes

1¾ lbs. lamb, cubed
Salt and pepper
1 small onion, peeled and chopped
2 Tbsp. vegetable oil
½ cup boiling water
1 Tbsp. tomato paste
1 cup beef broth
1½ cups dried prunes, pitted
2 tsp. sugar
2 tsp. vinegar
Pinch cinnamon
½ tsp. crushed cloves
½ tsp. minced dill

Sprinkle lamb with salt and pepper. Sauté onion in oil and add lamb. Pour in boiling water and braise for ½ hour. Blend in tomato paste and broth and simmer on low heat. Allow prunes to soak for 30 minutes in boiling water to cover. Drain off water and add prunes to lamb. Cook for 40 minutes. Add sugar, vinegar, cinnamon, cloves and dill; simmer for 5 minutes and taste for seasoning. Can be served with flat boiled noodles or white rice. *Serves 4.*

breast of lamb
with caraway seeds

7 cups water
1 breast of lamb (about 3 lbs.)
1 tsp. salt
1 medium carrot, sliced
4 sprigs parsley
1 stalk celery, sliced
1 medium onion, peeled and quartered
5 peppercorns
2 tsp. caraway seeds
1 tsp. sugar
1 tsp. white vinegar
1 Tbsp. butter
1 Tbsp. flour

Cut lamb into pieces so that it will easily fit into a Dutch oven. Add salt, carrot, parsley, celery, onion, and peppercorns to water and bring to a boil; simmer 5 minutes and add lamb. Cook until lamb is done, about 45 minutes. Remove from heat and skim fat from broth. Add 1 tsp. caraway seeds, sugar and vinegar to sauce. Melt butter. Add flour, and whisk in 2½ cups broth. Puree sauce in blender until smooth. Add remaining caraway seeds, pour over lamb, heat through, and serve. *Serves 4–6.*

shashlyk

This Georgian dish has become a part of Russian cuisine. The meat can be alternated on skewers with onion quarters, cherry tomatoes, slices of green bell pepper or mushroom caps, and should be served with lemon wedges on a bed of rice. If desired, the shashlyk may be sprinkled with finely minced scallions.

3 lbs. lamb, cut from leg, cubed

M A R I N A D E 1
1 tsp. salt
½ tsp. black pepper
¼ tsp. nutmeg
¾ cup vegetable oil
½ cup water
1 Tbsp. chopped parsley
1 medium onion, peeled and minced
1 bay leaf
Pinch ground cloves
Pinch thyme

M A R I N A D E 2
¾ cup vegetable oil
3 Tbsp. lemon juice
1 Tbsp. chopped parsley
1 Tbsp. chopped dill
2 cloves garlic, peeled and crushed
½ tsp. salt
¼ tsp. pepper

M A R I N A D E 3
⅔ cup red wine vinegar
⅓ cup vegetable oil
¼ cup water
½ cup red wine
1 medium onion, peeled and chopped
2 cloves garlic, peeled and chopped
½ tsp. salt and ¼ tsp. pepper
Optional: pinch cinnamon

For each marinade, combine all ingredients in a glass bowl and put in cubed meat. Let meat stand in marinade for at least 5 hours. The dish will be even better if the meat marinates overnight. Before placing on skewers, dry the meat well and sprinkle lightly with salt and, if desired, a little pepper. Thread on skewers with vegetables (see above), and broil over high heat; a hibachi-type grill, barbecue, or even broiler is fine. The meat and vegetables should be removed from the skewers and placed on rice just before serving, or this can be done at the table. *Serves 6.*

VEAL

veal "hacked" cutlets (pozharskie kotlety)

NABOKOVA

2 lbs. boneless veal shoulder or veal stew
3 large dry rolls or equal quantity of dry white bread
2 egg yolks
2 egg whites, beaten stiff
½ lb. butter (approximately)
1 tsp. salt
1 cup small ice chips
Bread crumbs

Place the rolls or bread in a deep bowl, cover with cold water and let soak for about ¼ hour. Finely grind the veal. Squeeze water gently out of the rolls or bread and add bread to veal. Work in egg yolks and salt. Mix very thoroughly until quite smooth. Carefully add beaten egg whites and shape into small oblong croquettes. Make a hole in the middle of each, put in a small piece of butter and ice chip. Close the opening tightly, pinching the edges of the croquette together. Roll the croquette in crumbs and flatten with a large kitchen knife. Quickly fry in remaining butter. *Makes 16–18 croquettes.*

fricassee of ground veal

2 lbs. ground veal
1 medium onion, peeled and finely chopped
¾ cup bread crumbs
1 tsp. salt

½ tsp. pepper
5 Tbsp. butter
½ lb. mushrooms, peeled and sliced
1 Tbsp. flour
½ cup beef broth
1 cup sour cream
1 tsp. lemon juice
1 Tbsp. chopped parsley
1 Tbsp. chopped dill
Optional: 2 egg yolks

Combine veal, onion, bread crumbs, salt and pepper, and form into small 1½-inch meatballs. Fry in 3 Tbsp. butter on all sides until browned. Sauté mushrooms in 1 Tbsp. butter until soft. In a separate saucepan melt remaining 1 Tbsp. butter. Add flour, and whisk in beef broth. Add sour cream, and season with salt and pepper to taste. Stir in lemon juice, dill and parsley. Blend mushrooms and sauce with meat, and allow to simmer 10 minutes. Just before serving, remove from heat and add egg yolks, well beaten, to ½ cup of sauce. Pour back into pan, taking care that the mixture does not boil and the yolks do not curdle. *Serves 4–6.*

veal scallops

PENDILL

2 lbs. veal scallops
Flour
2 Tbsp. olive oil
3 cloves garlic, peeled and minced
½ lb. mushrooms, sliced
½ cup dry Riesling or rosé wine
Salt and pepper
1 1-lb. can tomatoes
1 Tbsp. chopped fresh parsley

Pound veal scallops flat between 2 pieces of wax paper. Dredge lightly with flour. Sauté quickly on both sides in olive oil. Add garlic and mushrooms, and cook 5 minutes. Sprinkle with salt and pepper. Drain tomatoes and add; simmer another 5 minutes. Add wine and simmer 5 minutes or more. Sprinkle with chopped parsley and serve. *Serves 3.*

breast of veal with mushrooms

7 cups water
3–3½ lbs. breast of veal
1 large onion, peeled and quartered
2 sprigs parsley
1 stalk celery, sliced
1 carrot, peeled and sliced
Salt and pepper
½ lb. mushrooms, sliced
2 Tbsp. butter
1½ Tbsp. flour
Optional: 1 tsp. caraway seeds
1 tsp. lemon juice
⅔ cup light cream

Cut veal into pieces which will easily fit into a Dutch oven. Boil water, onion, parsley, celery, carrot, salt and pepper together for 5 minutes; add veal. Bring back to boil. Reduce heat and simmer 45 minutes to 1 hour until veal is tender. Sauté mushrooms in 1 Tbsp. butter. Separately, heat remaining Tbsp. butter; stir in flour; whisk in 2 cups of strained liquid in which veal was cooked. Add caraway seeds, lemon juice, and cream, and simmer 10 minutes. Cut veal meat from bones, and add to sauce along with mushrooms. Simmer on very low heat for 10 minutes. *Serves 4–6.*

veal with macaroni

2 lbs. stewing veal, cubed
2 Tbsp. vegetable oil
4 Tbsp. butter
Salt and pepper
¾ cup water
½ cup elbow macaroni
1 egg
2 Tbsp. grated Parmesan cheese
½ cup shredded ham
1 Tbsp. flour
1 tsp. lemon juice

Heat oil and 2 Tbsp. butter. Sauté veal on all sides until browned. Sprinkle with salt and pepper. Add ¾ cup water and simmer covered on low heat 30 minutes. Boil macaroni until just done. Combine macaroni, well drained, with 1 Tbsp. butter, well beaten egg and grated cheese. Add shredded ham and mix well. Remove veal from the pot, reserving pan juices and put in baking dish with 3 Tbsp. of juices. Cover with macaroni mixture and bake in a 350-degree oven for 25 minutes. Melt remaining 1 Tbsp. butter, stir in 1 Tbsp. flour, and add remaining juices from pan plus enough water to make 1 cup. Stir until thick and add lemon juice. Pour over veal mixture and continue to bake for another 25 minutes. *Serves 4–6.*

veal stew

GERSTMAN

2 lbs. veal, cubed
3 Tbsp. vegetable oil
Salt and pepper
3 cloves garlic, peeled and crushed
1 cup tomato juice
1 cup dry white wine

Fry veal in oil. Sprinkle with salt and pepper. Add garlic and stir. Blend in juice and wine, and simmer, partially covered for 1½ hours. Taste for seasoning. Serve with peas, rice or asparagus. *Serves 4.*

❖ veal stew with mushrooms

TUMARKIN

This recipe shows the influence of French cuisine. Boiled new potatoes make an excellent accompaniment

2 lbs. veal, cut into 1-inch cubes
1 Tbsp. + 1 tsp. salt
1 qt. water (approximately)
12 small white onions
3 medium carrots, peeled and coarsely sliced
1 stalk celery, coarsely sliced
1 leek (white part only, coarsely sliced)
3 sprigs parsley
1 bay leaf
1 clove garlic, peeled and crushed
3 peppercorns, crushed
Pinch thyme

1 lb. white mushrooms, sliced
½ cup milk
Juice of ½ lemon
3 Tbsp. butter
3 Tbsp. flour
¾ cup light cream
2 egg yolks, beaten

Bring veal to a boil in water to cover. Keeping water simmering, add 1 Tbsp. salt, onions, carrots, celery, leek, parsley, bay leaf, garlic, peppercorns, and thyme. Partially cover and simmer on medium low heat for 1 hour, until meat is tender. Remove meat, onions and carrots with a slotted spoon. Raise the heat and boil rapidly to reduce the broth by one third, and then remove the celery, leek, parsley and bay leaf.

Heat the milk, lemon juice and ½ tsp. salt in a pot and add the mushrooms. Bring to a boil and simmer for five minutes. Then remove the mushrooms from the heat and allow them to steep in the liquid for a few more minutes; strain, reserving the mushroom liquid. Melt the butter and stir in flour to form a golden brown roux. Add the mushroom liquid and all but a tablespoon or two of the meat broth, whisking until smooth, and cook the sauce on very low heat for 15-20 minutes, stirring to keep lumps from forming.

Cool the sauce slightly. While it is cooling, heat the meat, onions, carrots and mushrooms in the remaining broth to serving temperature (you can do that over medium low heat or by heating in a microwave for a minute or two). Blend yolks and cream, and slowly add to the sauce on very low heat, taking care that the mixture does not reach a boil, as that will cause the yolks to curdle. Correct the seasoning and strain the sauce.

Place the meat in a serving dish or casserole and cover with the mushrooms, onions and carrots. Pour the sauce over the veal and vegetables and serve immediately. *Serves 4-6*

veal with squash

2 lbs. veal for stew, cubed
2 Tbsp. vegetable oil
2 Tbsp. butter
2 Tbsp. tomato paste
¼ tsp. crushed red pepper
1½ cups water
3 small yellow squash (zucchini), sliced
1 Tbsp. chopped dill
Salt and pepper

Fry veal in 1 Tbsp. oil and 1 Tbsp. butter until browned. Add tomato paste and red pepper, and stir. Add water. Simmer for about 45–50 minutes until veal is tender and most of liquid is absorbed. In a separate pan sauté squash in remaining oil and butter, and add to meat. Sprinkle on dill and salt and pepper to taste and cook 10–15 minutes on low heat. *Serves 4.*

veal with tomatoes and mushrooms

2 lbs. veal, cubed
4 Tbsp. butter
½ lb. mushrooms, chopped
Salt and pepper
2 tomatoes
1 clove garlic, peeled and minced
Water
½ tsp. caraway seeds
1 Tbsp. flour
½ cup peas, fresh, frozen or canned

Fry mushrooms in 1 Tbsp. butter. Sprinkle with salt and pepper. Add tomatoes, cut in thin slices, and simmer for 5 minutes. Add garlic. Sprinkle veal with salt and pepper. Put 2 more Tbsp. butter in pan with vegetables, and add veal. When veal is browned, add water to partially cover meat, and simmer, covered, for 50 minutes. Sprinkle in caraway seeds. Melt remaining Tbsp. butter; add flour, and blend in pan juices plus enough water to make 1 cup. Return sauce to meat and simmer for 15 minutes. Add peas and simmer until heated through. Taste for seasoning. *Serves 4.*

roast of veal

B. Vinogradova

1 4-lb. roast of veal
1 clove garlic, peeled
1 Tbsp. paprika
1 Tbsp. salt
2 tsp. lemon juice
1 cup chicken broth or 1 vegetable broth packet
    dissolved in 1 cup hot water
1 onion, peeled and coarsely sliced

Rub veal thoroughly with garlic, paprika, salt and lemon juice. Cover with aluminum foil and place in lightly greased roasting pan in preheated 425-degree oven. Immediately lower heat to 350. Roast 15 minutes, lift foil and baste with broth. Scatter onion around veal. Roast for 1 to 1½ hours, basting every 15 minutes with pan juices, adding chicken broth if necessary. May be served with boiled potatoes. *Serves 6–8.*

veal with caviar sauce

1 4-lb. roast of veal
Salt and pepper
3 Tbsp. butter
1 small onion, peeled and sliced into rings
1 turnip, peeled and sliced
1 stalk celery, sliced
2 sprigs parsley
1 tsp. grated lemon rind
1 cup dry white wine
½ cup water
2 Tbsp. black lumpfish caviar
2 tsp. lemon juice

Rub veal with salt and pepper. Brown lightly on all sides in 2 Tbsp. butter. Add onion, turnip, celery, parsley, and brown for 2–3 minutes. Sprinkle meat with lemon rind and salt and pepper to taste. Pour in wine and water and braise, covered, for about 1¾ hours on low heat. Remove veal. Skim off fat and strain sauce. Add caviar, lemon juice, and 1 Tbsp. butter to sauce; pour over veal. Serve with boiled potatoes and a green salad. *Serves 6–8.*

POULTRY

chicken kotlety I

NABOKOVA

1½ lbs. ground chicken
2 pieces dry white bread,
    soaked in ½ cup cold water and squeezed dry
2 eggs, separated
½ tsp. salt
¼ lb. butter (approximately)
½ cup small chunks of ice
1 cup bread crumbs

Combine ground chicken with soaked bread, egg yolks, and salt. Beat whites and blend gently into chicken. Form small oblong croquettes and make a small hole in the center of each; insert a small (½ tsp.) piece of butter and a small piece of ice in each croquette, being sure the opening is well closed. Roll *kotlety* in bread crumbs, patting with the flat of a blade to be sure the coating adheres. Fry in butter until golden on both sides. Serve with peas and boiled potatoes. *Serves 4.*

chicken kotlety II
YAVITZ

6 chicken breasts
5 pieces white bread, crusts removed
1 cup light cream
2 egg yolks
2 egg whites, beaten
1½ sticks butter (¼ lb. + 4 Tbsp.)
Salt and pepper
1 Tbsp. chopped dill

Put chicken breasts through grinder. Soak bread in cream and squeeze dry. Combine meat, bread, yolks and 1 stick butter and blend thoroughly. Add salt, pepper, and dill to taste. Beat whites separately and carefully fold in. Form the mixture into small oval patties (about 2½ inches long), and fry in remaining butter until golden. *Serves 6–8.*

chicken kotlety III
MRS. L.

2 chicken breasts
1 piece white bread
4 cup milk
1 egg, beaten
Salt
¼ tsp. white pepper
¼ tsp. nutmeg
1 Tbsp. chopped dill
3 Tbsp. heavy cream
Butter
Oil

Soak bread in milk and squeeze dry. Grind chicken breasts and combine with bread, egg, salt, pepper, nutmeg, dill and heavy cream. Form into small oval croquettes about 2½–3 inches long. Fry in half butter-half oil until golden. *Serves 3–4.*

chicken and veal loaf

ODESSER

½ lb. ground chicken
½ lb. ground veal
1 egg
1 medium onion, peeled and grated
4 pieces white bread, crusts removed
⅓ cup milk
¼ cup chicken broth
1 tsp. salt
¼ tsp. pepper
1 Tbsp. chopped dill

Soak bread in milk and squeeze dry. Combine meats, egg, onion, and bread and mix well. Add broth, salt, pepper, and dill. Place in lightly greased loaf pan and bake for 50 minutes to 1 hour at 350 degrees. *Serves 4.*

cutlets maréchal

NABOKOVA

This chicken breast with truffles is an elegant version of Chicken Kiev

6 chicken breasts
5 truffles, canned or fresh
½ lb. butter
⅔ cup flour
2 eggs, beaten
1 cup bread crumbs
Salt and pepper

Bone and skin breasts. Remove small inner fillets. (The butcher can do this for you.) Pound both large and small fillets flat with a meat cleaver or the flat of a blade, being careful not to tear the meat. Season fillets with salt and pepper. (If truffles are fresh, peel and cook for a few minutes in a little white wine.) Cut truffles into thin round slices and place in center of large fillets. Cover with very thin tiny slices of butter, and then cover with small fillet. Roll up into an oblong cutlet and secure with toothpick. Dip cutlet into flour, then into beaten eggs, and then roll in bread crumbs. Fry in remaining butter, turning after about 5 minutes. Cover pan and place in oven. Can be kept warm at 300–325 degrees for no more than 20 minutes. Serve with small peas and boiled potatoes or rice. *Serves 6.*

Note: For Chicken Kiev the recipe is identical but very cold cylinders of butter are used, and the truffles omitted. The butter may be seasoned to taste with parsley and dill. It is advisable to keep the cutlets refrigerated for ½ hour before frying; they may be then kept warm in the oven for 10–20 minutes.

fried chicken breast cutlets (otbivnye kotlety)
ODESSER

4 chicken breasts
4 pieces white bread, crusts removed
1 tsp. salt
½ tsp. pepper
1–2 eggs, beaten
¼ lb. + 1 Tbsp. butter

Have the butcher bone the chicken breasts. Pound flat with the side of a meat cleaver. Crumb white bread very fine in blender and add salt and pepper. Dip breasts in beaten egg, then coat with bread crumbs and pat firmly to be sure the crumbs adhere. Fry in 5 tablespoons butter until light golden brown. Remove to a lightly greased baking dish. Slice remaining 4 Tbsp. butter thinly on top of cutlets. Bake in 350-degree oven for 15 minutes or until dark golden brown. Good with fresh or frozen peas cooked in a little lemon juice and chicken fat or bouillon. *Serves 4.*

chicken in wine
PENDILL

1 3½–4 lb. chicken, cut into serving pieces
Salt and pepper
3 Tbsp. butter
1 small onion, peeled and chopped
½ lb. mushrooms, sliced
½ cup Riesling or rosé wine
½ cup heavy cream

Rub chicken with salt and pepper. Brown quickly on all sides in butter. Add mushrooms and onion and cook for another 5 minutes. Transfer to baking dish and bake for 35–45 minutes at 350 degrees. Remove chicken pieces to platter. Add wine to baking dish, stir and simmer till reduced by half. Stir in cream, simmer for a few minutes until sauce thickens. Return chicken to pan and heat until chicken is warmed through. Serve with rice. *Serves 4.*

❖ my special chicken dish

CHERNYAKHOVSKAYA

The combination of flavors makes for an unusual and tasty dish

3 cups cubed (1-inch cubes) cooked chicken
2 Tbsp. olive oil
1 medium onion, peeled and coarsely sliced
2 carrots, peeled and coarsely sliced
8 oz. mushrooms, sliced
¼ cup raisins, softened in hot water
1 ½ Tbsp. butter
2 Tbsp. flour
1 ½ cups chicken broth
Salt and pepper
1 cup sour cream
½ cup grated cheese (Swiss or mixed Swiss and Parmesan)

Note: You can boil a chicken and remove the meat from the bones; in that case, use the chicken broth formed by boiling the chicken, adjust the seasoning for the broth, and skim the fat. Otherwise, you can use leftover cooked chicken and readymade chicken broth.

Fry the onion and carrots in 1 Tbsp. olive oil until the onions are dark golden brown and the carrots are soft, adding a little oil if needed to keep the mixture from burning. Fry the mushrooms in a separate pan in the other tablespoon of oil, stirring, until cooked through.

Combine the chicken, onion, carrots and mushrooms, and mix well. Add the drained raisins. Melt the butter and add flour, stirring to form a thick roux. Pour in the chicken bouillon and whisk until the sauce thickens. Blend the chicken mixture into the sauce and taste for seasoning, adding salt and pepper as needed (be careful with the salt, since the amount needed will depend on the salt in your chicken broth). Stir in the sour cream and blend well.

You can either place the mixture in a single casserole or divide it up between 6-8 small clay pots/casseroles. Sprinkle the casserole(s) with the grated cheese and bake at 350 for 20 minutes until chicken is very hot and the cheese is melted and lightly browned. For a crisp topping, after the dish has baked in the oven for 15 minutes run it under the broiler for 3-4 minutes, taking care that the cheese does not burn. *Serves 6-8.*

chicken in white sauce

B. VINOGRADOVA

1 3–4 lb. chicken, cut into serving pieces
4 Tbsp. butter
2 carrots, peeled and cut into large chunks
1 medium onion, peeled and coarsely sliced
½ tsp. salt
⅛ tsp. pepper
¼ tsp. thyme
1 Tbsp. paprika
2 cloves garlic, peeled and crushed
½ cup dry white wine
½ cup chicken stock
1½ Tbsp. flour
1¼ cups light cream

Melt 3 Tbsp. butter and sauté carrots and onion in it for 5 minutes. Sprinkle with salt, thyme, pepper, paprika, and garlic, and cook another 5 minutes. Put in chicken and sauté until golden. Add wine and chicken stock, and simmer 15 minutes. Melt 1 Tbsp. butter. Stir in 1½ Tbsp. flour, whisking until smooth; add cream, boil up, and stir till thick. Add sauce to chicken and blend well. Simmer on low heat for 45 minutes. Serve with noodles. *Serves 4.*

chicken with rice

7 cups water
1 4–lb. chicken
2 medium carrots, peeled and sliced
2 medium onions, peeled and quartered
1 stalk celery, sliced
3 sprigs parsley
1 tsp. salt
Pinch pepper
Pinch thyme
1 Tbsp. butter
1½ Tbsp. flour
½ cup light cream
½ cup sour cream
2 Tbsp. chopped scallions (green and white parts)
2 cups boiled rice

Cut chicken into serving pieces. Place in a pot with giblets, carrots, onions, celery, parsley, salt, pepper, and thyme, and 7 cups water. Bring to a boil and then reduce heat, partially cover, and simmer for about 45 minutes until chicken is done. Strain broth. Melt 1 Tbsp. butter. Sprinkle in flour, and whisk in 1½ cups of strained chicken broth. Add light cream, salt and pepper to taste, and simmer 5 minutes. Whisk in sour cream but do not boil. Stir scallions into rice. Pour sauce over chicken and simmer 5 minutes. Serve chicken over rice. *Serves 4.*

chicken barbecue style

B. VINOGRADOVA

1 3½-lb. chicken (broiler-fryer), cut into serving pieces
¼ cup vegetable oil
1 large onion, peeled and sliced into rings
½ stalk celery, chopped
1 cup ketchup
1 cup water
¼ cup lemon juice
2 Tbsp. brown sugar
1 tsp. mustard
Salt and pepper

Brown chicken pieces slowly in oil until golden. Remove chicken and add onion and celery to pan; simmer until tender. Add ketchup, water, lemon juice, sugar and mustard, and blend well. Season to taste with salt and pepper and simmer 10 minutes. Skim off excess fat. Place chicken in 11 x 7-inch baking dish and pour sauce over it. Bake uncovered in 325-degree oven for 1 to 1½ hours, basting occasionally. *Serves 4.*

chicken with fruit and kasha

1 6–7 lb. roasting chicken
1 cup cooked kasha
2 apples, peeled, cored and chopped
1¼ cups pitted prunes, chopped
¼ cup dark raisins
2 hardboiled eggs, peeled and chopped
½ cup sour cream
Salt to taste
2 Tbsp. butter, melted

Pat chicken dry with paper towels, and remove giblets; save for another purpose. Combine kasha, apples, prunes, raisins, eggs, sour cream and salt and stir until smooth. Stuff chicken with kasha and fruit mixture and close with skewers or toothpicks, or sew up. Place chicken in a roasting pan and brush with melted butter. Roast at 350 degrees for 20 minutes per pound (approximately 2 hours for a 6-pound chicken). If there is extra stuffing, place it in a corner of the roasting pan. Baste every 15–20 minutes with pan juices. Cover with foil if drumstick and wing tips start to burn. Do not turn chicken. Prick top of drumstick to check if chicken is cooked; when the bird is done juices will run yellow instead of pink and leg joint will easily move away from body. *Serves 6.*

chicken with grapes
ODESSER

1 3½-lb. chicken
1 tsp. salt
Pinch pepper
1 Tbsp. lemon juice
1½ Tbsp. butter
½ cup water or chicken stock
½ cup dry white wine
1 cup seedless green grapes

Rub chicken with salt, pepper and lemon juice. Rub ½ Tbsp. softened butter over grapes and stuff chicken. Truss, or close with large toothpicks. Place in roasting pan with water or stock, remaining butter, and wine. Roast at 350 degrees for 1 hour, basting occasionally and adding more stock and wine as needed to keep chicken from burning. A half-teaspoon sugar may be added to the pan juices before serving. *Serves 4.*

chicken stuffed with mushrooms and bread crumbs
ODESSER

1 4-lb. chicken
¼ lb. mushrooms
¼ lb. + 1 Tbsp. butter
Salt and pepper
1 clove garlic, peeled and crushed
2 slices white bread, crusts removed
1 cup chicken broth
½ tsp. dried tarragon
1 egg

Chop mushrooms; sauté for 2–3 minutes in 1 Tbsp. butter. Rub chicken with salt, pepper and garlic. Make bread crumbs in blender. Combine mushrooms, bread crumbs, salt, pepper, ¼ cup chicken broth, tarragon and egg, and blend well. Stuff chicken with mixture and truss or secure opening with toothpicks. Rub chicken with 2 Tbsp. butter and place in roasting pan. Melt remaining butter and combine with remaining bouillon. Pour over chicken. Bake at 350 degrees for 1 hour, basting periodically, and adding broth if necessary to keep chicken from burning. *Serves 4.*

cornish hens with fruit

VENGEROVA

The unusual combination of flavors makes for a tasty and appealing dish

2 Cornish hens, with giblets (omit liver)
⅓ cup dry sherry
⅓ cup lemon juice
½ tsp. salt
Pinch pepper
1 apple, peeled, cored and diced
1 orange, peeled and quartered
8 medium potatoes, peeled and quartered
5 Tbsp. butter
1 medium onion, peeled and sliced
⅓ cup Madeira wine
1 tsp. soy sauce
½ tsp. paprika

Combine sherry, lemon juice, salt and pepper. Marinate hens in this mixture for 2–3 hours, turning occasionally. Mix apple and orange pieces and stuff hens, closing opening by trussing or with large toothpicks. Place in roasting pan and scatter onion, potatoes and giblets around hens. Rub birds with 2 Tbsp. butter and put the remaining butter, Madeira and soy sauce in the pan around hens. Sprinkle hens with additional salt, pepper, and paprika. Bake at 350 degrees for 45 minutes to an hour, depending on size of hens, basting occasionally. Add more butter or water mixed with Madeira if necessary. Turn potatoes occasionally to keep from burning. Taste sauce for seasoning before serving. *2 servings of whole Cornish hens or 4 halves.*

turkey cutlets in dark cherry sauce

1½ lbs. ground turkey
1 slice white bread
½ cup milk
1 egg, beaten
1 tsp. salt
¼ tsp. pepper
2 tsp. Madeira
5 Tbsp. butter

Soak white bread in milk and squeeze until dry. Combine turkey, egg, bread, salt, pepper and Madeira and mix until smooth. Form into 8–9 small oval patties, and fry over medium heat on both sides in very hot butter until browned.

SAUCE:
1 1-lb. jar dark Bing cherries in syrup
2 cloves, crushed
½ tsp. ground cardamom
½ tsp. cinnamon
Optional: 3 tsp. sugar

Pit cherries. In saucepan, combine cherries, syrup, cloves, cardamom, cinnamon and sugar if desired. Cook over low heat for 5–10 minutes. Remove patties from pan to warm platter, and boil down juices, scraping bottom of pan, until reduced to about 3 Tbsp. Puree cherry mixture in blender until smooth and add to pan juices. Simmer 5 minutes, pour over cutlets and serve. *Serves 4.*

duck with apples

1 5-lb. duck
Salt
2 small apples, peeled, cored and chopped
4 Tbsp. butter
1 cup water
10 small potatoes, peeled
½ cup sour cream

Rub duck inside and outside with salt. Prick skin in several places. Sprinkle apples with a little salt and stuff duck, sewing opening or securing with toothpicks. Dot with 2 Tbsp. butter. Place duck in roasting pan. Heat oven to 400 degrees and add a few Tbsp. water. Immediately turn down to 375. After duck has roasted for ½ hour, surround with potatoes and remaining butter. Baste with pan juices, adding water as needed. Roast for 1 hour or until duck is tender. Skim fat from pan juices, blend in sour cream, and taste for seasoning. Good with sauerkraut. *Serves 4.*

duck stuffed with macaroni and mushrooms

1 5-lb. duck, with giblets
½ cup elbow macaroni
¼ lb. mushrooms, sliced
2 Tbsp. butter
1 tsp. salt
Pinch pepper
4 cloves, crushed
1 medium carrot, peeled and sliced
5 sprigs parsley
1 turnip, peeled and sliced
1 medium onion, peeled and quartered
1 stalk celery, chopped
1 bay leaf
2 cups water

SAUCE:
1½ cups sour cream
¼ cup flour
Few drops lemon juice
Salt and pepper
2 Tbsp. butter
¼ lb. mushrooms, sliced

Wash duck and dry throughly with paper towels. Cook macaroni according to package directions until just barely done. Fry mushrooms in 2 Tbsp. butter, sprinkle with salt and pepper and combine with drained macaroni. Pull excess fat from duck cavity, stuff duck with macaroni mixture and sew up. Rub duck with salt, pepper and crushed cloves. In a roasting pan place duck, giblets, carrot, parsley, turnip, onion, celery, bay leaf, and 2 cups water. Heat oven to 450 degrees and immediately turn down to 350 degrees. Put in duck and roast about 20–25 minutes per pound. After ½ hour, add ½ cup water, and baste. Add more water if needed. Strain pan juices and skim fat. Add water if needed to make 1 cup broth. For sauce, mix 1½ cups sour cream with ¼ cup flour until smooth; add a few drops of lemon juice, salt, pepper, 1 cup duck broth and the sliced mushrooms, cooked in 2 Tbsp. butter. Stir till smooth and simmer 10 minutes. Taste for seasoning. Thin with a little water if necessary. *Serves 4.*

roast goose

YAVITZ

1 12-lb. goose (or 7-lb. gosling)
4 cups chopped apples
4 cups pitted prunes
1 cup chopped orange peel
1½ tsp. salt
½ tsp. pepper
10 medium potatoes, peeled

Prick goose in several places to release fat. Heat oven to 350 degrees. Roast goose for 15 minutes; remove from oven, pour out fat, prick skin again, and return for 15 minutes. Again remove goose, pour off fat, and prick skin. Repeat once more and this time when goose is removed from oven, stuff with the mixed apples, prunes, orange peel, salt and pepper. Allow 30 minutes to the pound for roasting. Baste goose occasionally, and pour off fat as it accumulates. Fifty minutes before goose is done, add potatoes to pan. *Number of servings will depend on size of bird.*

OTHER MEATS

sausages in tomato sauce

6 frankfurters, thickly sliced
3 Tbsp. butter
1 Tbsp. flour
2 Tbsp. tomato paste
1 cup beef broth
2 tsp. Madeira
Salt and pepper

Fry frankfurters in 2 Tbsp. butter until pink. Melt remaining Tbsp. butter, add flour and tomato paste, and when thick, stir in beef broth. Add sausages and Madeira. Simmer 5 minutes. Taste for seasoning and add salt and pepper as needed. *Serves 4 as a first course, and 2 as a main course.*

sausages and sauerkraut
CHEOSKY

2 Tbsp. vegetable oil
¼ lb. salt pork, diced
2 onions, diced
2 lbs. sauerkraut
Water
2 lbs. frankfurters or kielbasa, sliced
Pinch sugar
1 small apple, peeled, cored and diced

Brown salt pork in oil in large skillet. Add onions, and cook till golden. Squeeze sauerkraut dry, reserving liquid, and add to pan. Simmer on very low heat for 1 hour, adding reserved liquid, checking to be sure that the mixture is always moist; add water if necessary. Put in sausage, sugar and apple and cook 35 minutes on low heat. *Serves 8.*

baked ham
KHAZANOV

1 3-lb. boiled canned ham
12 cloves
1½ tsp. coarsely ground black pepper
1 cup brown sugar
3 Tbsp. mustard
1 orange, thinly sliced

Stud ham with cloves, making small incisions if necessary so that the cloves will adhere. Sprinkle ham lightly with pepper. Bake at 350 degrees for 30 minutes. Remove ham from oven and allow to cool slightly. Combine mustard and sugar and cover ham with mixture. With toothpicks, cover surface of ham with thin slices of orange. Return to 400-degree oven for 20 minutes. *Serves 6.*

liver in sour cream and juniper

2 lbs. liver (beef or calf)
1 cup milk
2 Tbsp. butter
3 Tbsp. vegetable oil
1 small onion, peeled and chopped
1 medium carrot, peeled and sliced
1 stalk celery, sliced
2 sprigs chopped parsley
1 bay leaf
1 tsp. salt
½ tsp. pepper
⅓ cup + 1 Tbsp. flour
1 Tbsp. juniper berries, crushed
1 cup beef consommé
½ cup sour cream

Soak liver in milk for 2 hours. In 1 Tbsp. butter and 3 Tbsp. oil sauté onion, carrot, celery, parsley and bay leaf until vegetables are soft. Mix salt, pepper and ⅓ cup flour together and dredge liver. Push vegetables to one side of pan and add liver. Fry on both sides until meat loses red color. Sprinkle with salt. Remove liver from pan; add juniper berries, and simmer 5 minutes. Melt remaining Tbsp. butter. Add 1 Tbsp. flour, and stir in beef consommé and sour cream, blending till thick. Add to pan juices, and simmer 3–5 minutes. Slice liver into strips. Strain sauce. Return meat and sauce to pan and heat through. Serve with noodles. *Serves 4–5.*

liver stroganoff

1½ lbs. liver (beef or calf)
4 Tbsp. butter
1 large onion, peeled and chopped
1 Tbsp. flour
Salt
½ cup sour cream
1 tsp. Worcestershire sauce
2 tsp. Dijon-style mustard
2 tsp. chopped dill

Cut liver into thin strips, and fry in 2 Tbsp. hot butter. Sprinkle lightly with salt. In a separate pan melt remaining 2 Tbsp. butter, and sauté onion until golden. Sprinkle with salt and flour. Add sour cream, Worcestershire sauce, mustard and dill. Simmer 5 minutes. Pour over liver and simmer for another 5 minutes. *Serves 4.*

chicken livers in cognac

1½ lbs. chicken livers
⅓ cup + 1 Tbsp. flour
Salt and pepper
6 Tbsp. butter
2 scallions, chopped (white part only)
½ lb. mushrooms, sliced
1 cup chicken stock
2 Tbsp. heavy cream
2 Tbsp. cognac

Combine ⅓ cup flour with salt and pepper. Dredge livers in this mixture. Melt 5 Tbsp. butter and sauté scallions and mushrooms. Add livers, and sauté over fairly high heat for 45 minutes. In a separate pan melt remaining Tbsp. butter. Add 1 Tbsp. flour, and stir in chicken stock and heavy cream. Add to pan and simmer for a few minutes. Stir in cognac, simmer 2–3 minutes, taste for seasoning, and serve. Can be served over rice or noodles. *Serves 4.*

kidneys in madeira

5 lamb kidneys
Salt and pepper
4 Tbsp. butter
1½ Tbsp. flour
½ lb. mushrooms
¾ cup beef broth
2 Tbsp. Madeira

Clean kidneys and run cold water over them. Slice very thinly and sprinkle with salt and pepper. Melt 3 Tbsp. butter; cook kidneys over high heat for 10 minutes. Add mushrooms, reduce heat, and sauté for another 5 minutes. In separate pot melt remaining Tbsp. butter; add flour, broth, and stir till thick; pour in Madeira. Put in kidneys and simmer 10 minutes. *Serves 4.*

kidneys in sour cream

1 beef kidney
4–6 Tbsp. butter
3 medium potatoes, peeled and cubed
1 medium carrot, peeled and sliced
1 medium turnip, peeled and sliced
1 medium onion, peeled and sliced into rings
2 tomatoes, chopped
1 small cucumber, peeled, seeded, and diced
1 small dill pickle, diced
1 clove garlic, peeled and crushed
Salt and pepper
1¾ cups sour cream
1 Tbsp. chopped parsley

Clean kidney. Place in cold water to cover; bring to a boil, pour off water and replace with fresh water; repeat three times. Boil for 20 minutes. Remove kidney, and slice thinly. Melt butter; fry kidney, potatoes, carrot, turnip, onion and tomatoes on low heat until soft, about 20 minutes, stirring to keep from burning. Place in casserole; add cucumber, pickle and garlic; season to taste with salt and pepper. Stir in sour cream and bake, covered, in 350-degree oven for 30 minutes. Sprinkle with fresh parsley. *Serves 6.*

kidneys in whisky

KHAZANOV

The whisky flavor is absorbed into the sauce and gives this dish a unique aroma

1½–2 lbs. lamb kidneys
1/3 cup vegetable oil
½ tsp. salt
Pinch pepper
1½ tsp. lemon juice
2 Tbsp. Scotch whisky

Clean kidneys of all fat and chop into small pieces. Heat oil until very hot and fry kidneys on very high heat for 5 minutes, stirring constantly until they are no longer pink. Drain off excess oil, leaving about ¼ cup in pan. Add salt, pepper and lemon juice. Cook 5–6 minutes. Just before kidneys are done add whisky and continue to stir until sauce is reduced and slightly thickened. Check for seasoning and add lemon juice, salt or whisky to taste. This dish is excellent with mashed potatoes, or served on toast as an appetizer or lunch dish. *Serves 4.*

kidney-potato stew

Water
2 tsp. lemon juice
1 beef kidney (about 1 lb.)
¼ lb. smoked bacon, coarsely chopped
6 medium potatoes, peeled and cut in bite-sized pieces
1 medium onion, peeled and chopped
1 Tbsp. vegetable oil
1 Tbsp. butter
Pepper
Salt
1 12-oz. bottle light beer

Put kidney in pot with water to cover and lemon juice and bring to a boil. Drain off water, refill pot with water, and again bring to a boil; simmer 15 minutes. Drain off water. In a Dutch oven, melt oil and butter; fry onion until soft and add bacon; cook 5 minutes. Add potatoes, peeled and sliced kidney, and cook another 5 minutes, stirring well to be sure that mixture does not burn. Add pepper. Pour in beer, cover and cook for 40 minutes on low heat. Pour off any excess liquid. Skim off fat and add salt and pepper if needed. Serve with a green salad and beer. *Serves 4.*

vegetable, grain, egg, & cheese dishes

vegetable, grain, egg, and cheese dishes

Vegetables and greens have always played an important role in traditional Russian cooking, though in the USSR there were frequent shortages of these products because of agricultural problems. Cabbage has always been a staple of the Russian peasantry, and is frequently mentioned in medieval manuscripts. Cucumbers and pickles appear in the earliest chronicles and pumpkin, too, was known to medieval Russia. Eggplant and squash made their way into Russian recipes through Bulgarian and Turkish cooking.

The uses of vegetables have changed considerably over the years. Radishes were formerly served as a garnish to meat dumplings; during the time of Peter the Great green beans were considered to be decorative plants for estate gardens, and were only used for food later in the eighteenth century. The tomato and the potato were introduced to Russia, as they were to the rest of Western Europe, about two hundred years ago. Today it is hard to imagine Russian cooking without the potato. I have seen people eat three or four hot boiled potatoes smothered in sour cream and butter as an appetizer before proceeding to a lavish table of *zakuski*. Though the potato was allegedly introduced to Russia by Peter the Great (who supposedly sent a sack of them from Rotterdam to St. Petersburg), it in fact had come to Russia somewhat before that via Kamchatka, Siberia, and the Urals. A famous Russian botanist, Andrei Bolotov, conducted intensive research on the best ways of growing and cooking this new staple of the Russian diet. In the eighteenth century the potato replaced the turnip, which until that time had been baked, boiled, steamed, stewed, fried, and was even used in making the fermented drink *kvas*.

Mushrooms, on the other hand, have always been a Russian passion and most Russians can identify at least twenty different common types. Mushroom picking (which is at its best at four or five a.m.) is a national sport in Russia, and the fact that there are so few varieties available in American markets is a constant source of disappointment to Russian émigré cooks. Marinated mushrooms and mushrooms in sour cream are classic dishes of Russian cooking.

Vegetables are baked into a pudding called *zapekanka*, a heavier version of the western soufflé, consisting of mashed or finely chopped vegetables blended with a cream sauce and stiffly beaten egg whites. Also made with kasha, cheese, and fish, a *zapekanka* with a white sauce base is known as "Russian style" while a pudding with a sour cream base is called "Moscow style." Modern Russian cooking also features a wide variety of cabbage-based vegetable stews.

Millet was the most widely grown grain in old Russia, followed by rye, while rice appeared only in the seventeenth century when it was known as "Saracen grain." Today buckwheat groats, or kasha, are probably the most widely used grains in Russian cooking. Kasha can be served plain, with fried mushrooms and onions, or baked with cottage cheese into a sweet pudding.

Cheese and egg dishes have always been particularly popular in Russia because of the numerous meatless fast days, but are delicious served at any time of year for lunch or a light supper. Unlike France, Russia does not produce a great number of cheeses, and the majority of Russians are accustomed to two or three native varieties and to a few foreign imports such as Swiss or Camembert, though today more varieties are available in Russian stores.

The cheese dishes usually call for *tvorog*, the Russian version of cottage cheese. American cottage cheese can be substituted, though it tends to be much more liquid than the Russian, and should be lightly wrapped in cheesecloth and set in a strainer with a weight over it to drain off excess moisture for a few hours before use. Farmer cheese is a very acceptable substitute, but cream cheese should not be used because its texture is too rich to work well in most of these recipes. If the cottage or farmer cheese is sieved before being combined with other ingredients, the finished dish will have a much smoother texture. Cheese and egg puddings can be served with sugar, sour cream or jam to taste.

vegetable solianka

This casserole can accompany meat dishes or
stand on its own as a supper dish

½ medium cabbage, shredded
4½ Tbsp. butter
2 medium carrots, peeled and sliced
3 sprigs parsley, minced
2 medium onions, peeled and sliced
2 Tbsp. tomato paste
1 dill pickle, chopped
1 Tbsp. flour
1 bay leaf
1 Tbsp. capers
⅔ cup beef broth
½ tsp. sugar
Salt and pepper
1 Tbsp. grated cheese
2 hardboiled eggs, peeled and sliced

Cook cabbage in hot water to cover until just tender. Drain well. Melt 4 Tbsp. butter, and sauté carrots, parsley and onions until soft. Add tomato paste and pickle and blend. Sprinkle flour over mixture and stir until thick. Add cabbage, bay leaf, capers and beef broth, stirring until smooth. Cook 5–10 minutes. Add sugar and salt and pepper to taste. Place mixture in lightly greased casserole, sprinkle with cheese and dot with remaining butter. Bake 10–12 minutes in 375-degree oven until top is bubbly. Remove from oven and cover top with sliced hardboiled eggs. *Serves 4.*

beets in sour cream

1 1-lb. can sliced beets, with liquid
1 Tbsp. butter
1 Tbsp. flour
1 Tbsp. sugar
Pinch salt
2 tsp. red wine vinegar
½ cup sour cream
1 Tbsp. chives, chopped

Drain beets, reserve liquid and chop coarsely. Melt butter. Add flour; stir, blending in sugar, salt and vinegar. Stir in beets and cook for a few minutes. Add ¼ cup reserved beet juice and sour cream. Simmer for 5 minutes. Sprinkle with chopped chives just before serving. *Serves 4.*

beet zapekanka (pudding)

A nice accompaniment to beef or chicken

5 thin slices pumpernickel or very dark rye bread, cut in ½-inch cubes
1 8-oz. can beets, diced
⅓ cup raisins
3 eggs
⅓ cup white bread crumbs
Sour cream

Soak bread cubes in a bowl with water just to cover for 5 minutes, and squeeze dry. In another bowl beat 1 egg, combine with diced beets and raisins, and mix well. Butter an 8-inch casserole and sprinkle lightly with bread crumbs. Place half of bread cubes on bottom of casserole, cover with beet mixture, and top with the rest of the bread. Beat the remaining 2 eggs well and pour over the casserole. Bake at 350 degrees for 35–40 minutes. Serve with sour cream on the side. *Serves 6–8.*

beets and apples

An excellent accompaniment to chicken or pork

1 8-oz. can beets, drained and chopped
1 large apple, peeled, cored and coarsely chopped
1 Tbsp. margarine or butter
½ cup orange juice
¼ tsp. lemon juice
¼ tsp. salt
¼ tsp. cinnamon
¼ tsp. powdered cloves
1½ Tbsp. dry red wine

Combine beets and apple. Melt margarine or butter in a medium-size pot and stir in beets and apple; cook on low heat for a few minutes until apple begins to soften. Add orange juice, lemon juice, salt, cinnamon, and cloves and bring to a boil; reduce heat, cover and simmer on low heat for 10 minutes. Stir in wine, stir and simmer for another 5 minutes. Taste for seasoning. This dish should be served warm or at room temperature, but not piping hot. *Serves 4.*

eggplant with mushrooms and sour cream au gratin

NABOKOVA

This can make an excellent buffet or lunch dish as well as a vegetable side dish

2–3 medium eggplants (about 3–4 lbs.)
½ cup flour
½ lb. butter (approximately)
½ cup corn oil
1 lb. mushrooms
1 quart sour cream mixed with 1 Tbsp. flour and 3 Tbsp. milk
¼ lb. grated Parmesan or Swiss cheese
1 Tbsp. salt

Wash, dry and peel eggplants, and slice into ½-inch thick rounds. Salt lightly and dust in flour. Fry in half-butter and half-oil until lightly browned on both sides. Put slices into well-greased oblong baking dish. Wash, drain and dry mushrooms. Slice them, salt lightly and sauté in butter. Distribute mushrooms over eggplant rounds. Cover the entire surface of vegetables with sour cream and sprinkle with grated cheese. Bake in oven at 375 degrees for about 20 minutes until a light crust forms on pan. Serve from baking dish. *Serves 8–10.*

eggplant and potatoes

3 medium potatoes, peeled and thinly diced
1 medium eggplant, peeled, halved, and thinly sliced
3 Tbsp. tomato paste
2/3 cup sour cream
4 Tbsp. butter
Salt and pepper
Optional: ½ small green bell pepper, seeded, deribbed and finely chopped

Combine all ingredients and bake in 350-degree oven for 35–45 minutes until all vegetables are very tender. Taste for seasoning, and add salt or pepper as needed. *Serves 4–6.*

stuffed eggplant

2 medium eggplants
3 medium onions, peeled and chopped
2 medium carrots, peeled and chopped
1 stalk celery, chopped
2 sprigs parsley, minced
½ cup shredded cabbage
3 tomatoes, peeled, seeded and chopped
½ cup vegetable oil
Salt and pepper to taste

SAUCE:
¼ cup vegetable oil
1 clove garlic, peeled and minced
¼ cup tomato paste
⅔ cup tomato sauce
⅔ cup beef broth
1 tsp. flour
½ tsp. sugar
2 scallions, minced (white and green parts)
Salt and pepper

Slice eggplants in half lengthwise, and carefully remove pulp, leaving a shell at least ½-inch thick. Cut pulp into ½-inch thick slices. Sprinkle with salt and allow to rest for 45 minutes. Then chop pulp coarsely, and fry in oil together with onions, carrots, celery, parsley, cabbage and tomatoes, adding oil as needed to keep mixture from burning. Simmer on very low heat for 10–15 minutes; add salt and pepper to taste. In a separate saucepan, sauté garlic in oil. Add tomato paste, tomato sauce and beef broth and blend until smooth. Sprinkle with flour, and stir to blend well. Add sugar, scallions, salt and pepper, and simmer 5 minutes. Stuff eggplant shells with eggplant and vegetable mixture. Pour tomato sauce over top. Place on lightly greased baking sheet or in shallow casserole and bake in 350-degree oven for 20 minutes. Serve hot. *Serves 4.*

stewed carrots

B. VINOGRADOVA

7–8 large carrots, peeled
1 large onion, peeled
¼ lb. butter
1 tsp. salt

Cut carrots in coarse chunks; slice onion. Melt butter, add onion and carrots, and sprinkle with salt. Simmer partially covered on low heat for 25–30 minutes until vegetables are very soft. Taste for salt and add more if needed. *Serves 4.*

carrot cutlets

8 large carrots, peeled
1 cup milk
½ tsp. sugar
1½ tsp. salt
5 Tbsp. butter
½ cup of very thick cream of wheat,
cooked according to package directions
3 egg yolks, beaten
1 whole egg, beaten
⅔ cup fresh bread crumbs
4 Tbsp. vegetable oil
Sour cream

Grate carrots or chop in blender or food processor. Do not puree. Heat milk, sugar, ½ tsp. salt and 1 Tbsp. butter. Stir. Add carrots and cook over low heat until carrots are soft and mixture is thick (about 20–30 minutes). Make sure mixture does not burn.

Add cream of wheat. Cover and simmer over low heat for 10 minutes. Remove from heat, cool slightly, and add egg yolks. Allow to cool. Form into small 2-inch oval croquettes; dip each into beaten egg and then into bread crumbs mixed with remaining salt. Fry on both sides in mixture of 4 Tbsp. butter and 4 Tbsp. oil until golden brown. Drain on absorbent paper towels and serve with sour cream on the side. *Serves 4–6.*

peas and mushrooms

YAVITZ

This is particularly good with chicken

1 1-lb. can tiny peas, drained or 1 10-oz. package frozen peas
1 cup chicken broth
½ lb. mushrooms
1 small onion, peeled and chopped
3 Tbsp. butter
½ cup sour cream
Salt and pepper
Few drops lemon juice

Simmer peas in chicken broth for 3–4 minutes. Wash and slice mushrooms; sauté with onion in butter until onion is golden and mushrooms are soft. Add to peas; sprinkle with salt and pepper to taste and cook 3–4 minutes. Bring to a boil and add sour cream. Simmer for a few minutes, add lemon juice and taste for seasoning. May be served in small vol-au-vent shells. *Serves 4.*

mushrooms in sour cream

May be served on toast points as a lunch dish

1 lb. mushrooms, washed and sliced
4 Tbsp. butter
⅔ cup sour cream
2 Tbsp. flour
1 tsp. lemon juice
Salt and pepper
2 tsp. minced dill

Fry mushrooms in butter for 5–10 minutes until very soft. Mix sour cream with flour and add to mushroom mixture, blending well. Add lemon juice, salt, pepper and dill, and taste for seasoning. Serve very hot. *Serves 4.*

mushrooms po-russki
PETIT

½ lb. mushrooms, coarsely chopped
2 Tbsp. butter
1 tsp. minced parsley
2 scallions, chopped (white part only)
½ tsp. crushed fennel seeds
¼ tsp. nutmeg
½ tsp. salt and pinch pepper
⅔ cup sour cream
2 Tbsp. flour
2 Tbsp. milk

Fry mushrooms in butter for 5–10 minutes until soft. Add parsley, scallions and fennel, stirring well. Sprinkle with nutmeg, salt and pepper, and taste for seasoning. Combine sour cream, flour and milk and stir till thick; add to mushrooms, and blend well. Serve very hot. *Serves 2–4.*

mushroom and rice croquettes

2 cups water
¼ lb. mushrooms
1 medium carrot, peeled and sliced
1 stalk celery, sliced
2 sprigs parsley, minced
1 scallion, minced (green and white parts)
Salt and pepper
Pinch nutmeg
1 cup boiled rice
3 Tbsp. butter
1 small onion, peeled and chopped
2 Tbsp. flour
1 cup milk
1 cup fresh bread crumbs
Oil

In 2 cups water boil mushrooms, carrot, celery, parsley and scallion until vegetables are tender (about 15 minutes). Drain and season with salt, pepper, and nutmeg. Chop mixture very fine. Add rice and mix well. Sauté onion until golden in 1 Tbsp. butter and add to rice-mushroom mixture. Melt remaining 2 Tbsp. butter; add flour, and blend; stir in milk and cook until sauce is very thick. Add to mushroom mixture, and stir. Allow to cool. Form into 2-inch small oval croquettes. Roll in bread crumbs and fry on both sides in oil until golden brown. *Serves 4.*

baked mushrooms
PETIT

1 lb. mushrooms
½ cup + 2 Tbsp. flour
1 tsp. salt
2 Tbsp. butter + 3 Tbsp. melted butter
1 cup sour cream
1 Tbsp. milk
½ tsp. dried fennel
⅓ cup fresh bread crumbs

Wash mushrooms. Remove caps from stems, and reserve them for another use. Combine ½ cup flour and salt. Roll caps lightly in flour mixture, and fry in 2 Tbsp. butter until soft, turning occasionally. Combine sour cream, remaining 2 Tbsp. flour, and milk. Stir until smooth and blend into mushroom mixture. Add fennel and simmer 2–3 minutes. Place in ovenproof casserole. Sprinkle top with bread crumbs and drizzle melted butter over casserole. Bake at 350 degrees for 20 minutes until top is browned. *Serves 4.*

mushroom solianka

1 lb. mushrooms
2 medium onions, peeled and chopped
6 Tbsp. butter
Salt and pepper
1 large dill pickle, chopped
Water
½ lb. sauerkraut, drained
2 Tbsp. chopped parsley
1 large carrot, peeled and sliced
1 Tbsp. flour
1 Tbsp. tomato paste
½ cup pickle juice
¼ cup fresh bread crumbs
1 Tbsp. grated Parmesan cheese
1 Tbsp. chopped dill

Cut up mushrooms into rough pieces. Fry with onions in 4 Tbsp. butter. Sprinkle with salt and pepper. When vegetables are soft (about 8 minutes) add pickle and simmer. In water to cover, bring sauerkraut, parsley, and carrot to a boil. Simmer 10 minutes; drain, reserving liquid. Melt 1 Tbsp. butter. Add flour and tomato paste and stir until smooth. Add 1 cup of reserved cabbage broth and pickle juice. Add salt and pepper to taste. Place ½ of vegetable mixture in greased casserole. Cover with mushroom and onion mixture, and then with a top layer of remaining cabbage mixture. Pour sauce over all. Sprinkle with breadcrumbs and cheese, and dot with remaining Tbsp. butter. Bake for 20 minutes in 375-degree oven. Just before serving, sprinkle with dill. *Serves 4–6.*

Note: Use salt sparingly in this dish since the sauerkraut is very salty.

cauliflower in sour cream

1 10-oz. package frozen cauliflower,
    or florets from 1 small head of fresh cauliflower
⅔ cup salted water
1½ Tbsp. butter
2 Tbsp. flour
1 cup sour cream
⅛ tsp. nutmeg
1 tsp. lemon juice
½ tsp. salt
½ tsp. pepper

Cook cauliflower in boiling salted water 6–10 minutes, until tender. Drain. Melt butter. Add flour, and stir till smooth. Stir in sour cream and beat with whisk. Add nutmeg, lemon juice, salt and pepper and taste for seasoning; add more salt if necessary. Put cauliflower in sauce. Boil up, simmer 2–3 minutes and serve. *Serves 3–4.*

cauliflower zapekanka (pudding)

1 head of cauliflower, cut into florets
4 small potatoes, peeled, boiled and mashed
1 Tbsp. butter
2 Tbsp. flour
1¾ cups milk
1 egg yolk
¼ cup grated Swiss cheese

½ tsp. salt or to taste
Pinch black pepper
2 tomatoes, thinly sliced
2 hardboiled eggs, peeled and chopped

Boil cauliflower florets for 6–7 minutes, until partially cooked but not too soft. Drain well and chop any large florets into smaller pieces. Melt the butter, sprinkle in flour and add milk, stirring constantly until sauce thickens. Add grated cheese and stir until cheese melts; remove from heat and blend in egg yolk. Blend half a cup of the sauce with the potatoes, and spread on the bottom of a 9–10-inch buttered ovenproof casserole. Cut tomato slices in half and layer them on top of the potato mixture. Sprinkle with the hardboiled eggs and cover with a few tablespoons of sauce. Place the cauliflower on top of the eggs and cover with remaining sauce. Bake in a 350-degree oven for 25–30 minutes. *Serves 6.*

cabbage in cream

1 medium cabbage
1 Tbsp. butter
1 Tbsp. flour
1¾ cups light cream
Salt and pepper
⅓ cup bread crumbs

Wash cabbage. Boil in salted water until tender (about 30–35 minutes). Drain and chop well. In saucepan melt butter. Add flour, blend in cream and stir until sauce is thick. Season with salt and pepper. Add cabbage, and simmer 5 minutes. Place in casserole: sprinkle top with bread crumbs and bake in 350-degree oven for 10 minutes. *Serves 4–6.*

squash in sour cream

3 large zucchini
2 cups sour cream
2 Tbsp. flour
1 tsp. salt
Pepper
2 Tbsp. lemon juice
Butter
2 Tbsp. grated Parmesan cheese

Wash and scrape zucchini, but do not peel. Cut into 1¼-inch thick slices and boil in salted water for 12 minutes; zucchini should be soft. Drain thoroughly. Mix sour cream, flour, salt, pepper and lemon juice. Cover bottom of casserole thickly with butter; put in a layer of half of the zucchini. Cover with half of the sour cream. Put in another layer of zucchini and then the rest of the sour cream. Sprinkle top with grated cheese. Bake for 15 minutes in 325-degree oven until cheese is browned. *Serves 4.*

squash–apple zapekanka

This dish tastes so sweet that it could pass for a dessert

1 lb. squash (such as zucchini)
3 Tbsp. butter
¾ cup milk
2 large apples
¾ cup bread crumbs
½ cup sugar
Pinch salt
2 eggs, separated
Sour cream

Clean and slice squash. Cook for a few minutes in 2 Tbsp. butter and add ½ cup hot milk. Cook on low heat till squash is very soft, about 12 minutes. Peel, dice and core apples, and add to squash. Soak ½ cup bread crumbs in ¼ cup milk for 10 minutes, and add mixture to pot. (Do NOT squeeze dry; add the whole mixture.) Remove from heat and stir well. Beat egg yolks well and gradually beat in sugar and salt. Add to apple-squash mixture. Beat egg whites stiff and add. Grease an ovenproof casserole and line with ¼ cup bread crumbs. Pour in apple-squash mixture and dot with 1 Tbsp. butter. Bake at 350 degrees for 45 minutes. Serve warm with sour cream. *Serves 4–6.*

hot coleslaw

1 small cabbage, shredded
2 small carrots, peeled and sliced
1 medium onion, peeled and chopped
8 Tbsp. butter
3 small apples, peeled, cored and diced
1 cup sour cream
1 Tbsp. flour
1 tsp. sugar
½ tsp. salt
½ tsp. lemon juice

Boil cabbage in salted water to cover until tender, about 10 minutes. Fry onion and carrots in 4 Tbsp. butter until soft, about 10–15 minutes, and add remaining butter. Combine drained cabbage, onion and carrot mixture and apples, and simmer over low heat for 5 minutes, taking care that mixture does not burn. Add more butter if necessary. Combine sour cream with flour, sugar, salt and lemon juice. Add to vegetables, and simmer 5 minutes. Taste for seasoning and serve hot. *Serves 4–6.*

braised endives

GREY

Water
1 tsp. salt
1 lb. endives
4 Tbsp. butter
1 tsp. sugar

Boil endives in salted water to cover for 5 minutes. Drain well. Melt butter. Add endives and sauté over low heat for about 10 minutes, until tender. Sprinkle with sugar, turn on all sides and simmer another 2–3 minutes. *Serves 4.*

braised cucumbers

3 large cucumbers
1 Tbsp. salt
3 Tbsp. butter
1 medium onion, peeled and chopped
½ cup chicken broth
Salt and pepper
1 Tbsp. chopped dill
1 Tbsp. chopped parsley
½ tsp. lemon juice
½ tsp. sugar
2 Tbsp. sour cream

Peel and dice cucumbers thinly. Sprinkle with salt and allow to sweat for an hour. Drain off liquid. Melt butter, sauté onion, and add cucumbers, chicken stock, salt and pepper to taste, dill, parsley, lemon juice and sugar. Stir and simmer on low heat for 15 minutes, checking to be sure that mixture does not burn. Just before serving blend in sour cream. *Serves 4.*

lentils with dried apricots

1 cup lentils
½ cup dried apricots
1 large onion, peeled and chopped
2 Tbsp. vegetable oil
Salt and pepper
2 Tbsp. ground walnuts
2–3 Tbsp. butter
Chopped parsley

Wash lentils. Boil in 4 cups water until tender (about 1 hour). Chop apricots and soak for 15 minutes in warm water. Drain. Fry onion and apricots in oil; simmer 10 minutes, until apricots are soft, adding oil if necessary. Combine with drained lentils, and sprinkle with salt and pepper to taste. Add walnuts and just enough butter to keep mixture from burning. Simmer on low heat 10 minutes. Serve sprinkled with chopped parsley. *Serves 4.*

celery and apples

An excellent accompaniment to duck

5 Tbsp. butter
4 stalks celery, sliced
2 apples, peeled, cored and coarsely chopped
Pinch salt
⅓ cup sugar
2 cups apple juice

Melt butter; sauté celery and apples until soft. Sprinkle with salt and sugar. Add apple juice and bring to a boil. Simmer 10 minutes and serve. *Serves 4.*

hearts of palm

PENDILL

3 1-lb. cans hearts of palm, cut in 1-inch pieces
3 Tbsp. butter
2 Tbsp. flour

1½ cups milk
Dash Tabasco sauce
½ cup grated Swiss cheese
½ cup heavy cream
Salt and pepper
½ cup grated Parmesan cheese

Melt 2 Tbsp. butter. Stir in flour, add milk and blend until thick. Add Tabasco, Swiss cheese, cream, salt and pepper, stirring until cheese melts. Place hearts of palm in a greased baking dish and pour sauce over them. Sprinkle with Parmesan cheese and dot with 1 Tbsp. butter. Bake in 400-degree oven for 10–12 minutes until cheese is browned. *Serves 4–6.*

baked mashed potatoes
KALDOR

6 Idaho potatoes, baked in skins
8 Tbsp. butter
1 tsp. salt
Pepper

Carefully scoop potato pulp out of slightly cooled baked potatoes, leaving a ¼-inch shell. Mash pulp with 6 Tbsp. butter, salt and pepper. Put back in shells. Dot with remaining 2 Tbsp. butter. Bake at 400 degrees for 10 minutes. Serve very hot. *Serves 6.*

❖ garlic baked potatoes with cheese
CHERNYAKHOVSKAYA

6 Idaho potatoes
Butter
3 Tbsp. heavy cream
3 Tbsp. butter
Salt and pepper to taste
2 cloves garlic, peeled and mashed
2 Tbsp. minced parsley
2 Tbsp. minced dill
3 Tbsp. grated Swiss or Parmesan cheese

Wash potatoes well and rub with butter; bake until well done but still firm. Carefully remove tops of potatoes and scoop out pulp, leaving a ¼-inch shell. Mash pulp well with cream, butter, salt and pepper, garlic, dill and parsley. Return pulp to shells and sprinkle some of the cheese over each. Bake for approximately 15 minutes in a 350-degree oven until potatoes are hot and cheese forms a crust. *Serves 6.*

baked potatoes with mushroom
ODESSER

6 Idaho potatoes
¼ lb. mushrooms, chopped
¼ lb. butter
½ cup sour cream
½ tsp. lemon juice
½–1 tsp. salt
¼ tsp. pepper
3 Tbsp. grated Parmesan cheese

Bake potatoes in skins until well done but still firm. Cut thin slice off top of each potato, carefully scoop out pulp, and reserve. Fry mushrooms in 2 Tbsp. butter until soft. Add ¼ cup sour cream, and simmer 2–3 minutes. Add to potato pulp. Stir in lemon juice, salt and pepper, and blend well. Gradually add the remaining sour cream, and 2 more Tbsp. butter. Pack mixture back into potato shells; dot with remaining butter and sprinkle with grated cheese. Bake 10–15 minutes in 325-degree oven until potatoes are hot and cheese is melted. *Serves 6.*

Note: If made with very small potatoes, these may be served as individual hot *zakuski.*

baked potatoes with cheese and eggs

6 large potatoes
6 Tbsp. butter
4 Tbsp. grated Parmesan cheese
3 egg yolks
½ cup sour cream
Salt and pepper

Bake potatoes until well done but still firm; carefully cut a slice off top of each and scoop out pulp. Put potato pulp through sieve and cool slightly. Blend in butter, 3 Tbsp. grated cheese, egg yolks, and sour cream. Add salt and pepper and taste for seasoning. Return pulp mixture to shells. Sprinkle with remaining 1 Tbsp. grated cheese and bake for 15 minutes in 350-degree oven, until cheese melts. *Serves 6.*

baked potatoes with meat

6 large potatoes
½ small onion, peeled and chopped
3 Tbsp. butter
½ lb. ground chuck
1 tsp. fresh chopped dill
Salt and pepper
⅓ cup beef bouillon
1 egg
1 cup sour cream
1 Tbsp. flour
1 Tbsp. tomato paste

Bake potatoes until just firm. Carefully scoop out insides of each and reserve pulp. Fry onion in butter until just soft. Add chuck, dill, salt, pepper and beef bouillon, stirring to break up meat. Cook until meat loses pink color. Simmer 10 minutes. Beat egg into potato pulp. Add meat mixture and blend well. Taste for seasoning. Put potato pulp back into shells and place in baking dish. Blend sour cream with flour and tomato paste; heat through. Pour sauce over each potato, and bake in 375-degree oven for 10 minutes. *Serves 6.*

baked potatoes with herring or sardines

6 large potatoes
½ large onion, peeled and chopped
1 Tbsp. butter
1 large herring fillet or 4 sardines, chopped
1 egg
Pepper
1 cup sour cream

Bake potatoes until well done but still firm. Carefully cut slice off the top of each and remove pulp. Fry onion lightly in butter. Mix onion and herring or sardines with potato pulp. Add egg, pepper, and ½ cup sour cream and taste for seasoning. Pack mixture back into shells, and cover each with some of remaining sour cream. Bake in 375-degree oven for 15 minutes. *Serves 6.*

potato casserole with herring or anchovies

1 medium onion, peeled and sliced into rings
2 scallions, minced (white part only)
2 Tbsp. butter
6 large potatoes, boiled and peeled
1 herring fillet, or 8 anchovies, chopped
2 egg yolks
½ cup sour cream
¼ cup light cream
Pepper

Fry onion and scallions in butter until soft. Slice potatoes and toss with onion mixture. Place potato mixture in greased casserole and sprinkle with chopped fish. Combine egg yolks, sour cream, light cream, and pepper, and pour over potatoes. Bake for 20–25 minutes at 350 degrees. *Serves 6.*

potatoes with herring and onion

6 potatoes
3 fillets Matjes herring
4 Tbsp. vegetable oil
1 small onion, peeled and finely chopped
Pinch pepper
2 Tbsp. fresh bread crumbs
2 Tbsp. melted butter
1 Tbsp. chopped parsley

Boil potatoes, unpeeled, for about 20 minutes. Drain, peel, and cut in cubes. Chop herring finely. Fry onion in 1 Tbsp. oil and combine with herring. Add potatoes, pepper and more oil and fry for about 5–8 minutes, until potatoes are crisp. Transfer to a buttered casserole; top with bread crumbs and melted butter, and bake for 10 minutes at 350 degrees until top is browned. Sprinkle with parsley. *Serves 6.*

potatoes with mushrooms and onions

½ lb. mushrooms, thinly sliced
Salted water
8 medium potatoes, peeled and thinly sliced
Butter and oil
2 onions, peeled and coarsely chopped
Salt

Boil mushrooms in salted water for 3 minutes. Drain. Fry potatoes in half butter and half oil until they just start to color. Add mushrooms and onions, sprinkle with salt, and continue to fry on fairly high heat until potatoes are crisp. Drain off excess fat. *Serves 6.*

potato-mushroom bake

3 large potatoes, peeled and very thinly sliced
10 oz. mushrooms, washed and thinly sliced
2 medium onions, peeled and chopped
2 Tbsp. chopped parsley
2 Tbsp. chopped dill
⅔ cup sour cream
¼ cup white bread crumbs
⅓ cup grated Swiss or Gruyère cheese
6 Tbsp. butter
Salt and pepper

Heat 3 Tbsp. of the butter in a large frying pan and sauté potatoes until soft. In another pan heat 2 Tbsp. of the remaining butter and sauté onions until soft and golden. Add mushrooms and cook for 5–8 minutes; add parsley and dill, and stir as mushrooms give off liquid. Butter a medium-size (9 x 9-inch) oven-proof casserole and layer half the potatoes on the bottom. Sprinkle lightly with salt and pepper. Place the onion and mushroom mixture on top, and layer the rest of the potatoes on the vegetables. Sprinkle with more salt and pepper. With a spatula spread the sour cream over the mixture. Combine the bread crumbs and grated cheese and sprinkle over the sour cream. Dot with the remaining tablespoon butter. Bake in a 350-degree oven for 25–35 minutes until the top of the casserole is well browned. The dish can be covered with waxed paper, refrigerated, and reheated in a 300–325-degree oven. *Serves 6.*

potatoes with apples and tomatoes

6 medium potatoes, peeled and cut into thin strips
3 apples, peeled, cored and cut into strips
Butter and oil
½ lb. mushrooms, washed and coarsely sliced
4 tomatoes, cleaned and thinly sliced
1 small onion, peeled and finely chopped
Salt and pepper
1 cup sour cream
2 Tbsp. grated Parmesan cheese

Fry potatoes and apples together in half butter-half oil until golden. Sprinkle with salt and pepper. Drain and remove to casserole. Fry mushrooms and tomatoes in half butter and half oil. Drain. Place potato mixture in a casserole and top with tomatoes. Sprinkle with salt and pepper. Fry onion lightly in butter and oil; drain, and mix with sour cream. Pour over vegetables, sprinkle with salt, pepper, and grated cheese, and bake for 30 minutes at 350 degrees. *Serves 6–8.*

potato kotlety

MARTIN

4 large potatoes
2 Tbsp. milk
1 egg
1 Tbsp. butter
½ to ¾ cup flour
Salt and pepper
Butter for frying

Boil potatoes in skins; cool and peel. Mash potatoes together with milk, egg, 1 Tbsp. butter, salt, pepper and enough flour to form a dough that holds its shape. Form into small 2½ inch oval cutlets; dust with flour and brown in butter until golden on both sides. *Serves 4.*

potato soufflé

3 cups cooked mashed potatoes
3 Tbsp. butter, softened
1 cup sour cream
2 Tbsp. sugar
4 eggs, separated

Mix all ingredients except eggs. Heat gently, but do not boil. Add egg yolks, and beat. Remove from heat. Whip egg whites until stiff and fold in. Bake in well greased baking dish at 350 degrees for about 25 minutes until puffed and browned. *Serves 6.*

potato zapekanka
MARTIN

6 large potatoes
2 eggs, separated
3 Tbsp. butter
¼ cup milk
Salt and pepper

Boil potatoes, cool slightly, peel and mash. Add egg yolks, 2 Tbsp. butter, milk, salt and pepper. Beat whites stiff and gently fold in. Grease dish with remaining butter; pour in potato mixture and bake in 350-degree oven for 30 minutes until puffed and brown. *Serves 6.*

rice baba
B. VINOGRADOVA

1 medium onion, peeled and chopped
¼ lb. butter
1 cup rice, washed
1 tsp. cumin seeds
Salt and pepper
1 tsp. sugar
1 large carrot

Fry onion in 1 Tbsp. butter until soft. Mix with rice and place in pot; cover with water to depth of 1 inch over rice. Simmer on low heat until rice is soft. Stir in cumin, salt and pepper. Add 3 Tbsp. butter, and mix. Place rice in well-greased baking dish and dot with rest of butter. Bake in 300-degree oven for 50 minutes until crust forms on top of rice. Sprinkle with sugar and with carrot curls (made with vegetable peeler). *Serves 6.*

rice with lima beans

A good accompaniment to stews

2 cups water
1 cup rice
1 cup frozen or canned lima beans
2 tsp. dill
½ tsp. salt
4 Tbsp. butter

Bring water to a rolling boil and add rice. Cover and simmer until rice is tender. Add beans, dill, salt and butter, and mix. Continue to simmer, adding a little water if necessary to prevent mixture from burning. Drain off any excess liquid before serving. *Serves 6.*

kasha and mushrooms

4 cups beef broth
2 cups kasha (buckwheat groats)
¼ lb. mushrooms, sliced
6 Tbsp. butter
1 tsp. salt
1 Tbsp. chopped parsley
1 Tbsp. chopped dill

Cook kasha according to package directions, but use beef broth instead of water. Fry mushrooms in 1 Tbsp. butter. Melt remaining butter; combine with mushrooms, kasha and salt. Place in greased casserole and bake in 300-degree oven for 10 minutes. Sprinkle with parsley and dill, and top with an additional piece of butter. May be served with sour cream on the side. *Serves 6–8.*

kasha and cottage cheese pudding

1½ cups kasha (buckwheat groats)
2 cups water

5 Tbsp. butter
2 cups cottage cheese, drained
2 Tbsp. bread crumbs
3 eggs
4 Tbsp. sugar
1⅓ cups sour cream
½ tsp. vanilla extract
Pinch salt

Cook kasha according to package directions, using 2 cups water. Add 4 Tbsp. butter. Put cottage cheese through sieve and add to kasha. Grease casserole with remaining 1 Tbsp. butter and line with bread crumbs. Place kasha and cheese mixture in casserole. Combine eggs, sugar, sour cream, vanilla and salt. Pour over kasha. Bake in 350-degree oven for ½ hour. May be served with additional sour cream. *Serves 6.*

string bean omelet

B. VINOGRADOVA

1 lb. cooked French-cut string beans
1 large onion, peeled and sliced into thin rings
3 Tbsp. butter
4 eggs
Salt and pepper
2 tomatoes, sliced

Cut onion rings in half. Sauté onion in 2 Tbsp. butter until transparent. Beat eggs well. Add onion, string beans, salt and pepper. Melt remaining Tbsp. butter. Pour egg and bean mixture into pan and allow to set, turning omelet once. Garnish with sliced tomatoes. *Serves 3–4.*

❖ fruit omelet

CHERNYAKHOVSKAYA

An unusual breakfast or brunch dish, excellent with brioche or challah
2 eggs
2 Tbsp. milk
1 apple, peeled and cut into fairly large ¼" thick slices
1 banana, peeled and thinly sliced
Salt and pepper
2 Tbsp. butter

Beat eggs well with milk, and add salt and pepper to taste. Heat butter until hot but not smoking, and gently fry apple and banana slices until soft, adding more butter as needed.

Pour in egg and milk mixture, and cook over low heat until eggs are set, lifting up edges to allow runny eggs to cook. Serve as soon as eggs are set. *Serves 2.*

sausage omelet
GEOFFREY

¼ lb. hard salami, thinly sliced
6 eggs
3 Tbsp. water
Salt
1½ Tbsp. butter

Cut each slice of salami in half. Beat eggs with water and salt. Add salami. Melt butter and pour in salami-egg mixture. Allow to set and turn once. *Serves 3.*

eggs with potato puree

6 large potatoes
3 Tbsp. butter
½ tsp. salt
2 Tbsp. hot milk
2 Tbsp. bread crumbs
3 Tbsp. grated Swiss cheese
4 eggs

Boil potatoes in salted water. Peel and mash. Add 1 Tbsp. butter, ½ tsp. salt and milk. Beat. Place in buttered casserole and sprinkle with bread crumbs and grated cheese; drizzle with 2 Tbsp. melted butter. Bake for 10 minutes at 350 degrees. Remove from oven and with a tablespoon hollow out 4 dents on top of mixture. Break an egg into each hollow and return to oven for 3–5 minutes until eggs are set. *Serves 4.*

egg croquettes

5 eggs, hardboiled and peeled
2 egg yolks
1 egg white
1 Tbsp. butter
1 Tbsp. flour
1 cup milk
1 Tbsp. chopped dill
1 Tbsp. chopped parsley
Salt
½ cup bread crumbs
Butter for frying

Coarsely chop hardboiled eggs. Melt 1 Tbsp. butter, add flour and blend. Whisk in milk, stirring until sauce is smooth. Turn off heat. Add the 2 yolks and beat. Combine sauce with chopped eggs, dill, parsley and salt. Form into small egg-shaped croquettes and dip into slightly beaten egg white. Roll in bread crumbs and fry in butter until golden. *Serves 4.*

lapshevnik (egg and noodle casserole)
RASKIN

2 cups broad, flat noodles
5 cups salted water
1 egg
6 Tbsp. butter

Boil noodles in salted water, drain, rinse with cold water and cool. Beat egg with softened butter, and mix with noodles. Place in greased casserole and bake for 20 minutes at 350 degrees until top is crisp. *Serves 4–6.*

drachena
(egg pudding)

*An airy, soufflé-like egg pudding that can be served
on its own or with sugar, jam or sour cream*

4 eggs, separated
2 Tbsp. sour cream
Pinch salt
2 tsp. flour
½ cup milk
1 Tbsp. butter

Beat yolks and mix with sour cream. Add mixed salt and flour by spoonfuls. Stir in milk
and beat. Beat egg whites stiff and carefully fold into mixture. Pour into greased
1-quart ovenproof casserole. Melt 1 Tbsp. butter and pour over top. Bake at 350
degrees for about 20 minutes until puffed and brown. *Serves 4.*

syrniki

TRIFUNOVICH

2 eggs
1 lb. cottage cheese
2 Tbsp. flour
2 Tbsp. potato flour
1 Tbsp. butter

Beat eggs well. Be sure the cottage cheese is not too liquid; if necessary, place it in a
sieve and press lightly with a wooden spoon to remove excess moisture. Mix cottage
cheese and eggs, then add flour and potato flour and blend. Heat a teaspoon of
butter in a small skillet and when it is very hot, drop in batter by the tablespoonful.
Fry quickly on both sides until golden brown. Add remaining butter if necessary.
Keep warm in the oven.

Some people like to add ¼ cup sugar to this batter, but I find it too sweet.
Sugar, jam, whipped cream or sour cream may be served on the side. A few raisins
may be added to the sour cream or sprinkled into the batter before frying. *Makes 16
small syrniki.*

❖ t v o r o z h n i k i

CHERNYAKHOVSKAYA

These fluffy cheese cakes or fritters are an excellent brunch dish

½ lb. farmer cheese
1 egg
Pinch salt
¼ tsp. baking soda
¼ tsp. white vinegar
¾ cup flour
2 Tbsp. sugar
Pinch lemon rind
Butter and oil for frying
Sour cream or applesauce

Using the back of a wooden spoon, press the farmer cheese through a sieve. Add the egg and salt, and beat well. Dissolve the baking soda in the white vinegar, and after it has stopped foaming add it to the flour and mix well. Slowly beat the flour mixture into the cheese until it begins to form a dough. Add the sugar and lemon rind, and form the dough into a long "sausage" 2 inches in diameter, rolling it in flour as you do so. Cut off pieces to form 2 1/2 inch long patties, about 1/2 inch thick; roll lightly in flour, and allow them to rest for 5-10 minutes.

In a large frying pan, heat equal amounts of oil and butter (to a depth of about 1/2 inch) on a fairly high flame until very hot. Carefully lower in patties, and cook for a few minutes on each side until golden. Remove from pan and drain off excess fat on paper towels.

Serve with sour cream or applesauce on the side. *Makes 10-12 tvorozhniki.*

p o t a t o   a n d
c h e e s e   c a k e s

2 cups cottage cheese
3 medium potatoes
1 egg
6 Tbsp. flour
Pinch salt
Butter for frying
Sugar
Sour cream

Put cottage cheese through sieve. Boil, peel and mash potatoes. Cool slightly. Combine potatoes with cottage cheese, egg, flour and salt, adding a bit more flour if needed to make the dough hold its shape. Form into small 2½-inch cakes. Fry in butter on both sides until crisp; then bake in a 325-degree oven for 5 minutes. Sprinkle with sugar and serve with sour cream on the side. *Serves 6.*

cottage cheese pudding

2¼ cups cottage cheese
2 Tbsp. flour
4 Tbsp. sugar
Pinch salt
½ tsp. vanilla extract
1 Tbsp. butter
1 Tbsp. bread crumbs
1 egg
½ cup sour cream

Put cottage cheese through sieve. Add flour, sugar, salt, and vanilla, and blend well. Grease casserole with butter and line with bread crumbs; pour in cottage cheese mixture. Combine egg and sour cream and pour over top of pudding. Bake at 350 degrees for ½ hour. Serve with sour cream or melted butter. *Serves 4.*

sugared cheese

This dish is very popular in Russia as a snack; it makes a novel breakfast idea

1 cup cottage cheese
1 cup sugar (approximately)
½ cup raisins
1 cup sour cream
Cinnamon

Combine cottage cheese and about half of sugar, or to taste, mashing very well with a fork. Mound cottage cheese in individual small bowls. Mix raisins, sour cream and remaining sugar, and pour over cheese. Sprinkle with cinnamon if desired. *Serves 2.*

desserts

desserts

I have never met a Russian who did not have a sweet tooth. Dessert, for Russians, marks not the end of a dinner but the beginning of a kind of second meal, a selection of cakes, cookies, and candies to accompany the inevitable and repeated cups of steaming hot tea. Russians like to linger over dessert, slowly savoring cake and conversation. Even the heaviest of meals usually ends with a huge round of sweets.

Cakes are the greatest glory of Russian cooking, and the choice of which recipes to include and which to omit was a painful one. Light and puffy nut cake, fruit cake, almond cake with apricot jam and white wine blended into an intoxicating mixture, velvety chocolate cake, Mrs. Gellman's lemon-almond cake, pineapple cream cake soaked in rum—all are sumptuous endings for the most elegant dinner. Easter is always celebrated with the tall, feathery *kulich* and the rich white cheese *paskha*, and birthday gatherings often feature a *krendel*, a raised pretzel-shaped cake. Frostings are usually light—a dusting of confectioner's sugar, a puff of whipped cream, a glaze of jam. The cakes tend to be light in texture, a tribute to the days when nothing but the freshest eggs, butter, and cream were used.

And the cookies! Mint *prianiki* (little biscuits), cookies with nuts, jam, poppy seeds, candied fruits, dates, meringues, crescents, prune and jam pastries—the list goes on and on. Then there are the other desserts—strawberry and cream cheese pie, delicate lemon cream, a Grand Marnier-flavored orange mousse, a rice dessert with vanilla and candied fruit, a banana ice cream, apple and bread pudding, and Livonian cake, a rich pancake concoction with a sweet cheese filling. Mousses and pudding exist in two forms—the light, airy French mousses and the heavier Russian bread-based puddings. The fruit puddings and *kissels* are a good way of using any kind of summer fruit and berries, and provide lighter endings to heavy meals. Indeed, there are so many desserts that this section of the book is the largest of all.

CAKES

russian pound cake

GELLMAN

½ lb. butter
7 eggs, separated
1 cup + 2 Tbsp. sugar
1½ cups flour
⅓ cup potato flour
1 tsp. baking powder
½ cup almonds, blanched

Cream butter with egg yolks. Beat in sugar, then flours and baking powder. Grind almonds and add to mixture. Beat whites stiff and fold in gently. Bake in a lightly greased 10-inch round springform pan at 375 degrees for about 40 minutes or until sharp knife inserted in center comes out clean. *Serves 8–10.*

❖ old russian vanilla or almond pound cake

MILLER

½ lb. sweet butter, cold and cut into pieces
1 ⅔ cups sugar
2 cups unbleached flour
5 eggs
1 tsp. lemon juice
1 Tbsp. vanilla extract or 1 Tbsp. almond extract
Confectioner's sugar

Cream butter, and gradually beat in sugar. Add 3 eggs one by one, beating after each addition. To produce a really fluffy cake it is important to keep beating the batter for at least 5-7 minutes; use an electric mixture on medium-medium high speed. Then add 2 Tbsp. flour, and the last two eggs, beating after each addition. Beat in the remaining flour, and the vanilla or almond extract.

Pour batter into a well buttered and floured tube pan (or large loaf pan), and bake at 300 degrees for 1 hour 20 to 1 hour 30 minutes, checking on the cake from time to time. It is done when firm to the touch and golden on the top/bottom.

Allow to cool before removing from pan. Then sift confectioner's sugar over the top and sides. *Makes 18 servings.*

mother's lemon cake
BELSKY

¼ lb. butter
½ cup sugar
3 eggs
¼ cup milk
2 cups flour
1 Tbsp. lemon juice
⅓ cup raisins

Cream butter with sugar. Add eggs one by one, beating well after each addition. Blend in milk and flour, alternating by tablespoonfuls, until absorbed; stir in lemon juice. Sprinkle top with raisins. Bake in greased 8 x 8 x 2-inch pan for 30 minutes in 350-degree oven. *Makes 16 small squares.*

mother's raisin cake
BELSKY

1 cup milk
1 envelope dry yeast
1 cup + 2 Tbsp. sugar
4 eggs
½ lb. butter, softened
3¾ cups flour (approximately)
1 cup raisins, soaked for 20 minutes in warm water
2 Tbsp. light rum

Scald and cool milk. Dissolve yeast and sugar in milk and allow to stand for 20 minutes. Add eggs and butter, stirring constantly. Work in flour and then raisins and rum. Allow to rise in a warm place for 45 minutes. Knead dough until elastic, and bake in a greased and floured 10-inch round springform pan at 375 degrees for 45–50 minutes until a sharp knife inserted in center comes out clean. *Serves 10.*

dr. mazner's torte

BELSKY

¼ lb. sweet butter
1 cup sugar
1 envelope dry yeast
¼ cup warm water
2 eggs
1 cup buttermilk
1¾ cups sifted flour
1 tsp. vanilla extract

Cream butter with sugar until light. Dissolve yeast in ¼ cup warm water. Add eggs one at a time to butter and sugar mixture while beating. Scald buttermilk very lightly and cool. Add yeast to buttermilk and combine with egg mixture. Stir in flour. Beat until smooth and add vanilla. Allow to rise for 45 minutes in a warm place. Bake in greased and floured 11 x 7-inch pan for 35 minutes at 375 degrees. *Serves 6–8.*

streusel torte

BELSKY

A crumb cake

⅓ cup milk
1 envelope dry yeast
½ cup + 1 Tbsp. sugar
Pinch salt
4 Tbsp. butter, melted and cooled
1 egg
1¾ to 2 cups flour

Heat milk until warm. Cool. Add yeast and stir until dissolved. Blend in sugar, salt and cooled melted butter. Beat egg well and add to mixture. Gradually blend in flour. Roll out on floured board to ½-inch thickness; place rectangle of dough (about 8 x 12 inches) on greased and floured baking sheet. Strew with a mixture of:

¼ lb. butter
½ cup flour
½ cup sugar

Combine all three ingredients and drop in small crumbs over cake. Bake at 350 degrees for about 30–40 minutes. *Serves 6–8.*

s a n d   c a k e
RASKIN

½ lb. sweet butter
1 cup + 1 Tbsp. sugar
6 eggs, separated
½ cup flour
½ cup potato flour or potato starch
Juice of ½ lemon
1 Tbsp. grated lemon peel

Cream butter with sugar. Gradually add egg yolks, beating well after each addition. Stir in flours, then lemon juice and peel. Beat whites until they form stiff peaks and carefully fold into mixture. Bake in greased and floured 8 x 8 x 2-inch pan for about 45 minutes at 350 degrees. *Makes 16 small squares.*

k o v r i z h k a
BOGRASH

⅔ cup sugar
1 egg, beaten
⅔ cup strong brewed tea
2 Tbsp. oil
2 Tbsp. honey
1¾ cup flour
1 tsp. baking soda mixed with ⅛ tsp. cider vinegar

Beat sugar and egg together in electric mixer until light; add tea, oil and honey. Combine flour and soda, and gradually add to liquid mixture. Bake in a buttered and floured 9-inch square pan at 350 degrees for 30–35 minutes, until cake is golden brown, springs back to touch, and a cake tester comes out clean. Cool and cut into squares. *Makes 16 squares.*

cake with coffee

RASKIN

1 egg, separated
⅓ cup sugar
½ cup milk
1 cup flour
½ tsp. baking soda
1½ Tbsp. strong black coffee
1 Tbsp. white vinegar

Beat yolk well, and blend in sugar. Mix flour and baking soda. Alternately add milk and flour and soda to yolk mixture, beating after each addition. Add vinegar and coffee. Beat egg white stiff and fold into mixture. Bake in a buttered 8 x 8 x 2-inch dish at 350 degrees for 15–25 minutes. *Serves 16 (small squares).*

almond and lemon cake

GELLMAN

1¼ cups almonds, blanched
½ tsp. cinnamon
½ tsp. grated lemon rind
2 egg whites
1 cup + 2 Tbsp. sugar
2 Tbsp. lemon juice

Grind almonds, but not too fine. Mix with cinnamon and lemon rind. Beat egg whites with sugar until stiff. Fold in lemon juice and nuts, and add egg whites. Bake in lightly greased 8-inch round springform pan at 275 degrees for 45–50 minutes, until a sharp knife inserted in center comes out clean. *Serves 6.*

almond–walnut cake

2 eggs
1 cup sugar
¾ cup dried currants
½ cup coarsely chopped walnuts
½ cup chopped blanched almonds
1 cup flour

1 tsp. baking powder
¾ cup raspberry jam

Beat eggs until light and stir in sugar. Add currants, walnuts and almonds and stir well. In separate bowl mix together flour and baking powder; add to nut mixture. Spoon into buttered and floured 9 x 9-inch baking pan and bake at 350 degrees for approximately 25 minutes, until dough springs back to the touch and a cake tester comes out clean. Cool slightly and spread with jam. Cut into squares. *Makes 9 large or 16 small squares.*

rektor nut cake

BELSKY

A light, fluffy, no-flour walnut cake

6 egg yolks
¾ cup sugar
1 whole egg
1¾ cups walnut halves

Grind nuts finely. Cream egg yolks with sugar. Add whole egg. Beat until light. Add ground nuts and stir to mix well. Bake in greased and floured 8 x 8 x 2-inch pan at 350 degrees for 30–40 minutes, until a sharp knife inserted in center comes out clean. *Makes 16 squares.*

❖ nut cake with coffee

YAVITZ-VINOGRADOVA

Both Mrs. Yavitz and Mrs. Vinogradova made variations on this recipe.

3 eggs, separated
½ cup sugar
4 oz. walnuts, coarsely ground
½ tsp. baking powder
1 tsp. lemon juice
1 Tbsp. matzo meal

1 cup raspberry jam
            or
1 cup heavy cream
1 tsp. instant coffee powder
1 tsp. coffee liqueur such as Kahlua or Tia Maria

Beat egg yolks until lemon-colored, and add sugar; continue to beat until mixture is thick and smooth. Stir in lemon juice. Add walnuts and mix well. Combine baking powder and matzo meal, and blend into mixture.

Beat egg whites until stiff, and carefully blend into batter. Pour into a lightly greased 10-inch round cake pan (you can coat with matzo meal or flour). Pour in batter, and bake for 30 minutes at 350 degrees, until a cake tester inserted in the center comes out clean. Allow to cool completely.

Either spread cake with raspberry jam, or make coffee cream:

Beat cream until soft peaks form, and blend in coffee and liqueur; beat until stiff peaks form. Cover top and sides of cake with coffee cream and chill until time to serve. *Makes 10 servings*

nut torte

NABOKOVA

A walnut cake with coffee cream

DOUGH:
8 eggs, separated
2 cups sugar
1 cup ground walnuts
1 cup freshly ground bread crumbs

CREAM:
½ lb. sweet butter
⅓ cup strong black coffee
3 egg yolks
1½ cups sugar
1 vanilla bean, grated

FOR DECORATION:
½ cup ground walnuts
1 cup shelled walnuts, broken in half
4 Tbsp. sugar
1 Tbsp. water
Butter

For the dough: Cream the 8 egg yolks with the sugar until white. Add ground walnuts and ¾ cup bread crumbs, stirring well. Beat whites very stiff and gently fold into dough. Grease a 10-inch springform pan and sprinkle with remaining ¼ cup crumbs. Pour in batter and bake at 250 degrees for 15 minutes; then increase heat to 350 degrees and continue baking for 30 minutes or until a sharp knife inserted in center comes out clean.

Cream: Cream butter with coffee until fluffy and light. Cream yolks with sugar and vanilla until white, and then add to butter mixture. Cut cooled cake into 2 layers, and spread both with cream. Place top layer on bottom layer and decorate as follows:

Decoration: Thickly grease a large plate with butter. Heat sugar and water until sugar is dissolved and mixture is very hot. Toss walnut halves in sugar mixture for a few minutes until well coated; remove from heat and place walnuts on greased plate. Allow them to cool. Sprinkle top of cake with remaining ground walnuts, and then decorate with cooled walnut halves. *Serves 8–10.*

almond cake with apricot-wine filling

NABOKOVA

5 large eggs, separated
1¼ cups sugar
1 cup (about 5 oz.) ground blanched almonds
¾ cup fine white bread crumbs
12 oz. (about 1 cup) apricot jam
¾ cup white wine
2 tsp. vodka
1 tsp. lemon juice combined with 1 tsp. sugar
10–15 blanched almond halves for garnish
1½ Tbsp. butter for greasing form

Cream egg yolks with sugar until white. Add ground almonds and mix well with wooden spoon. Add bread crumbs and mix. Beat egg whites and carefully fold in. Thickly grease a 9-inch springform pan with butter and pour in mixture. Allow mixture to rise for about 40 minutes in 110-degree oven or an oven that has been heated to 300 degrees, then turned off and allowed to cool for 15 minutes, Raise heat to 300 and bake 30–40 minutes until toothpick comes out clean. The top should be brown, and the dough springy to the touch. When the cake is cool, split into 2 layers. Spread 1 layer with apricot jam. Cover with top layer and spread remaining jam on top and sides.

Pour wine, vodka, lemon juice and sugar into a small pot and stir on low heat until sugar melts. Pour this mixture over cake (including edges and sides) and let the cake absorb the mixture in the refrigerator for at least 3 hours. Then decorate with reserved almond halves. *Serves 6–8.*

jam cake
WOLHEIM

3 egg yolks, hardboiled
¾ cup flour
6 Tbsp. butter
⅓ cup sugar
⅓ cup ground blanched almonds
½ tsp. cinnamon
1 tsp. grated lemon peel
1½ cups strawberry jam

Put egg yolks through a sieve. Combine flour, butter, sugar, almonds and egg yolks, and knead to form a stiff dough. Add cinnamon and lemon peel, kneading well. Allow dough to rest for 30 minutes. Divide into 3 parts. Press ⅓ into the bottom of a greased and floured 8-inch springform pan. Form the second piece of dough into a thin frankfurter-like roll and press around sides of pan, joining edges with dough on bottom. Cover dough with jam; make a roll of the third part of dough and form into a lattice work on top of jam. Bake for 30 minutes at 350 degrees. *Serves 8.*

jam pie

1 cup sour cream
3 egg yolks
1¾ cups flour
½ lb. sweet butter, softened
1½ cups apricot jam

Blend sour cream with 2 of the egg yolks. Gradually sprinkle in flour alternating with bits of butter, and knead until dough is smooth. Roll into a ball and chill overnight in refrigerator. Roll out ⅔ of dough into a ½-inch thick rectangle and place on greased and floured baking sheet. Spread jam across rectangle, leaving a 1-inch border. Roll out remaining dough, cut into long strips and form a lattice across jam, pinching ends of strips into border of dough. Beat remaining egg yolk with 2 tsp. water and brush on dough. Bake at 350 degrees for about 30 minutes, until golden brown. Cool and cut into squares. *Serves 8–10.*

the guests are at the door cake

BOGRASH

Tatyana Bogrash gave the cake this name because it is so quick and easy to prepare

1½ sticks + 1 Tbsp. butter (13 Tbsp.), softened
¾ cup sugar
2 eggs
1½ cups flour
½ tsp. baking soda mixed with 3 drops cider vinegar
1 cup fruit preserves (raspberry, strawberry, plum, etc.)

In an electric mixer beat butter until light and add sugar; beat in eggs one at a time. Combine flour and soda and gradually add to butter mixture. Towards the end of the mixing process the dough will become quite thick; use your hands instead of the mixer to blend in the last ½ cup of flour. Pat dough into a 1½-inch thick layer into a 10-inch round buttered and floured pan (you can use a springform pan), reserving about ⅓ cup of dough. Using a spatula, cover top with a generous layer of jam. Pat remaining dough into small round pieces about an inch wide and ¼-inch thick and arrange on top of jam. This is not a lattice pattern; you will not have enough dough for that, and the arrangement need not be symmetrical. The dough will spread during the baking process and form a thin, uneven and crusty layer with jam showing through.

Bake in a 350-degree oven for about 40–45 minutes, until patches of dough on top of cake are a deep golden brown. Cool before slicing. *Serves 8.*

bobes'

BELSKY

A cookie-like dough with nuts and jam

¼ lb. sweet butter
⅓ cup sugar
1 egg yolk + 1 whole egg, beaten
1¼ cups flour
Pinch salt
¼ cup chopped blanched almonds
¼ cup raisins
½ cup strawberry jam

Cream butter and sugar together until light and fluffy. Add eggs. Sift flour with salt and add to egg mixture. Place in greased and floured 9-inch round cake pan. Combine nuts, raisins and jam, and spread evenly over dough. Bake for 40 minutes in 325-degree oven. *Serves 6–8.*

Alexander torte I

GELLMAN

A flaky open pastry with black currant jam

¼ lb. sweet butter
½ cup sugar
1 cup flour
1 cup black currant jam

Cream butter and sugar. Add flour, and work until dough holds shape. Chill for 1 hour. Roll out dough into 2 thin (¼-inch) rectangular-shaped layers. Place bottom layer on greased baking sheet. Spread with jam and place second layer on top. This dough is extremely delicate and should be handled as little as possible. Bake in a 300-degree oven for 20–25 minutes until light golden brown. Cut into squares with a small and very sharp knife. *Makes 14–16 squares.*

Alexander torte II

TUMARKIN

A heavier dough gives this pastry a different texture

¼ lb. butter
¼ cup sugar
Pinch salt
½ cup solid vegetable shortening such as Crisco
3 Tbsp. milk
¼ tsp. vanilla extract
2 cups flour
1 cup raspberry jam

Cream butter. Add sugar and salt, and beat until light. Blend in shortening, milk, vanilla, and flour. Form into a ball and chill for 1 hour. Divide into 3 equal pieces, and roll out into 3 equal rectangles, about ½-inch thick. Bake all 3 on ungreased baking sheet in a 400-degree oven for 10 minutes. When cool spread 2 layers with raspberry jam.

Place 1 layer on top of other, and place layer with no jam on top of the other two. Trim edges to even rectangles. Ice with:

¼ cup confectioners' sugar
1 Tbsp. water
½ tsp. vanilla extract

Blend all ingredients. Dribble over top of Alexander torte and chill for ½ hour before serving. *Makes about 10 squares.*

my chocolate cake
BELSKY

This light and creamy cake tastes like a chocolate mousse

6 eggs, separated
1 cup + 2 Tbsp. sugar
½ lb. butter
6 oz. (squares) grated bittersweet or sweet chocolate + 2 oz. for the top of cake
½ cup flour
1 cup heavy cream

Beat egg yolks with sugar until light. Combine 6 oz. grated chocolate with butter and blend until smooth. Add butter mixture to egg yolk-sugar mixture and beat until very smooth. Gradually add flour. Whip egg whites and carefully but thoroughly fold into mixture. Bake in lightly greased and floured 8-inch springform pan at 325 degrees for about 40 minutes until cake shrinks slightly from the sides of the pan and a sharp knife inserted in the center comes out clean. Cool. Whip the cream and fold in 2 oz. grated chocolate. Cover top and sides of cake and refrigerate for at least 1 hour. *Serves 6–8.*

chocolate torte
YAVITZ

A no-flour mocha cake made with Grand Marnier

CAKE:
½ lb. bittersweet chocolate
1 Tbsp. instant coffee, dissolved in 2 Tbsp. water
½ lb. sweet butter
1 cup sugar
6 eggs, separated
3 Tbsp. bread crumbs
2 Tbsp. Grand Marnier liqueur

TOPPING:
1 cup heavy cream
1 Tbsp. confectioners' sugar
¼ tsp. powdered instant coffee

Melt chocolate, coffee and butter in a double boiler, stirring until smooth. Beat yolks with ½ cup of the sugar, and add to slightly cooled chocolate. Beat whites with remaining sugar and add. Place ⅓ of mixture in a separate bowl and add Grand Marnier; chill. Add bread crumbs to remaining batter and blend well. Pour into a buttered and crumbed 8-inch springform pan and bake at 350 degrees for 35–40 minutes, until a knife inserted in the center comes out clean. Check to be sure cake does not burn. Cool to room temperature and cover with Grand Marnier mixture.

Whip cream with confectioners' sugar and coffee and spread on top of cake. *Serves 6–8.*

chocolate cake

ODESSER

A light whipped-cream cake made with bitter chocolate

12 eggs, separated
¾ cup sugar
4 oz. bittersweet chocolate, melted
¼ lb. sweet butter, softened
1 cup heavy cream

Beat yolks with sugar and chocolate until thick. Add butter and keep beating. Whip egg whites stiff and gently fold into mixture. Divide batter into 3 equal parts. Pour 2 of the parts into two 9-inch round, lightly buttered and floured springform cake pans, and bake at 350 degrees for 15–20 minutes, until a knife inserted in center comes out clean. Cool and remove from pans. Spread remaining batter on 1 layer and top with second layer. Whip cream and spread over top of cake. *Serves 6–8.*

brenner chocolate

BELSKY

A chocolate almond pastry

5 oz. dark chocolate
4 eggs, separated
¾ cup sugar
¼ lb. + 1 Tbsp. sweet butter, softened
½ cup unblanched, ground almonds

Melt chocolate; beat egg yolks with sugar and when chocolate is slightly cooled, add to mixture. Blend in butter, and then almonds. Beat egg whites stiff and carefully fold in. Pour into a greased and floured 9-inch round or square springform pan and bake for 55–60 minutes at 325–350 degrees. *Makes 16 squares.*

marble cake
RASKIN

¼ lb. sweet butter
1 cup + 1 Tbsp. sugar
Juice and grated peel of 1 lemon
⅓ cup + 1 Tbsp. milk
2 eggs, separated
1½ cups flour
½ tsp. baking powder
2 oz. sweet chocolate

Cream butter and sugar. Add lemon juice and peel and beat well. Blend in ⅓ cup milk, egg yolks, flour and baking powder. Beat whites stiff and fold in carefully. Divide mixture into 2 halves. Melt chocolate with 1 Tbsp. milk and add to half of batter. Line an 8 x 8 x 2-inch pan with buttered wax paper. Pour in white batter, then chocolate batter, and make a few swirls with a knife to cut across the layers. Bake for 40–50 minutes at 350 degrees. *Makes 16 squares.*

niura's chocolate-date cake
BELSKY

4 egg whites
1 cup sugar
1¼ cups ground blanched almonds
3½ oz. sweet chocolate, ground
1 cup dates, pitted and finely chopped

Beat egg whites with sugar until very stiff. Fold in almonds and chocolate, then dates. Bake in a lightly greased 9 x 9 x 2-inch pan at 350 degrees for 20–30 minutes or until a sharp knife inserted in the center comes out clean. *Makes 16 squares.*

❖ date squares

This cake is very light and keeps well; wrap tightly and store in a cool, dry place

¾ cup dates, pitted
¼ lb. + 2 Tbsp. butter, softened
¾ cup sugar
4 eggs, separated
1 cup flour

Grind the dates or chop finely (you can do this in a food processor). Cream the butter until light, and beat in the sugar. Add the egg yolks one by one, and beat until mixture is lemon-colored and thickens. Stir in the flour by tablespoonfuls, beating well, and then add the dates.

Whip egg whites until stiff but not dry, and gently fold in to the batter. Bake at 325 degrees in a lightly greased and floured 8 x 8 x 2 pan for about 40 minutes, or until the top is well browned and a cake tester inserted in the center comes out clean. Allow to cool before removing from pan and cutting into squares. May be served with sweetened, whipped cream. *Makes 16 small squares*

cottage cheese cake

BELSKY

1 cup + 1 Tbsp. sugar
2 eggs, separated
1 lb. (2 cups) cottage cheese
½ cup almonds, blanched
4 Tbsp. raisins
½ tsp. vanilla extract
¼ cup ground macaroons or mandelbrot

Beat yolks with sugar until mixture is light and forms a thick ribbon when dropped from spoon. Put cottage cheese through sieve and add to yolks. Beat until smooth. Stir in ground almonds, raisins, vanilla and ground cookie crumbs. Beat egg whites until stiff. Very gently fold into mixture. Bake in greased and floured 8 x 8 x 2-inch pan at 350 degrees until light brown on top, about 40 minutes. Cool in pan. Cake will have the consistency of a thick pudding. This cake does not need any frosting. Makes 16 squares.

strawberry cream cheese cake

MARTIN

CRUST:
2 cups Graham cracker crumbs
5 Tbsp. butter, softened
⅓ cup sugar

FILLING:
12 oz. cream cheese
2 eggs
½ cup sugar + 2 Tbsp. sugar
½ tsp. vanilla extract
1 cup sour cream
1 quart strawberries, cleaned
1 Tbsp. confectioners' sugar

Combine Graham cracker crumbs, butter and ⅓ cup sugar with a fork, and press evenly to line the bottom and sides of a 10-inch pie plate.

In a large mixing bowl combine cream cheese and eggs, beating well (low speed should be used for an electric mixer). Gradually add ½ cup sugar and vanilla. Beat until very smooth and pour into prepared crust. Bake at 350 degrees for 20 minutes.

Blend sour cream with remaining 2 Tbsp. sugar. When pie has baked for 20 minutes, turn off oven and spread sour cream over top of pie. Return pie to turned-off oven and bake 4 minutes. Cool slightly and chill in refrigerator. Just before serving, garnish top with whole strawberries and sprinkle with confectioners' sugar. *Serves 8*.

cheese cake

BRODSKY

1 lb. cottage cheese
2 eggs
3 Tbsp. uncooked farina
2 Tbsp. sugar
1 tsp. vanilla extract
½ tsp. white vinegar
¼ tsp. baking soda

Put cottage cheese through sieve. Combine with all other ingredients and beat very well. Pour into a greased and floured 8-inch springform pan and bake for 30–35 minutes at 350 degrees. *Serves 6–8.*

apple cake with nuts
GELLMAN

½ lb. sweet butter
½ cup + 2 Tbsp. sugar
1 egg yolk
2¼ cups flour
6 large apples, peeled, cored and chopped
½ cup finely chopped almonds
4 Tbsp. melted butter

Blend butter and ½ cup sugar; add egg yolk and when mixture is smooth add flour to form a stiff dough. Refrigerate for 1 hour. Pat onto a greased and floured 11 x 7-inch pan. Combine apples with 2 Tbsp. sugar and sprinkle over dough. Strew with almonds over the top, and then pour melted butter over cake. Bake for 30–35 minutes in a 350-degree oven. *Serves 10.*

apple cake with fruit puree
TRIFUNOVICH

2 cups + 1 Tbsp. flour
1 tsp. baking powder
6 Tbsp. margarine or vegetable shortening
4 Tbsp. sour cream
1 cup sugar
4 egg yolks, beaten
1 8-oz. can fruit cocktail, drained
1 8-oz. jar applesauce
½ tsp. vanilla extract
½ tsp. cinnamon

Sift flour with baking powder. Cream shortening with sour cream and sugar; blend in egg yolks. Combine with flour mixture, and chill for 2 hours in refrigerator. Roll out and form a large (approximately 11 x 7-inch) rectangle. Place on greased and floured baking sheet. Combine fruit cocktail, applesauce, vanilla and cinnamon. Bring to a boil, simmer 10 minutes and cool. Spread on top of dough, and bake for 20–25 minutes at 275 degrees, until lightly browned. *Serves 10.*

apple cake with currants

RASKIN

1 egg
1 egg yolk
¼ lb. butter + 1½ Tbsp. butter
½ cup sugar + ¼ cup sugar
1 Tbsp. rum
1 cup flour
½ tsp. baking powder
3 large apples, peeled, cored and thinly sliced
¼ cup dried currants
¼ cup finely chopped almonds

Beat egg with egg yolk. Cream ¼ lb. butter, add ½ cup sugar; beat until fluffy; add eggs and rum. Mix flour and baking powder and combine with egg mixture to form a stiff dough. Place dough in a well-greased 9-inch springform pan. Cover with a layer of apples; sprinkle with currants, and then with nuts. Sprinkle ¼ cup sugar on top of the cake and dot with 1½ Tbsp. butter. Bake for 10 minutes at 375 degrees, turn down oven to 325 degrees and continue baking for about 35 minutes, until lightly browned. *Serves 8.*

russian apple pie

GELLMAN

5 Tbsp. sugar
1 cup flour
½ lb. butter
3 Tbsp. ice water
3 large apples, peeled, cored and thinly sliced
1 tsp. cinnamon

Mix 3 Tbsp. sugar with flour. Crumble butter into flour until mixture is like cornmeal. Working quickly, pour in water and knead just until a soft dough is formed. Roll out into a 9-inch pie pan. Place sliced apples on dough and sprinkle with remaining sugar and cinnamon. Bake for 30 minutes at 325 degrees. Remove from oven. Roll out thin strips from remaining dough and make a lattice on top of pie. Return to oven and bake for another 25 minutes until golden. *Serves 6.*

cherry cake

RASKIN

A meringue-topped fruit cake

¼ lb. sweet butter
3 Tbsp. sugar
1 egg
1½ cups flour
1 1-lb. can dark Bing cherries, pitted and drained
3 egg whites
1 Tbsp. confectioners' sugar

Cream butter and sugar until fluffy. Add egg. Beat until smooth and blend in flour to make a fairly stiff dough. Roll out and place in a greased and floured 11 x 7-inch pan and cover dough with cherries. Bake at 350 degrees for 30–35 minutes. Remove from oven. Beat egg whites with confectioners' sugar and spread over cherries. Return to oven, and bake at 325 degrees for about 20 minutes until meringue is firm and slightly browned. *Serves 10.*

fruit cake

BELSKY

Almost any fruit can be used for this cake

1½ sticks butter (¼ lb. + 4 Tbsp.)
1 cup sugar
3 eggs
1¼ cups flour
3 large apples, pears or peaches, peeled, cored or
    pitted and coarsely chopped, or 6 plums, pitted and chopped

Cream butter and sugar. Add eggs one by one and continue to beat. Blend in flour, and when dough is smooth work in fruit. Bake in a greased and floured 8 x 8 x 2-inch pan for 45 minutes in a 350-degree oven. *Makes 16 squares.*

candied fruit cake
RASKIN

4 eggs, separated
½ cup sugar
¼ lb. butter
1¾ cups flour
½ tsp. baking powder
½ cup milk
Juice and grated peel of 1 lemon
½ cup chopped raisins
½ cup ground blanched almonds
½ cup mixed chopped candied fruit
1 Tbsp. rum

Beat egg yolks with sugar until light. Work in butter, then flour mixed with baking powder and then milk. When well blended, add lemon juice, peel, raisins, almonds, candied fruits and rum. Beat egg whites stiff and gently fold in. Bake in a greased and floured 9-inch springform pan at 350 degrees for 45 minutes or until a sharp knife inserted in the center comes out clean. *Serves 6–8.*

ladyfinger cake
ODESSER

3 packages ladyfingers (3 dozen)
¼ lb. butter
¼ cup sugar
½ cup ground blanched almonds
½ cup strong black coffee
1 cup sour cherry jam or red currant jam
1 cup heavy cream, whipped

Place 1 package of ladyfingers in a single layer on a large plate, cut side facing up. Sprinkle with coffee. Cream butter with sugar and ground blanched almonds until smooth, and spread over ladyfingers. Cover with a second row of ladyfingers, also cut side up. Spread the jam over this layer, and top with the third layer. Cover the top layer with whipped cream (may be flavored with liqueur such as Grand Marnier if you wish) and refrigerate for at least 2 hours. *Serves 10.*

torte napoleon

TRIFUNOVICH

A delicate 10-layer custard cake

This cake is best made the evening before serving to allow the cream to soak into the cake overnight; 24 hours of refrigeration is even better.

DOUGH:
2 Tbsp. butter
2 eggs, beaten
2 Tbsp. sour cream
1½ cups flour

Combine butter, eggs and sour cream, and work in flour to make a very stiff dough. Divide the dough into 10 equal pieces, and roll each out into a very thin (1/8-inch) circle with a diameter of about 7 inches. Bake at 350 degrees for about 5 minutes until stiff and dry. Be careful not to overbake. Cool.

CREAM:
¼ lb. butter
1 cup flour
2 cups milk
1 cup sugar
4 eggs
2 tsp. vanilla extract

Blend butter and flour until smooth. Heat milk and sugar together until mixture boils. Then add butter-flour combination and return to the boil stirring constantly. Stir and simmer for 3–4 minutes more and allow to cool slightly. Off heat beat in eggs 1 at a time, stirring after each addition until mixture regains thickness. Add vanilla. Allow cream to chill. Place 1 of the dough circles in the center of a cake plate and spread with cream. Cover with the next circle, then more cream, and continue alternating dough circles and cream, ending with a layer of cream on top. Chill very thoroughly for at least 12 hours. *Serves 8.*

pineapple cream torte

TRIFUNOVICH

DOUGH:
10 eggs, separated
10 Tbsp. sugar
10 Tbsp. flour

Beat egg yolks well with sugar until light. Carefully fold in flour and then stiffly beaten egg whites. Divide mixture equally between 2 round 8-inch greased and floured cake pans and bake at 325 degrees for 25–30 minutes. Cool and cut each layer in two.

SYRUP:
1 cup water
1 cup sugar
3 Tbsp. rum

Boil water and sugar until slightly thickened; add rum.

CREAM:
1 8-oz. can pineapple chunks, with liquid
3 cups heavy cream
½ cup confectioners' sugar
¾ cup rum
1 envelope gelatin
½ cup warm water

Whip cream with confectioners' sugar. Combine pineapple liquid and rum. Dissolve gelatin in warm water, add to juice mixture and let thicken.

Cover each layer of cake with sugar-water-rum syrup and allow to sit for a few minutes. Mix juice-gelatin blend with whipped cream and pineapple and cover each layer with this cream. Place layers on top of each other. The top layer may be decorated with additional pieces of pineapple and chopped nuts. *Serves 8.*

"russian salad" cake

TRIFUNOVICH

*The nuts, candied fruit and raisins in this cake are like
the finely chopped ingredients of a Russian salad*

CAKE:
12 egg whites
12 Tbsp. sugar
6 Tbsp. ground blanched almonds
6 Tbsp. flour
6 egg yolks, beaten

FILLING:
1½ cups heavy cream, whipped
¼ cup finely chopped blanched almonds
¼ cup raisins, soaked for 20 minutes in ¼ cup rum
¼ cup chopped mixed candied fruit
¼ cup fruit jelly candies, chopped
2 Tbsp. confectioners' sugar

Beat egg whites with sugar until stiff. Fold in almonds, flour, and egg yolks. Bake in a greased and floured deep 9-inch springform pan for 40 minutes at 350 degrees. Cool. Hollow out the cake dough from the center forming a shell with thick sides. Combine cream, almonds, raisins, candied fruit, jelly candies, and confectioners' sugar. Fill cake shell and chill for at least 1 hour. *Serves 8.*

rum torte
BELSKY

1 recipe for "Russian Salad Cake" batter
¼ cup + 2 Tbsp. rum
¼ cup warm water
½ lb. + 3 Tbsp. butter
½ lb. confectioners' sugar
1 cup heavy cream
1 cup fresh raspberries or strawberries, cleaned and slightly crushed

Make cake batter as in "Russian Salad Cake" recipe, but divide between two 8-inch round layer cake pans, and then bake as indicated. Allow to cool. Combine ¼ cup rum and ¼ cup warm water, and pour evenly over each layer. Mix butter, sugar and remaining rum, and spread ⅔ of it over 1 cake layer. Place second layer on top and spread it with remaining butter cream. Whip heavy cream and fold in berries. Place on top of cake, spreading evenly, and refrigerate for at least 2 hours before serving. *Serves 8.*

mazurek

10 hardboiled egg yolks
⅓ cup melted butter
½ cup sugar
Peel of ½ lemon, grated

2 raw eggs
¾ cup flour
1 cup red currant or raspberry jam

Put egg yolks through sieve and cream with butter until smooth. Add sugar, lemon peel, and raw eggs, blending well. An electric mixer will do this nicely. Add flour, and continue to beat. Pour into a buttered 10-inch cake pan, and spread jam on top. Bake at 375 degrees for 25–30 minutes until the cake is golden and shrinks from the sides of pan. *Serves 10.*

krendel'

This pretzel-shaped coffee cake often makes an appearance at Russian birthday parties

⅓ cup milk
2 envelopes dry yeast
6 Tbsp. sugar
Pinch salt
3 eggs
6 Tbsp. sweet butter, softened
3 cups flour
½ tsp. baking soda
½ tsp. almond extract
½ tsp. powdered cardamom
½ cup raisins
½ cup blanched chopped almonds
½ cup chopped candied fruit

Scald milk until small bubbles appear around rim; cool. Combine yeast, sugar, salt and hot milk and allow to rest for 10 minutes. Add eggs and beat well. Work in softened butter, flour and soda, then almond extract, cardamom, raisins, almonds and candied fruit. Cover with a damp kitchen towel and allow to rise in a warm place for 1 hour. Punch down and allow to rise again for 35–45 minutes. The dough will be soft. Form into a long pretzel shape (a large capital letter "B") and place on a greased and floured baking sheet. Allow to rest in a warm place for 20 minutes. Bake for 25–35 minutes until golden in a 350-degree oven. Store tightly covered to keep from hardening. *Makes 25–35 small servings.*

kulich

NABOKOVA/TRIFUNOVICH

Traditional Russian Easter cake

2 envelopes dry yeast
½ cup warm water
2 cups milk
2½ cups sugar
About 8–10 cups flour
12 egg yolks
½ lb. + 4 Tbsp. butter, melted
1 cup chopped candied fruit
1 cup sultana raisins
⅓ cup chopped blanched almonds
1 Tbsp. rum
2 vanilla beans, finely minced
Peel of 1 lemon, grated
Pinch salt

Dissolve yeast in ½ cup warm water. Let it rest for 15 minutes. Scald the milk. Combine 1 cup sugar and 1½ cups flour, and pour in hot milk, stirring until the mixture acquires the texture of sour cream. If it is too thick add an extra ½ cup milk. Allow mixture to cool slightly and add yeast. Beat egg yolks with remaining sugar until light. Add melted butter to yeast mixture, and then egg yolks with sugar. Gradually beat in remaining flour. The dough will be soft, elastic, and should not stick to hands. Add candied fruit, raisins, almonds, rum, vanilla, lemon peel and salt, and knead very well, about 30 minutes. Allow dough to rise for at least 3 hours in a warm place, free from drafts, covered by a kitchen towel. After the dough has risen, place in greased and floured *kulich* tins or coffee cans. (Greased tins may be lined with greased brown paper or parchment.) Be sure not to fill the tin or can more than ⅓ full. Allow the *kulich* to rise another 30–45 minutes. Bake for about 1–1½ hours at 250–300 degrees until puffed and golden. *Makes 3–5 kulichs, depending on the size of the tins.*

cinnamon roll

KORENEVA

The dough from this recipe will make both the cinnamon roll and the lemon cake below. This is a good recipe for a party, as the 2 cakes will serve a large group. They both also freeze well.

DOUGH:
1 envelope yeast
1 tsp. salt
1 Tbsp. sugar
½ cup milk
2½ sticks (½ lb. + 4 Tbsp.) butter, melted
1 cup yogurt
2 Tbsp. + 3½ cups flour

FILLING:
1 cup sugar
2 tsp. cinnamon
4 Tbsp. butter

In a small bowl combine yeast, salt and sugar. Heat milk until bubbles just form around the edge of the pot and mix into yeast, stirring constantly. Allow to sit for 10 minutes, add 2 Tbsp. flour, and mix well. In a large bowl combine melted butter and yogurt, and beat well. Add yeast mixture, beating well, and gradually mix in flour, working the mixture first with a spoon and then with your hands until the dough is elastic, forms a ball and does not stick to hands. (The dough may require a bit more or less than 3½ cups.) Allow the dough to rise for 1 hour in a warm, dry place (a turned-off oven is fine), covered by a damp dish towel.

Combine sugar and cinnamon. Roll half of the dough out on a lightly floured board to form a 13 x 17-inch rectangle. Place very thin slices (a cheese slicer is good for this) of butter along the center of the rectangle, leaving a 1½-inch border unbuttered. Sprinkle the sugar-cinnamon mixture over the buttered area and roll up along the long side to form a roll. Twist the ends together and pinch the dough along the seam to tightly close the roll. Place seam side down on a buttered baking sheet and bake in a 350-degree oven for 40–50 minutes, until roll is golden brown. Do not worry if some of the filling seeps out during baking. Cool completely before slicing. *Makes 12–14 slices.*

Note: Remaining half of dough can be used for lemon cake (or, by doubling the filling ingredients, for a second cinnamon roll).

open lemon cake

KORENEVA

This kind of open pastry is known as a Siberian shanga

½ recipe for cinnamon roll yeast dough
2 lemons
1¾ cups sugar

Cut lemons in quarters and pit them. Put pieces in food processor and process until mixture is finely chopped but not pureed. This is not a mistake: do not peel the lemons. Put entire pieces with peel into processor. (You can grate the lemons on the large holes of a grater instead of using the processor, but this is very time-consuming. If you do this, however, put the lemons in the freezer for 40 minutes before grating; it will make the process easier.)

Roll out dough to form a 12 x 9-inch rectangle and spoon filling onto the center, leaving a 1½-inch border. Pinch together edges of border to form a 1-inch high ridge to keep filling from spilling out during baking. Bake in a 350-degree oven for about 40–45 minutes, until edges of dough are golden brown. Cool completely before slicing. *Makes 12–16 squares.*

cinnamon bulochki

KALDOR/JOFFE

These are really sweet rolls rather than cakes

1 envelope dry yeast
¼ cup milk
¼ cup + 2 Tbsp. sugar
¼ tsp. salt
2 eggs
¼ cup melted butter
¼ cup raisins
2¼ cups sifted flour
2 Tbsp. cinnamon

Scald milk; combine with ¼ cup sugar, yeast and salt. Allow to stand in a warm place until the yeast dissolves (about 20–25 minutes). Add eggs, butter and raisins and beat well. Mix in half of the flour, continuing to beat; then add the remaining flour. Knead well and allow to rise in a warm place, covered, until dough doubles in size (about 45 minutes). Knead dough again, and allow to rise a second time. Roll out into a narrow rectangle, and sprinkle with remaining 2 Tbsp. sugar and cinnamon. Roll up, jelly roll fashion, and cut into small 2-inch pieces. Place in a shallow flat pan and allow to rise. Bake on a greased baking sheet for about 35 minutes at 350 degrees. *Makes about 12 rolls.*

COOKIES

lemon cookies

GELLMAN

¼ lb. butter
⅓ cup sugar
1 egg
½ tsp. vanilla extract
1 cup flour
Pinch salt
Peel of 1 lemon, grated
½ cup coarsely chopped walnuts

Cream butter and sugar. Add egg, and beat. Stir in vanilla. Mix flour, salt and grated lemon peel. Add to butter mixture and beat till smooth. Drop from teaspoon onto greased baking sheet. Sprinkle with walnuts and press nuts into cookies with spatula. Bake in a 325-degree oven for 10–12 minutes. *Makes 2 dozen cookies.*

liubochka's cookies

BELSKY

A yeast dough flavored with cinnamon

1 envelope dry yeast
½ cup milk
½ lb. butter, softened
1 egg, separated
2½ cups flour
½ cup sugar
1 Tbsp. cinnamon

Scald milk. Dissolve yeast in warm milk and allow to sit for 10–15 minutes. Cream butter with egg yolk, and add yeast mixture and flour alternately, beating well. Allow the dough to rise for 1 hour, covered with a kitchen towel, in a warm place. Roll out into a flat (11 x 7-inch) rectangle and sprinkle with sugar and cinnamon. Roll up jelly roll fashion and cut into slices ¼-inch thick. Place on a greased and floured baking sheet, and brush tops of the cookies with egg white. Bake for 30 minutes at 350 degrees. *Makes 3 dozen cookies.*

crescent cookies
LANG

Ground nuts and raisins make for flavorful cookies

¼ lb. sweet butter
½ cup sugar
1 cup flour
¼ cup ground blanched almonds
¼ cup raisins

Cream butter with sugar. Work in flour, nuts, and raisins until dough is smooth. Roll out on floured board. Form crescents, and bake on greased sheet. Be sure cookies are not too close to each other. Bake at 400 degrees for 8–10 minutes. Allow to cool before removing from sheet. *Makes 2–3 dozen cookies.*

vanilla cookies
WEINSCHENKER

3½ cups flour
1 tsp. baking powder
¼ lb. + 4 Tbsp. butter
½ cup white sugar
½ cup brown sugar
3 eggs
1 Tbsp. vanilla extract

Combine flour and baking powder. Cream butter and sugars until light and fluffy. Add eggs one by one. Beat well after each addition. Stir in vanilla and then flour mixture. Refrigerate dough for 1 hour. Form dough into a long, thin "sausage," 1½ inches in diameter, and cut into rounds ½-inch thick. Bake on greased and floured baking sheet for about 20 minutes at 350 degrees. Cookies should be browned. *Makes 4 dozen.*

l e p e s h k i

KHAZANOVA

Almond cookies

½ lb. butter
½ cup sugar
½ tsp. almond extract
2 cups flour
½ tsp. salt
½ cup almonds, blanched

Cream butter and sugar until light. Add almond extract. Combine flour and salt, and beat into butter-sugar mixture. Roll out on a floured board and cut into rounds 1½ inches thick. Press 1 almond or half an almond into the center of each cookie, and bake on a greased and floured baking sheet for 20 minutes at 300 degrees. Take care that the cookies do not burn. *Makes 2½–3 dozen cookies.*

m o o n   c o o k i e s

TRIFUNOVICH

½ lb + 6 Tbsp. sweet butter
1½ cups sugar
6 egg yolks
Peel of 1 lemon, grated
1 tsp. vanilla extract
4 cups flour
1 cup coarsely chopped walnuts (or blanched almonds)

Cream butter with sugar until fluffy and add egg yolks one by one, beating well. Add lemon peel and vanilla, and then work in the flour to form a smooth dough. Blend in nuts. Refrigerate dough for 2 hours. Roll out onto a floured board and cut into half-moon shapes. Bake at 375 degrees for 10 minutes, on a greased and floured baking sheet. Cookies will be soft; allow to harden before removing from sheet. *Makes 5 dozen cookies.*

proskaur
BELSKY

Lemon and orange cookies

¼ lb. butter
½ cup sugar
1 egg
1 Tbsp. orange juice
1 Tbsp. lemon juice
Peel of 1 lemon, grated
½ cup flour
1½ cups ground, blanched almonds

Cream butter; add sugar and keep beating. Add egg, juices and lemon peel. Stir in flour and fold in nuts. Dough will be soft. Drop by teaspoonfuls onto greased and floured baking sheet, and bake for 15 minutes in a 325-degree oven. Cookies will harden as they cool. *Makes 2 dozen small cookies.*

my siberian cookies
BELSKY

This old Siberian recipe produces tender nut cookies

3 eggs
1 cup sugar
4 oz. (about 1/3 cup) ground almonds
4 oz. (about 1/3 cup) ground walnuts
1 cup flour
1 Tbsp. melted butter
1 tsp. cinnamon

Beat eggs well and add sugar. Beat till sugar is absorbed, and add ground nuts. Gradually add flour, mixing with a spoon, then melted butter and cinnamon, mixing till well blended. Drop by teaspoonfuls onto a greased and floured cookie sheet. Bake for about 10 minutes at 350 degrees till edges are just slightly brown. Cookies will be soft. Remove from cookie sheet and allow to harden. *Makes about 3½ dozen cookies.*

nadia's dry cookies

BELSKY

Lemon, walnuts and almonds give these cookies lightness and flavor

¼ lb. butter
½ cup sugar
1 egg yolk
½ tsp. lemon juice
Peel of 1 lemon, grated
½ cup chopped blanched almonds
½ cup chopped walnuts
1¾ cups flour

Cream butter and sugar. Add egg yolk, lemon juice and peel, beating until smooth. Fold in nuts and flour. Roll between the palms to form long "sausages" about 1-inch thick. Cut sausages to form ½-inch thick cookies. Bake on a greased and floured baking sheet at 375 degrees for 10 minutes. *Makes 5 dozen cookies.*

liubochka's nut cookies

BELSKY

Nut meringues

6 egg whites
2¼ cups sugar
1 tsp. vanilla extract
1 Tbsp. lemon juice
1 cup ground, blanched almonds
⅓ cup ground walnuts

Grind almonds and walnuts together. Beat egg whites, gradually adding sugar, until stiff and shiny. Add vanilla and lemon juice and continue beating. Set 1 cup of the mixture aside and gently fold nuts into the remaining whites. Drop by spoonfuls onto a greased and floured baking sheet, far apart since the cookies spread during baking. Onto each drop ½ teaspoon of reserved egg white mixture. Bake at 250 degrees for about an hour, until firm and just starting to darken. *Makes 2–3 dozen cookies.*

vanilla horns
WOLHEIM

½ lb. butter
⅓ cup sugar
1¼ cups ground blanched almonds
3 cups flour
1 vanilla bean
½ cup confectioners' sugar

Combine butter, sugar and almonds and slowly work in flour. Dough will be stiff and crumbly; keep kneading vigorously until it forms a single ball and can be rolled in pieces between the hands (this will take 10–15 minutes). Form into small (1½-inch) crescents ("horns") and place on an ungreased baking sheet. Bake for 10–12 minutes at 350 degrees. Horns will be very light golden brown. Allow to cool on the sheet–they will crumble if moved while hot. Grate vanilla bean and mix with confectioners' sugar. When horns are cool roll them carefully in vanilla sugar. *Makes 3½ dozen.*

chocolate-cinnamon meringues
RASKIN

2 egg whites
1 cup sugar
1 cup ground almonds (unblanched)
2 oz. chocolate, grated
1 tsp. cinnamon

Beat egg whites with sugar until stiff. Fold in almonds, chocolate and cinnamon. Drop from a teaspoon onto a lightly greased baking sheet and bake for 30 minutes at 300 degrees. Allow to dry on pan before removing. *Makes 3 dozen cookies.*

mother's sandy cookies
BELSKY

½ cup milk
1 envelope dry yeast
1 cup sugar

¼ lb. butter
4 egg yolks
⅔ cup sour cream (at room temperature)
4 cups flour

Scald milk. Allow to cool and dissolve yeast in it; add ½ cup of the sugar and stir well. Allow to rest for 20 minutes. Cream butter with remaining sugar and add egg yolks one by one, stirring after each addition. Add sour cream, and then alternately work in yeast mixture and flour. Allow to rise for 1 hour. Roll out on a floured board and cut into 1-inch circles, or drop by teaspoonfuls and bake on a greased and floured baking sheet for 20 minutes in a 325-degree oven until the cookies are golden brown. *Makes about 5 dozen cookies.*

mother's rusks
BELSKY

1 envelope dry yeast
½ cup milk
¼ lb. butter
1 cup sugar
1 egg
1 tsp. vanilla extract
2¾ cups flour

Scald milk, allow to cool and dissolve yeast in it. Allow to rest for 10 minutes. Cream butter with sugar. Add egg and vanilla extract, beating well. Blend in, alternating, yeast mixture and flour. Allow the dough to rise for 40 minutes. Roll between the hands into 1-inch thick sausages, and cut into ½-inch rounds. Bake on a greased and floured baking sheet for 10 minutes at 375 degrees. *Makes about 5 dozen cookies.*

berta raskin's rusks

2 eggs
1 cup sugar
1 Tbsp. butter
½ cup ground almonds
⅓ cup raisins
½ tsp. cinnamon
½ tsp. baking soda
2 cups flour

Beat eggs with sugar until light; add butter, and then ground almonds and raisins. Mix cinnamon, soda and flour, and work into the egg mixture. Form into rounds 1 inch in diameter and bake for 16–18 minutes on a greased baking sheet at 325 degrees until golden brown. *Makes 2 dozen rusks.*

vanilla rusks
RASKIN

1 vanilla bean, grated
1¾ to 2 cups flour
¼ cup sugar
½ tsp. baking soda
½ cup milk
1 Tbsp. butter, softened
1 tsp. vanilla extract

Mix grated vanilla bean, flour, sugar and baking soda. Stir in milk, butter and vanilla extract, beating vigorously. Roll between palms to form 1½-inch long "sausages" and bake at 325 degrees for 10–12 minutes. Cookies will be brown on bottom but white on top. *Makes 3 dozen.*

pondin's cookies
BELSKY

These sour cream cookies have a brown sugar crumb topping

DOUGH:
¼ lb. butter
½ cup sour cream
1¾ cups flour

TOPPING:
1½ cups brown sugar
2 Tbsp. butter
2 eggs
1½ cups ground blanched almonds
½ tsp. vanilla extract

Work ¼ lb. butter, sour cream and flour together to form a soft dough. Roll out or pat into a greased and floured 8 x 8 x 2-inch square pan. Combine all other ingredients into a mixture with the texture of thick crumbs. Sprinkle over the top of the dough in a thick layer. Bake for 30 minutes at 350 degrees. Allow to cool before cutting into squares. *Makes 16 squares.*

poppy seed cookies
GELLMAN

¼ lb. butter
¾ cup sugar
2 eggs
½ cup sour cream
Pinch salt
3 cups flour
¾ cup poppy seeds

Cream butter and sugar. Add eggs and sour cream. Beat well. Combine with salt, flour, and then poppy seeds. Roll out and cut into very thin rounds, and bake for 6–10 minutes at 350 degrees on a greased baking sheet. *Makes 5 dozen cookies.*

poppy seed rusks
BELSKY

¼ lb. + 1 Tbsp. butter
½ lb. sugar
4 egg yolks + 1 whole egg
½ cup sour cream
½ cup poppy seeds
Pinch salt
3½ cups flour

Cream butter and sugar. Add egg yolks, whole egg and sour cream. Combine poppy seeds, salt and flour and blend into the butter-sugar mixture. Make small 1½-inch long "sausages" and bake on a lightly greased baking sheet at 350 degrees for 40 minutes. *Makes 5 dozen.*

cocoa-topped cookies
LANG

¼ lb. + 4 Tbsp. butter
1¼ cups sugar
2 eggs, separated
1½ cups flour
½ cup strawberry jam
2 Tbsp. cocoa powder
¼ cup chopped almonds

Cream butter and ½ cup sugar. Beat in egg yolks. Add flour and work to form a soft dough. Roll out and pat into a square 9 x 9 x 2-inch greased and floured pan. Bake for 15 minutes at 375 degrees. Remove from the oven and cool slightly. Spread with jam. Beat egg whites with remaining sugar and cocoa powder. Spread over the top of dough and strew with chopped nuts. Bake for another 5–7 minutes until meringue is set. Cool thoroughly and cut into squares. *Makes 16 squares.*

khvorost
TRIFUNOVICH

Fried ribbon cookies

2½ cups flour
2 Tbsp. sugar
½ tsp. salt
1 whole egg + 1 egg yolk
⅓ cup water
1 Tbsp. vodka
Vegetable oil (do not use olive oil)
Confectioners' sugar

Mix flour, 2 Tbsp. sugar and salt. Combine egg, egg yolk, water and vodka. Make a well in the center of the flour mixture, pour in liquid, and work to form a manageable dough. Roll out to ¼-inch thickness on a well-floured board and cut into strips 3 inches long and ½ inch wide. Fold over as shown:

In each strip, make a slit as shown in figure 1. Insert the end through this slit and gently pull it through as shown in figures 2 and 3. Heat the vegetable oil in a skillet to a depth of 1–1½ inches. When very hot, put in twisted strips and fry for 3–5 minutes until pinkish-golden. Remove with a slotted pancake turner and drain well on paper towels. While still hot, sprinkle generously with confectioners' sugar. *Makes about 3 dozen.*

prianiki
RASKIN

Honey biscuits

1½ cups flour
½ tsp. baking soda
½ cup honey
2 Tbsp. butter, softened
1 egg
2 cloves, crushed
¼ tsp. cinnamon
¼ tsp. ground cardamom
¼ tsp. ground ginger
Pinch nutmeg

Sift flour with soda. Place honey in a large bowl. Add butter, egg and spices and stir for a few minutes. Then blend in flour, and mix to form a soft dough. Drop from a teaspoon onto a greased and floured baking sheet and bake for 10–12 minutes at 300 degrees. *Makes 2½ dozen.*

mint prianiki
TRIFUNOVICH

These little cookies are very refreshing with tea

1 cup sugar
⅔ cup water
2 Tbsp. butter
3–4 drops mint extract
3 cups flour
½ tsp. baking powder

Boil sugar and water until sugar is dissolved. Add butter, stir to dissolve and cool. Add mint extract and flour mixed with baking powder. Stir well and let stand for 20 minutes. Roll out on a floured board to finger thickness. Cut in 1-inch circles and bake on a greased and floured cookie sheet in a 350-degree oven for about 10 minutes. Cookies will still be white on top, slightly brown on bottom. *About 2 dozen cookies.*

ponchiki I

Jelly doughnuts

1 cup milk
1 envelope dry yeast
3½ cups flour
3 egg yolks
1 Tbsp. sugar
¼ lb. butter, softened
Pinch salt
½ tsp. cinnamon
½ tsp. grated lemon peel
⅔ cup strawberry jam
Vegetable oil
Confectioners' sugar

Scald and cool milk. Dissolve yeast in it and allow to rest for 15 minutes. Add 1 cup flour and stir well. Allow to rest for 30 minutes. Add egg yolks, sugar, butter, salt, cinnamon and lemon peel, and work in remaining flour until dough is elastic and does not stick to hands. Knead well. Set aside for 45 minutes to rise. Roll out on floured board and cut into circles 1/2-inch thick and about 3 inches in diameter. In the center of 1 round place a teaspoonful of strawberry jam. Cover with a second round of dough and pinch edges together tightly. Place on a baking sheet and allow to rise in a warm place for 40 minutes. Fry in very hot oil on both sides for a few minutes until golden and puffed. Drain on paper towels and sprinkle with confectioners' sugar while still warm. *Makes about 16–18 ponchiki.*

ponchiki II

1½ cups sifted flour
½ tsp. baking soda
2 Tbsp. sugar
½ tsp. cinnamon
½ tsp. grated lemon peel
1 egg
½ cup milk
1 Tbsp. butter, softened
⅔ cup strawberry jam
Vegetable oil
Confectioners' sugar

Combine flour, soda, sugar, cinnamon and lemon peel. Stir in egg, milk and butter and knead well. Roll out ½ inch thick and cut into 2-inch rounds. In the center of 1 round place 1 heaping teaspoon of jam; cover with a second round and pinch edges tightly shut. Fry in hot oil on both sides until puffed and golden. Drain on paper towels and sprinkle with confectioners' sugar. *Makes about 12–18 ponchiki.*

z a v i t u s h k i

GELLMAN

Nut and jam roll-ups

¼ lb. butter
2 eggs
1–1¼ cups flour
½ cup orange marmalade
½ cup strawberry jam
⅓ cup ground blanched almonds

Cream butter. Add eggs, beating well, and then work in flour. Roll out on a floured board to ¼-inch thickness, and cut into 2-inch squares. In the center of each square place ½ tsp. of orange jam and ½ tsp. of strawberry jam, and sprinkle with a few ground blanched almonds. Fold up 2 of the opposite corners of the square as shown:

Fold up remaining corners and pinch together so that the filling will not spill out. Bake in a 350-degree oven for 20–25 minutes. *Makes 2 dozen.*

z a v i t u s h k i   w i t h   a l m o n d s

GELLMAN

Almond roll-ups

1 envelope dry yeast
½ cup milk
1 cup sugar
½ lb. butter
3 egg yolks
Pinch salt
½ tsp. vanilla extract
2½ cups flour
4 oz. (about ⅓ cup) chopped blanched almonds

Scald and cool milk. Dissolve yeast in it, add ¼ cup sugar, and let rest 10 minutes. Cream ⅔ of butter, blend in egg yolks, salt and vanilla. Add alternately with flour to yeast mixture. Roll out into a ½-inch thick rectangle. Cover with remaining butter, thinly sliced and sprinkle with chopped almonds and remaining ½ cup sugar. Roll up jelly-roll fashion and cut into ½-inch thick rounds. Make sure *zavitushki* do not touch each other. Bake on a greased and floured baking sheet at 275 degrees for 25 minutes. *Makes 2½ dozen*.

cherry jam cookies

¼ lb. sweet butter
¼ lb. farmer cheese
1 cup flour
⅔ cup cherry jam

Cream butter with cheese. Stir in flour and knead just until smooth. Roll into a ball and chill in refrigerator for 1 hour. Roll out ¼-inch thick. Cut into 2½-inch rounds. Put ½ teaspoon of jam in the center of each and pinch edges closed to form semi-circles. Bake on a greased and floured cookie sheet in a 350-degree oven for about 20 minutes, until just slightly golden. *Makes 2 dozen cookies*.

cherry jam sour cream squares

1 recipe cherry jam cookie dough (*see above*)
1 cup cherry jam
½ cup sour cream
1 egg yolk
2 tsp. sugar
Pinch cinnamon

Divide dough into 2 equal parts and chill in the refrigerator for 1 hour. Roll out half of dough into an 8 x 12-inch rectangle, and place on a greased and floured baking sheet. Cover evenly with jam, leaving a ½-inch border around the edges. Combine sour cream, egg yolk, sugar and cinnamon and beat well. Pour over jam, covering completely. Roll out remaining dough and cut into ½-inch strips. Make a lattice work over the jam rectangle, pinching edges to expose the lower layer of dough. Bake in a 350-degree oven for 30–40 minutes, watching to be sure the dough does not burn; the strips should be a light golden color. Cool and transfer to serving plate. Cut into squares. *Makes about 14–16 squares*.

jam rolls
RASKIN

¼ lb. butter
2 Tbsp. sour cream
2 Tbsp. sugar + ¼ cup sugar
1 cup flour
¼ tsp. baking soda
⅔ cup raspberry jam
2 tsp. cinnamon

Combine butter, sour cream, and 2 Tbsp. sugar. Work in flour and baking soda to form a smooth dough. Roll out into a ½-inch thick rectangle and spread with jam. Sprinkle with ¼ cup sugar and cinnamon. Roll up and cut into ½-inch thick rounds. Bake on a greased and floured baking sheet for 20 minutes at 350 degrees. *Makes 2½ dozen.*

pineapple, prune and apricot open squares
B. VINOGRADOVA

DOUGH:
2 cups flour
½ lb. butter
½ cup sour cream
1 tsp. vanilla extract

Cut butter into flour with a pastry blender or mix with 2 forks until the mixture is like cornmeal. Add sour cream and vanilla and mix well. Refrigerate for 1 hour.

PINEAPPLE FILLING:
1½ cups canned crushed pineapple, drained
1½ tsp. cornstarch
¼ cup water
½ cup sugar

Dissolve cornstarch in ¼ cup water. Then cook along with pineapple and sugar over medium heat, stirring constantly until thick and clear. Cool before using.

PRUNE FILLING:
½ lb. pitted prunes (1¼ cups)
1 cup water
2 Tbsp. sugar
¼ tsp. allspice
¼ tsp. grated lemon rind
1 Tbsp. lemon juice

Cook all ingredients together over medium to low heat for about 20 minutes until most of the liquid has evaporated. Beat with a wooden spoon until fluffy. Cool.

APRICOT FILLING:
½ lb. dried apricots
1 cup water
¼ cup sugar
3 Tbsp. lemon juice
¼ tsp. nutmeg

Cook all ingredients over low heat until tender, stirring to keep from burning. Whip with fork until light and fluffy. Cool before using.

Roll out dough ½-inch thick onto a floured board. The dough can either be cut into individual 2-inch squares and some of the filling placed on each or it can be rolled into an 11 x 7-inch rectangle, the filling placed on top, and the pastry cut into squares after baking. The squares should be baked on a greased and floured sheet at 350 degrees for about 25 minutes. Watch to keep them from burning. *One dough recipe and each of the fillings make about 15–20 squares.*

aratun — currant squares

GELLMAN

Moist and chewy, these easy-to-make, old-fashioned squares disappear quickly

¼ lb. butter
¼ cup sugar
2 egg yolks
½ tsp. vanilla extract
1 cup flour
1½ cups dried currants

Cream butter until smooth. Add sugar and continue beating. Add egg yolks and beat till smooth. Stir in vanilla. Put in flour by tablespoonfuls and work until blended. Blend in currants and work dough well to be sure the currants are evenly distributed. Turn out into a greased and floured 8-inch square pan, and bake for 20–25 minutes at 375 degrees until light brown at the edges and top. Carefully cut into squares and allow to cool in pan before removing. *16 squares.*

t r u b o c h k i
GELLMAN

Filled pastry horns

¼ lb. butter
½ cup sugar
4 eggs
2¾ cups flour
1 tsp. grated lemon peel
1 tsp. vanilla extract

Cream butter and sugar; add eggs one by one, beating well. Add flour, lemon peel and vanilla. Wrap dough around greased cannoli cylinders. Bake at 350 degrees for about 25 minutes. They can be filled with sweetened whipped cream or with flavored fillings (see below). *Makes about 2½ dozen.*

t a r t a l e t k i
(l i t t l e   f i l l e d   t a r t s)
GELLMAN

¼ lb. + 4 Tbsp. butter
½ cup sugar
1 cup ground blanched almonds
2⅓ cups flour
1 Tbsp. cognac

Cream butter and sugar. Gradually work in ground blanched almonds and flour, and then cognac. Knead dough well for 10–15 minutes until it forms a ball and can be rolled between the palms. Take a small ball of dough (about 2 inches in diameter), poke your thumb in the center to make a hole, being sure not to poke through the bottom of the ball, and press into greased and floured miniature tart pans. (Do not try to bake these on an ordinary baking sheet–they will collapse.) Bake at 350 degrees for 15 minutes until lightly browned. Allow to cool in pans or tarts will crumble. When cool, fill with one of the following creams. *Makes 2 dozen.*

fillings for trubochki and tartaletki

BELSKY

VANILLA CREAM:
3 egg yolks
2 Tbsp. sugar
½ cup heavy cream
2 Tbsp. flour
1 tsp. vanilla extract
½ tsp. rum

Beat egg yolks with sugar; add cream and stir well. Place over very low heat and stir in flour, then vanilla and rum, and simmer until the mixture just begins to thicken. Do not allow to boil. Remove from heat and chill for 2 hours before using.

MARZIPAN CREAM:
2 egg yolks
½ cup sugar
Juice of 2 lemons
¼ cup ground blanched almonds

Beat egg yolks with sugar until light. Add lemon juice and work in the ground blanched almonds. Beat to a smooth consistency and chill.

NUT CREAM:
1½ cups ground blanched almonds
¼ cup rum
1 egg white
½ cup sugar
¼ lb. + 4 Tbsp. butter

Soak nuts in rum for 10 minutes. Beat egg white with sugar, and stir in a double-boiler over low heat until glossy. Remove from heat, cool slightly, and add butter and nuts, blending to a smooth cream; this can be done in a food processor. Allow to cool completely before using.

Possible variations: add 2 oz. grated sweet chocolate to the butter or ¼ cup orange juice, the grated rind of 1 orange and 1 Tbsp. curacao.

LEMON CREAM:
2 egg yolks
½ cup sugar
1 Tbsp. sweet white wine
Juice and grated rind of 1 lemon
1 envelope gelatin
¼ cup water

Beat yolks with sugar until fluffy. Add wine, lemon juice and rind. Cook in double boiler until just thick. Do not allow to boil. Add gelatin dissolved in water and chill 45 minutes.

wartime truffles

ODESSER

*These are called "wartime truffles" because they are made
without butter, a rarity in World War II Russia*

½ cup flour
¾ cup milk, heated to boiling point
¼ cup sugar
½ cup powdered cocoa

In a teflon pan (this is essential), carefully fry flour over medium heat, stirring constantly with fork, until it turns brown. Immediately reduce the heat and CAREFULLY pour in hot milk (it will spatter). Stir briskly and add sugar. Beat until mixture forms a smooth mass in the center of the pan. Cook for 2–3 more minutes. Remove from heat. When just cool enough to handle, form into balls 1 inch in diameter and roll in powdered cocoa. Cool before serving. *Makes 16 truffles.*

OTHER DESSERTS

paskha I
NABOKOVA

3 lbs. unsalted farmer cheese
1 lb. sweet butter
1 vanilla bean
3 cups sugar
8 egg yolks
½ pint heavy cream

Put cheese through a sieve twice. Cream butter until white (preferably with an electric mixer). Cut up vanilla very fine and mix with sugar. Beat egg yolks well and add sugar, beating until almost white. Combine egg yolk mixture and butter and beat until smooth and well blended. Add butter-egg mixture to the cheese and beat with a wooden spoon. Whip cream and add it gently to the mixture, turning from bottom to top slowly to fold in the cream. Wrap *paskha* in cheesecloth (damp gauze may be used) and place it in a *paskha* form or a clean terra cotta flower pot with a hole in the bottom. Close cheesecloth or gauze over the top of the *paskha* and place either the wooden square of the *paskha* form or a weight on top (a small, heavy casserole or 2 or 3 cans will do.) Leave in the refrigerator on a plate for 1 day so that the liquid can drain off the *paskha*. Before serving, remove the *paskha* from the refrigerator, remove the weight, unwrap the cheesecloth ends, place a large round platter over the top, and quickly invert the *paskha* onto the platter. Remove cheesecloth. Makes 1 *paskha*. *Serves 15–20.*

Note: This dish is so rich that all but the most hardy (or gluttonous) are unable to eat more than a few spoonfuls.

paskha II
TUMARKIN

½ lb. sweet butter
2 cups sugar
4 egg yolks
1 cup sour cream
1 vanilla bean, finely chopped
1 Tbsp. grated lemon rind
1 Tbsp. grated orange rind
4 Tbsp. orange marmalade
½ cup Sultana raisins
½ cup chopped candied fruit
2 lbs. unsalted farmer cheese

Cream butter with sugar. Slowly beat in the egg yolks until fluffy. Add sour cream, and then vanilla, grated lemon and orange rind, orange marmalade, raisins and candied fruit. Put the farmer cheese through a sieve and blend with the mixture. Place in a mold as in the Nabokova *Paskha* recipe, and proceed in same way. *Makes 1 paskha (serves 10–15).*

paskha III
BAKER

2 lbs. pot cheese or farmer cheese
6 hardboiled egg yolks
½ lb. unsalted butter (very soft)
1½ cups sugar
1 cup sour cream
2 Tbsp. vanilla extract

OPTIONAL:
½ cup raisins
½ cup chopped candied fruit
¼ cup ground blanched almonds

Put cheese and egg yolks through a food mill or fine sieve 2 or 3 times until the mixture is free of lumps. Set aside. Beat butter, sugar and sour cream until light and fluffy. Add cheese mixture and vanilla and beat until mixture is very smooth. Mix in the other ingredients, if desired. Proceed as in the Nabokova *Paskha* recipe. *Makes 1 paskha (serves 10–15).*

paskha IV
MRS. L.

1½ lbs. farmer cheese
6 hardboiled egg yolks
1¾ cups sugar
¼ lb. sweet butter
2 cups heavy cream
¼ lb. chopped blanched almonds
½ cup chopped dark raisins
½ cup chopped candied fruit
1 vanilla bean, ground

Put cheese and egg yolks through a sieve. Gradually blend in sugar, butter and cream (do not whip cream.) Add almonds, raisins, candied fruit and vanilla bean. Proceed as in the Nabokova *Paskha* recipe. *Makes 1 paskha (serves 10–12).*

rice dessert
YAVITZ

1 cup raw rice
3 cups milk
½ vanilla bean
¼ lb. + 4 Tbsp. butter
¾ cup sugar
½ tsp. baking powder
5 eggs, separated
½ cup bread crumbs

Heat milk with vanilla to boiling. Throw in rice and simmer for 15–20 minutes until the rice is soft. Remove from heat and remove vanilla bean. Add butter, sugar, baking powder and egg yolks. Mix well. Beat egg whites stiff and carefully fold in. Bake in a buttered and crumbed ovenproof casserole at 375 degrees for 45 minutes. May be served with sweetened whipped cream. *Serves 8.*

rice cake with raisins
WEINSCHENKER

½ cup raisins
½ cup water
1 Tbsp. rum
¼ lb. + 4 Tbsp. butter, softened
1 cup boiled rice
4 eggs, separated
¾ cup sugar
1 tsp. vanilla extract
½ tsp. grated lemon rind
3 large apples, peeled, cored and chopped
½ cup raisins
½ cup bread crumbs
½ tsp. cinnamon

Soak raisins in warm water and rum. Combine ¼ lb. butter with boiled rice. Beat yolks with sugar, and add vanilla and lemon rind. Blend in chopped apples and raisins. Fold in buttered rice. Beat egg whites very stiff and gently fold into mixture. Generously butter an ovenproof casserole with half of the remaining butter. Sprinkle with half of the bread crumbs. Put in the rice mixture; dot with remaining butter and bread crumbs, and sprinkle with cinnamon. Bake for 25–30 minutes at 350 degrees. *Serves 6.*

rice impératrice
BELSKY

1 cup raw rice
2 cups water
1 cup milk
1¼ cups light cream
3 egg yolks
¾ cup sugar
1 envelope gelatin
¼ cup cold water
½ cup chopped blanched almonds
½ cup mixed candied fruit
1 tsp. vanilla extract
1 cup heavy cream

Cook rice for 10 minutes in 2 cups water. Drain, and continue to cook on low heat for 10 minutes in 1 cup milk. Watch carefully to be sure rice does not burn. No liquid should remain in the pot. Scald light cream and allow to cool slightly. Blend egg yolks with sugar; add scalded cream and cook over hot water until the mixture thickens (do not allow it to boil). Remove from heat and add gelatin, dissolved in ¼ cup cold water. Chill for 15 minutes. Add rice, almonds, candied fruit and vanilla, and mix well. Whip the cream and carefully fold into the rice. Chill for at least 5 hours. *Serves 8.*

cranberry kissel'
NABOKOVA

1 12-oz. box or bag fresh cranberries
7 cups water for the cranberries
2 cups sugar
¾ cup potato starch
1 cup water for the potato starch

Cook cranberries in 7 cups water for about 15 minutes. Drain them and sieve into a pan so that only hulls and seeds remain in sieve. Discard hulls and seeds. Add sugar to berry pulp and bring to a boil. In the meantime thoroughly blend the potato starch with 1 cup of cold water, stirring until the mixture is smooth. While stirring constantly, slowly pour the potato starch mixture into the pan with the cranberry pulp and heat until thickened and transparent. Serve hot or cold with heavy cream. *Serves 6–8.*

cranberry-raspberry kissel'

MARTIN

6 cups cranberry juice
½ cup Giroux raspberry or grenadine syrup
3 Tbsp. cornstarch
¼ cup water

Put juice and syrup in a saucepan. Dissolve cornstarch in water, add to juices, and bring to a boil. Reduce heat and cook until mixture becomes transparent. Chill and serve with fresh cream. *Serves 6–8.*

banana plombir

RASKIN

A rich ice cream

3 bananas
1 cup sugar
1¼ cups water
2 envelopes gelatin
1 cup heavy cream, whipped
Juice of 1 lemon

Puree bananas with sugar in blender or food processor. Dissolve 1 envelope gelatin in 1 cup water and add to bananas. Dissolve second envelope of gelatin in ¼ cup water and add to whipped cream. Add cream mixture and lemon juice to bananas and stir well. Place in freezer for 1 hour. Remove from freezer, mash well and return to freezer. Freeze for at least 3 hours. *Serves 6.*

bread pudding
RASKIN

3 eggs
1½ cups milk
2 Tbsp. sugar
1 loaf French bread
½ tsp. cinnamon
½ cup raisins
1 tsp. butter

Beat eggs well. Combine with milk and sugar. Remove white part from French bread and allow to soak in milk mixture for 10 minutes; then stir well. Add all other ingredients and mix well. Bake for 45 minutes in a buttered casserole at 325 degrees. *Serves 4–6.*

almond cream
RASKIN

1 cup heavy cream
1 envelope gelatin
¼ cup warm water
½ cup ground blanched almonds
½ cup sugar
1 tsp. vanilla

Scald cream. Dissolve gelatin in warm water and add slightly cooled cream. Fold in almonds, sugar and vanilla. Place in mold and chill for at least 4 hours. Unmold just before serving and spoon into individual dessert dishes. *Serves 4.*

chocolate cream
RASKIN

4 eggs, separated
¼ cup sugar
2 oz. chocolate, grated (preferably bittersweet)
1 envelope gelatin
¼ cup warm water

Beat yolks well and add sugar; beat until light. Add chocolate, and then gelatin dissolved in water. Beat whites stiff and carefully fold into the mixture. Chill in a mold for at least 3 hours. Unmold just before serving and spoon into individual dishes. *Serves 4.*

honey mousse

4 eggs, separated
1 cup honey

Beat egg yolks well and slowly add honey. Simmer over very low heat until mixture thickens. Cool. Beat whites and carefully fold in; allow to cool. Serve in individual dessert dishes. *Serves 6–8.*

Note: ¾ cup whipped cream can be substituted for the egg whites. In that case be sure the mixture is very cool before adding the cream. The mousse may need to be stirred before serving if the honey mixture has separated.

gurevskaia kasha

1 cup cream of wheat cereal, uncooked
6 cups light cream
2 egg yolks
⅔ cup sugar
½ lb. ground blanched almonds
¼ cup raisins
¼ tsp. almond extract
¾ cup chopped candied fruit
¾ cup peach or apricot jam

Cook cream of wheat in light cream, stirring constantly. Add egg yolks, sugar, almonds, raisins and almond extract. Do not boil. Place a layer of this mixture in a well-buttered casserole. Cover with candied fruit and a thin layer of peach jam. Put in another layer of cream of wheat mixture, candied fruit, and jam, and repeat once more. There should be 3 "kasha" layers. Sprinkle top with sugar. Bake for 20 minutes at 350 degrees. Serve warm. *Serves 6.*

zapekanka of apples and bread crumbs

3 eggs
2 cups milk
10 slices white bread, crusts removed
8 apples, peeled, cored and chopped
½ cup + 2 Tbsp. sugar
¼ lb. + 6 Tbsp. butter
¼ cup ground blanched almonds

Blend eggs with milk. Crumb bread in blender, and soak the crumbs in the egg-milk mixture. Mix apples with ½ cup sugar. Coat an ovenproof casserole with butter and bread crumbs. Place a layer of the milk-soaked crumbs in the casserole, and put thin slices of butter on top, then a layer of apples, then more crumbs and butter. Continue until all crumbs and apples have been used up. Melt remaining 6 Tbsp. butter and pour over top. Sprinkle with ground blanched almonds and remaining 2 Tbsp. sugar. Bake for 45 minutes in a 350-degree oven. *Serves 8.*

black bread charlotka

A pudding of black bread, cherry jam, apples, wine and spices

9 slices stale black bread
¼ lb. + 4 Tbsp. butter
1 tsp. cinnamon
3 cloves, ground
Peel of ½ lemon, grated
Peel of ½ orange, grated
2 Tbsp. Port wine
⅔ cup sugar
5 apples, peeled, cored and thinly sliced
1 cup cherry jam
Butter
White crumbs

Crumb stale bread. Melt ½ lb. butter, add bread and fry gently along with cinnamon, cloves, lemon peel, orange peel, wine, and ⅓ cup sugar. Butter an ovenproof casserole and sprinkle with some of the remaining sugar. Place a layer of white crumbs on bottom, then a layer of bread mixture, then apples. Sprinkle with some of the remaining sugar, then put in a layer of the bread mixture, a layer of cherry jam, apples, sugar and remaining bread. Smooth over top and sprinkle with any remaining butter, sugar and white crumbs. Bake at 325 degrees for 35 minutes. *Serves 6–8.*

orange cream
VENGEROVA

1 package powdered orange gelatin dessert
1½ cups boiling water
1 Tbsp. orange juice
2 tsp. lemon juice
2 tsp. Grand Marnier or rum
1 pint vanilla ice cream

Dissolve gelatin dessert in boiling water and chill until syrupy—about 45 minutes to 1 hour. Add juices and liqueur and stir. Soften ice cream, and beat into gelatin mixture with an electric mixer until smooth. Refrigerate for at least 5 hours until firm. Can be served with whipped cream. *Serves 4.*

lemon cream
NABOKOVA

2 envelopes gelatin
1 cup cold water
8 eggs, separated
2 cups sugar
Juice of 4 lemons
Grated rind of 1 lemon
1 cup heavy cream

Dissolve gelatin in 1 cup cold water. Beat sugar and yolks together until light and creamy. Add lemon juice and grated lemon rind, then heavy cream. Blend mixture thoroughly. Cover the bottom of a small pot with 2 Tbsp. water and bring to a boil. Add the gelatin, quickly stir until transparent and immediately remove from heat. Add to the egg yolk mixture, stirring thoroughly. Refrigerate. When the cream has attained the consistency of mayonnaise beat the whites stiff and fold in gently, stirring until completely smooth. Return to refrigerator and chill at least 5 hours. May be served with any kind of cookies. *Serves 10.*

pears à la crème

FRANKFURT

Water
4 ripe pears, peeled, cored and halved
1 8-oz. can evaporated milk
½ cup sugar

Boil pears in water until tender, about 25–40 minutes depending on the ripeness of the pears. Drain. In a separate pot, heat evaporated milk and sugar over low heat until mixture starts to thicken. Remove from heat, pour over pears and chill thoroughly. *Serves 4.*

pear pudding

12 pears, peeled, cored and coarsely chopped
½ cup sugar
½ tsp. cinnamon
3 cloves, ground
¼ cup water
¼ cup white wine
6 eggs, separated
1 Tbsp. butter
2 slices white bread, crusts removed
⅓ cup milk
1 tsp. grated lemon peel

Sprinkle chopped pears with ¼ cup sugar, cinnamon and cloves. Add water and wine, and bring to a boil in a covered saucepan. Reduce heat and simmer 10 minutes. Cool. Blend egg yolks with remaining ¼ cup sugar. Add butter, bread soaked in milk, and lemon peel, and mix well. Beat whites stiff and carefully fold into mixture. Place half of egg-bread mixture in buttered casserole; then put in pears, drained, in 1 layer. Cover with remaining crumbs. Bake at 350 degrees for 20–25 minutes, until browned. *Serves 6–8.*

raspberry dessert

MRS. YU.

1 lb. (2 cups) cottage cheese
4 Tbsp. confectioners' sugar
2 Tbsp. milk
1 cup fresh raspberries

Mix cottage cheese and sugar. Put through a sieve. Blend in milk and then raspberries, crushing lightly. Put into glass bowls and chill for 1 hour. May be decorated with a few whole raspberries. *Serves 4.*

livonian cake

PETIT

Thin pancakes layered with a sweet cheese mousse

6 blinchiki (See B. Vinogradova or J. Visson crêpe recipe, pp. 126, 129)
1 lb. unsalted farmer cheese
6 Tbsp. butter
¾ cup + 2 Tbsp. confectioners' sugar
Pinch of salt
4 egg yolks
2 egg whites
¼ cup raisins
¼ cup chopped candied fruit

Put cheese through a sieve and blend with butter and confectioners' sugar. Beat in salt and egg yolks. Put whole mixture through a sieve. Add raisins and candied fruit. Beat egg whites stiff and carefully fold in. Grease casserole well. Put in a pancake and cover with some of the cheese mixture; cover with another pancake and continue until the last pancake is used up. (Top should be a pancake.) Bake for 45 minutes in 350-degree oven. Serve warm with sour cream or whipped cream. *Serves 8.*

blinchatyi pirog s iablokami

Pancake cake with apples

6 blinchiki (See B. Vinogradova or J. Visson crêpe recipe, pp. 126, 129)
4 large apples, peeled, cored and chopped
¾ cup sugar
¼ cup butter, softened
2 eggs
½ cup sour cream

Mix apples with ½ cup sugar and butter. Place 1 *blinchik* in the bottom of a well-greased casserole; spread with apple mixture. Cover with another *blinchik* and continue until all apples are used up. The last pancake should be on top. Beat eggs with sour cream and remaining sugar. Pour over top and bake at 350 degrees for 25 minutes. Serve warm. *Serves 6–8.*

kut'ia iuzhnaia (southern kut'ia)
TRIFUNOVICH

1 lb. wheat
1 lb. walnuts
2 cups sugar
1 vanilla bean, grated
Peel of 1 lemon, grated
Confectioners' sugar

Shell walnuts. Soak wheat overnight in water to about 1 inch over the level of grain. Boil it for 2-3 hours. There should be just enough water in the pot to keep wheat from burning. Be sure that heat is low and watch very carefully. Add water if necessary. Pour off water and rinse with cold water. Pour off all liquid. Allow to dry for 2 hours spread out on kitchen towels. Put dried wheat through a meat grinder twice. Grind nuts and mix with ground wheat, sugar, lemon peel and vanilla. Place in a serving dish and serve sprinkled with confectioners' sugar. *Serves 6.*

sauces, jams & drinks

sauces, jams, and drinks

While Russian cooks do not rely on rich or complicated sauces they do use a number of flavorful accompaniments to meat and fish. Sour cream, mayonnaise and horseradish sauces garnish salads and fish, mustards accompany cold meats, black currant sauce is good with lamb and Georgian *tkemali* is traditionally served with *shashlyk*. Sometimes sauces are mixed into chopped meat leftovers for a quick casserole or sandwich filling.

With tea, Russians like to eat jam, which is often served in special little saucers with tiny spoons. In the old days, wild berries were gathered in the summer to be made into huge vats of preserves or were marinated for the winter months. Jam-making is still a popular pastime among Russians, and the preserves range from a single fruit to orange-lemon or even radishes in honey.

"The joy of the Russes is drinking," said St. Vladimir in the tenth century, and even today few would disagree with him. All kinds of reasons may drive a Russian to drink. In 1936 Communist Party leader Anastas Mikoyan asserted that, under the tsars, Russians drank from grief and poverty, while under Soviet power they drank from joy. Be that as it may, Russians do love to drink, and they brew quite a few excellent beverages, both alcoholic and non-alcoholic.

Meals in Russian émigré homes were always well lubricated and though many a glass of vodka was consumed, I cannot remember having ever seen anyone visibly drunk. The code was to drink only as much as one could comfortably handle, legendary drinking bouts and rounds of toasts to all present and absent notwithstanding. Vodka is usually drunk with *zakuski* and is gulped by the shot, for sipping vodka is guaranteed to give one a headache as well as a hangover. Many Russians believe that great quantities of butter will prevent intoxication no matter how much vodka is consumed. They also prefer to stick to vodka and do not switch to wine during the meal. Cognac may be drunk with *zakuski* instead of vodka.

From earliest times, Russians enjoyed *kvas*, a mildly fermented mixture of bread, mint, raisins, berries, spices and herbs. Bread *kvas* is still very popular in Russia today, both as a drink and as a base for cold soups. Mead, which probably came to the country from Scandinavia, enjoyed great popularity in medieval Russia. Wine was first introduced by the Greeks and Byzantines, and Peter the Great imported French vines and began growing them in the Crimea.

Honey drinks are traditional in Russia. The well-known samovar was origi-
nary used for *sbiten'*, a drink made with honey, and only several hundred years later
was used for making tea. Honey and spices were added to boiling water, and the coal-
heated, barrel-bodied samovar kept the drink hot. The traditional cylindrical samovar
appeared only in the eighteenth century. By the nineteenth century, at least fifty separate enterprises in the city of Tula, the samovar capital of Russia, were turning out
these economical devices which used very little fuel and gave out the pleasant gur-
gling sound which Russians associate with tea and sympathy.

Many Russians make their own flavored vodkas, which are easy to prepare.
The longer the flavoring is left to steep, the more intense it becomes. The principle is
simple: a piece of orange or lemon peel, a clove of garlic, or a hot red pepper is left
inside a bottle of vodka for about 2 weeks until flavors are blended. Mixed punches
(kriushon), sparkling and refreshing for festive occasions, are made with fruit, white
wine, champagne, and brandy. The preparation of fruit liqueurs is another Russian
custom, and a way of using ripe summer fruit. The time spent waiting for the liqueur to
ferment is well worth the result. As Elisavietta Ritchie Farnsworth's poem about her
grandmother's brewing of such cherry liqueur illustrates, the preservation of Russian
cooking is not only a gastronomic but also a literary endeavor.

SAUCES

garlic mayonnaise
KHAZANOVA

1 tsp. salt
1 tsp. sugar
2 egg yolks
1 clove garlic, peeled and minced
1 tsp. white vinegar
About 2 cups olive oil

Combine salt and sugar and beat into egg yolks. Add minced garlic and slowly beat in
oil until mixture thickens. Blend in vinegar. *Makes about 2 cups.*

salad dressing
ODESSER

This is particularly good on vegetable and cucumber salads

½ cup sour cream
⅓ cup buttermilk

½ tsp. salt
Pinch pepper
2 tsp. lemon juice
5 finely chopped scallions, white and green parts

Combine sour cream and buttermilk; add salt, pepper and lemon juice. Add scallions and taste for seasoning. Let rest for half an hour before using; stir thoroughly before pouring on salad. *Makes about 1 cup.*

sour cream—
mayonnaise sauce
ODESSER

½ cup mayonnaise
½ cup sour cream
½ tsp. lemon juice
Pinch salt and pepper
½ tsp. sugar

Mix all ingredients well. Good with salads or over cold fish. *Makes 1 cup.*

sour cream—
tomato sauce

1 small onion, peeled and finely chopped
1 Tbsp. butter
Pinch salt
2 Tbsp. tomato paste
1 Tbsp. flour
1½ cups beef broth
1 cup sour cream

Fry onion in butter until golden. Sprinkle with salt and add tomato paste while stirring constantly. Stir in flour. Add beef broth and whisk in sour cream. Simmer 30 minutes. Good with beef dishes or potatoes. *Makes 2 cups.*

sour cream—
horseradish sauce I

1 Tbsp. butter
1 Tbsp. flour
1 cup beef broth
⅓ cup sour cream
2 Tbsp. commercially prepared red horseradish
1 tsp. red wine vinegar
Pinch salt and pepper

Melt butter and add flour. Whisk in broth, stirring until smooth. Add all other ingredients and simmer 10 minutes. An extra teaspoon of butter may be stirred in at end of cooking. Good with leftover soup meat or cold meats. *Makes about 1 cup.*

sour cream—
horseradish sauce II

1 cup sour cream
2 Tbsp. commercially prepared white horseradish
2 egg yolks
1 tsp. Dijon-style mustard
1 tsp. white vinegar
½ tsp. sugar
½ cup beef broth
½ tsp. salt

Combine all ingredients and simmer gently for 5 minutes, being sure that the mixture does not boil. Good with cold ham, beef, chicken or fish. M*akes about 1 cup.*

beet—horseradish sauce

½ cup commercially prepared white horseradish
4 Tbsp. vegetable oil
Pinch salt
1 Tbsp. red wine vinegar
1 large beet, grated

Combine all ingredients and puree in blender or food processor. Can be used for salads (good on cold potato salad). *Makes 1 cup.*

onion sauce

2 Tbsp. butter
1 Tbsp. flour
⅔ cup beef broth
2 medium onions, peeled and finely chopped
2 Tbsp. tomato paste
1 Tbsp. red wine vinegar
1 small dill pickle, chopped
Pinch salt and pepper

Melt 1 Tbsp butter. Add flour, and whisk in beef broth until smooth. Fry onions in the remaining Tbsp. butter. Add tomato paste, vinegar, pickle, salt and pepper and cook 5 minutes. Add to broth and simmer 5 minutes. Puree in a blender or food processor. *Makes 1–1½ cups.*

mustard sauce

2 Tbsp. dry mustard
2 Tbsp. sugar
2 cloves, crushed
⅔ cup white vinegar

Mix mustard, sugar and cloves. Add vinegar and stir. Pour into a jar and cover with a kitchen towel. Allow to stand in a warm place for 3 days. *Makes 1 cup.*

russian tartar sauce

5 egg yolks
2 tsp. sugar
2 Tbsp. vegetable oil
½ cup white vinegar
⅓ cup commercially prepared white horseradish

Combine all ingredients and puree in a blender or food processor. If the mixture is too thick add oil as needed. *Makes 1 cup.*

pear mustard

4 large pears, peeled, cored and coarsely chopped
2 Tbsp. sugar
1 tsp. salt
⅓ cup white vinegar
½ cup Dijon-style mustard

Cook pears in water to cover until soft, being careful that the fruit does not burn. Drain and cool slightly. Add all other ingredients and puree in a blender or food processor until smooth. *Makes 1–1½ cups.*

berry sauce

3 Tbsp. blueberry or black currant jam
1 Tbsp. Port wine
½ tsp. orange juice
Grated peel and juice of 1 lemon
1 tsp. mustard
Pinch sugar
Pinch salt
1 tsp. shallots, finely chopped

Combine all ingredients in a blender and puree for 10–15 seconds on high speed. Good with venison, lamb or duck. *Makes ½ cup.*

tkemali sauce

½ lb. pitted prunes
Water
2 cloves garlic, peeled
2 Tbsp. chopped parsley
1 Tbsp. chopped fresh coriander or 1 tsp. powdered coriander
½ cup sour cream
½ tsp. salt
Pinch cayenne pepper
¼ tsp. basil
2 Tbsp. lemon juice

Cook prunes in water to cover until very soft (about 25 minutes). Drain off water, leaving ½ cup liquid in the pan. Put all ingredients (including prunes and ½ cup liquid) in a blender and puree on high speed until smooth. Place in a small saucepan and simmer on low heat for 10 minutes. Taste for seasoning and add lemon juice, salt and pepper as needed. Serve with *shashlyk. Makes 1½-2 cups.*

JAMS

citrus jam
BELSKY

4 oranges, cut in eighths, with rind, seeded
2 lemons, cut in eighths, with rind, seeded
Water
2 cups sugar (approximately)

Soak oranges and lemons in about 10 cups water for 24 hours. Bring to a boil in the same soaking water and simmer for 1½ hours on very low heat, adding water if necessary to keep from burning. Add sugar gradually, stir constantly, and taste. Keep adding sugar until desired sweetness and thickness are obtained. Cook for 30 minutes over very low heat. *Makes 2–3 cups jam.*

strawberry jam

1 lb. strawberries
1 lb. sugar
⅔ cup water

Clean and wash berries. If very big cut in half. Cook water and sugar over very low heat until sugar dissolves. Add berries, stir, and cook over very low heat for 30 minutes. *Makes 2–3 cups jam.*

raspberry jelly

¾ cup sugar
1½ cups water
1 cup raspberries
1½ tsp. lemon juice

Boil water and sugar to form syrup. Wash raspberries; add to syrup and simmer on low heat 15–20 minutes. Put through a sieve and add lemon juice; chill for 3–4 hours. *Makes 1–1½ cups jam.*

cranberry–pear relish

ODESSER

Water
2 cups raw cranberries
2 pears, peeled, cored and chopped
4 Tbsp. sugar
2 tsp. lemon juice

Boil cranberries and pears in water to cover until tender—almost no liquid should remain in the pan. Add sugar, lemon juice, and just enough water to keep the mixture from burning. Simmer 10 minutes. Taste for seasoning and adjust sugar and lemon juice to taste. Good with poultry and game. *Makes about 3 cups.*

lemon and carrot jam

1 lb. carrots
1 lb. sugar
Peel of 1 lemon, coarsely chopped
Water

Clean carrots; cut up into ½-inch slices. Boil carrots in water until tender, drain, and sprinkle with sugar. Cook lemon peel in boiling water for 1 minute; drain. Add to carrots. Add ⅔ cup water to the carrot mixture, and stir over very low heat. Add water to keep it from burning. Taste for seasoning, and add lemon juice or sugar as needed. Simmer until the syrup is thick and the carrots are almost transparent. Serve with beef. *Makes 3 cups jam.*

radish-honey preserves

RASKIN

Try and see if your guests can guess the ingredients of this very old recipe

1 bunch (6 oz.) radishes, grated
   (can be done in blender or food processor)

Water
1 cup honey
¼ cup sugar
¼ cup finely chopped blanched almonds
¼ tsp. powdered ginger

Boil radishes in at least 1 quart of water for half an hour. Drain thoroughly. Separately, boil together the honey, sugar and 2 Tbsp. water until the sugar is dissolved. Add radishes, ginger and almonds, and simmer on fairly low heat until the mixture has turned dark brown (10–15 minutes). Cool thoroughly and serve with tea and rusks. *Makes 1½ cups.*

DRINKS

nikolashka

This is not a drink hut an accompaniment to cognac. The name
is derived from Tsar Nicholas II, the last Tsar of Russia, who was
purported to be sweet on the outside, but sour on the inside . . .

Lemon wedges
Confectioners' sugar

Surround a mound of confectioners' sugar with a circle of lemon wedges. Dip wedges in sugar and eat between sips of cognac.

flavored vodka
RITCHIE FARNSWORTH

IN A BOTTLE OF VODKA PLACE EITHER:
2 slices of scraped lemon peel OR
1 large piece scraped orange peel OR
1 small hot red pepper
O R
10 raspberries and 1 tsp. confectioners' sugar

Put bottle in the refrigerator and allow to steep for at least 2 weeks. Drain raspberry vodka through a fine sieve lined with cheesecloth before serving. *Makes 1 bottle flavored vodka.*

cherry liqueur
MARTIN

1 quart cherries
Sugar
Vodka

Select perfect cherries and wash well. Do not remove stems. Prick the cherries with a pin in 2 or 3 places. Fill a large glass jar with proportional amounts of cherries and sugar (⅔ cherries to ⅓ sugar). Pour in vodka to fill the jar. Screw the top on the jar firmly. Let the jar stand (not refrigerated) for 3 months until the sugar has totally dissolved. Shake the jar every 2 or 3 days to redistribute contents. Strain before serving. *Yield: 1 fifth cherry vodka liqueur.*

fruit liqueur

1 basket raspberries
½ lb. apricots, pitted and halved
Sugar
1 bottle vodka

Place raspberries in a shallow dish. Cover with a thin layer of sugar. Place a layer of apricots on the raspberries, then cover with more sugar, then another layer of raspberries, and top with sugar. Cover with a thin layer of gauze or cheesecloth, and leave in a warm place for 2 weeks. Transfer to a large jar, pour in vodka, cover or cork tightly, and leave for 1 month. Then strain and cork. Leave for 1 week before drinking. *Makes 1–1½ bottles liqueur.*

liqueur ivanovich
BELSKY

Coffee Liqueur

4 cups very strong black coffee
2 cups sugar
1 cup water
2 cups vodka
1 tsp. vanilla extract

Boil sugar and water together; simmer until sugar has completely dissolved and the mixture is thick. Add coffee and simmer 5 minutes. Cool. Add vodka and vanilla. Pour into bottles and cork. Allow to stand for 3 days before using. *Makes 2 bottles.*

kriushon (punch)

1 very large melon (honeydew or catawba)
1 basket strawberries
½ cup sugar
½ bottle cognac
2 bottles white wine
2 bottles soda water
1 bottle champagne

Cut top off the melon, and hollow out, leaving a ¾"–1" shell. Cut the melon into balls and discard seeds, if any. Fill the melon with strawberries and sprinkle with sugar; cover with cognac, and put in the melon balls. Replace the top on the melon and allow to sit for 1 day in the refrigerator. Place the contents of the melon, white wine, soda water and champagne in a punch bowl. Add ice. *30–40 servings.*

apple kriushon

8 apples, peeled, cored and sliced
Juice and sliced peel of 2 lemons
9 cups cold strong tea
2½ cups sugar
1 bottle champagne

Cut up apples; place in a pot with lemon juice and peel, and pour in tea. Add sugar, cover, and place in refrigerator for 5–6 hours. Put in a punch bowl and add champagne and more sugar if needed. *About 25 servings.*

russian punch
PETIT

2 bottles champagne
1 pineapple, cut into small chunks
1 cup kirsch
⅓ cup sugar

Combine sugar and kirsch. Soak pineapple in kirsch for 3 hours. Drain. Put a piece of pineapple in each glass and fill with champagne. *About 15 servings.*

wine punch

RASKIN

1 bottle white wine
2 8-oz. bottles Giroux or other raspberry or grenadine syrup
1 8-oz. can dark, sweet Bing cherries, pitted, with juice
4 peaches, peeled, pitted and cut in quarters

Combine all ingredients and chill for 4–5 hours. *About 10 servings.*

sbiten' (honey drink)

This honey drink dates back to the 15th century and will warm up the coldest day! It can be "spiked" with brandy but is good plain

4 cups water
¼ cup sugar
¼ cup honey
½ tsp. ground cloves
½ tsp. cinnamon
½ tsp. ginger
½ tsp. cardamom
1 bay leaf, crumbled

Boil all ingredients on low heat for 15 minutes. Let the pot settle for 5 minutes, and strain through a very fine sieve. *Serves 4.*

Note: The *sbiten'* vendor of old was somewhat akin to today's Good Humor trucks. Figures of such vendors are frequently represented on old prints and engravings.

cold medok

2 eggs, separated
¾ cup honey
4 cups strong tea
Juice of 3 lemons
Grated peel of 1 lemon
1 cup sugar

Beat egg yolks with honey. Add warm tea and stir over heat, being sure the mixture does not boil. Stir in the juice of 2 lemons. Cool, pour into glasses and keep in the refrigerator. Just before serving, beat egg whites stiff with sugar; add the remaining lemon juice and peel, and divide equally among the glasses. *Serves 4.*

coffee glacé

FOR EACH CUP:
1 cup very strong black coffee
Few grains salt
1 tsp. sugar
1 Tbsp. milk
1 scoop rich coffee ice cream

Combine all ingredients except ice cream, and chill. Just before serving place a scoop of ice cream in each cup, and pour in the coffee mixture.

gogol'-mogol'

FOR EACH DRINK:
VARIATION I
1 egg
1 Tbsp. sugar
2 Tbsp. sweet white wine
Few grains salt
¾ cup milk

Combine all ingredients except milk. Beat in the milk, blend well and strain before serving.

VARIATION II
1 egg yolk
1 Tbsp. sugar
Few grains salt
¼ tsp. vanilla extract
¾ cup milk

Blend all ingredients, and strain before serving.

VARIATION III
1 egg
1 cup milk
3 Tbsp. honey
1 Tbsp. lemon juice

Blend all ingredients until smooth and pour into glass.

my father's vishnevka

The demijohn must be glass, he insists,
not a crock. Alternate
layers of cherries and sugar until
the whole jar is filled.
Then pour vodka over, one-hundred-proof –
though Babushka always argued:
Don't make it too strong!
She liked her drinks *doux et pas fort*,
but of course didn't drink at all.

Now tie a cloth over the top
to keep out the bugs,
and haul the full demijohn up to the roof
so it gets as much sun
as the sun is willing to give.
Leave it undisturbed . . . How long?
Between cherry-picking time and the fall.

Meanwhile, watch
the liquid turn redder and redder.
Babushka used to climb the rickety stairs
to the roof every day, just to check.
By the time the cherries were bled
the liquid level had dropped
perhaps by evaporation.
Babushka seemed especially cheerful.
She finally said it was ready.

Just pour the liquid into clean bottles.
No distillation involved.
Throw out the old fruit, now greenish and strong.
Sometimes the chickens get the old cherries –
Not, Daddy says, too good an idea.
In Florida now, he adds, we use local fruit:
you should try your Babushka's recent *kumquatka*.

Elisavietta Ritchie Farnsworth
George Artamonoff

appendices

sample menus

A HIGH TEA

Stuffed eggs with livers and cognac
Cream cheese and red caviar canapés
Herring snacks
Spiced cottage cheese
Mushroom salad
Ham pirozhki
Alexander torte
Niura's chocolate date cake
Lepeshki

A SPRING LUNCH

Stuffed celery
Stuffed cucumbers
Cold vegetable okroshka
Salat Olivier
String bean omelet
Raspberry dessert
Lemon cookies

A WINTER DINNER

Russian borshch
Pirozhki with yeast dough, meat filling
Chicken kotlety I
Kasha and mushrooms
Braised cucumbers
Cranberry kissel' with
Aratun (currant squares)

EASTER BUFFET TABLE

Green borshch
Smoked salmon and red caviar tort
Vinegret I
Tomato, apple, and scallion salad
Marinated mushrooms
Baklazhannaia ikra I
Assorted cold cuts
Mint prianiki
Kulich
Paskha

A QUICK MEAL

Cold summer beet soup
Veal scallops
Braised endives
Mother's lemon cake

contributors

Alexandra Baker–Born in a Russian family in Yugoslavia; retired Professor of Russian, Middlebury College, Vermont

Irene Balaksha–Daughter of White Russian Officer; retired lecturer in Russian, Columbia University

Eugenie Belsky–Singer, St. Petersburg opera

Tatyana Bogrash–Retired Moscow high school mathematics teacher, survived the World War II siege of Leningrad

Lia Brodsky–Moscow-born art historian

Catherine Cheosky–Russian-born cook and housewife

Leonora Chernyakhovskaya–Director, Moscow International School of Translation and Interpreting

Elisavietta Ritchie Farnsworth–Poet, writer, translator; granddaughter of Tsarist general

Mirra Frankfurt–Daughter of Mrs. Belsky; former actress

Sofia Gellman–Born in St. Petersburg; daughter of musician in Tsar's orchestra

Janna Geoffrey–Raised in Berlin; was famous for her cooking in New York Russian community

Maria Gerstman–Retired Russian-language verbatim reporter, United Nations

Jenny Grey–Singer in Paris Russian community; wife of the late Andrei Sedykh, editor of *Novoe Russkoe Slovo*

Anne Jalbert–Simultaneous interpreter

Riba Kaldor–Her mother, Anuta Joffe, left Russia in 1890, lived to age 100, and was one of the founders of Woodbine, NJ. émigré colony

Rosa Kavenoki–Born in St. Petersburg; lives in Monterey, California, translator and interpreter

Boris Khazanov–Moscow-born computer expert and folklorist

Marina Khazanova–Moscow-born ethnographer, teacher of Russian

Elena Koreneva–Retired Moscow marine geologist, botanist and homemaker

Oksana Kujbida–Former Program Officer, IREX, US-USSR academic exchange organization

Mrs. L.–Baku-born music patron

Olga Lang–Former Social Revolutionary; taught Russian at Swarthmore College

Victoria Martin–Paris-raised painter and expert cook

Professor M.–Department Head, Moscow State University

Frank Miller–Professor, Department of Slavic Languages, Columbia University

Sofia Nabokova–Cousin of writer Vladimir Nabokov; worked for George Balanchine

Mery Odesser–Dietician; lived for years in Brazil

Galina Pendill–Riga-born illustrator and interpreter

Rose Raskin–Taught Russian at Columbia University

Ariadna Sosinskaya–Daughter of Social Revolutionary Victor Chernov

Suzanne Tumarkin–Worked in import-export; collector of many Russian recipes

Vera Vengerova–Daughter of Sofia Gellman; lived in Ecuador.

Alla Vinogradova–Moscow economist and amateur chef

Bertha Vinogradova–Expert at cooking for large groups; lived in Iran

Jacqueline Visson–Married to my Russian uncle; taught French at US. Foreign Service Institute

Lynn Visson–Raised in Russian family; taught Russian at Columbia University; simultaneous interpreter; author of books on Russian language and culture

Mirra-Renée Visson–Author's mother; born in St. Petersburg, lived in Paris; formerly with French Cultural Services, New York

Vivian Weil–Senior Research Associate, Center for the Study of Ethics in the Professions, Illinois Institute of Technology

Tamara Weinschenker–Fashion and bridal consultant, New York

Irene Wolheim–Viennese housekeeper for author's family; superb cook

Catherine Woronzoff–Raised in Russian family in France

Manya Yavitz–Superb Russian-born cook

Mrs. Yu.–Wife of Soviet diplomat formerly stationed in the U.S.

index